1990

THE
ESSENTIAL
PLOTINUS

REPRESENTATIVE TREATISES
FROM THE ENNEADS

THE
ESSENTIAL
PLOTINUS

REPRESENTATIVE TREATISES
FROM THE ENNEADS

SELECTED AND NEWLY TRANSLATED
WITH INTRODUCTION AND COMMENTARY BY
ELMER O'BRIEN, S. J.

This republication, spring 1975, is dedicated by the
publisher in memorium to
JOHN W. KUNHARDT 1928-1974
FRANCIS D. WHITE   1923-1974

The editor wishes to thank Basil Blackwell & Mott Ltd.,
Oxford, and Harvard University Press, Cambridge, for
their kind permission to use selections from *Ancilla to
the Pre-Socratic Philosophers,* Kathleen Freeman's translation of
Die Fragmente der Vorsokratiker.

This edition of *The Essential Plotinus* is a facsimile reproduction
of the first printing, April, 1964, of The New American
Library edition.

Reprinted by HACKETT PUBLISHING COMPANY, INC.
          P.O. Box 55573
          Indianapolis, Indiana 46205

Distributed in Canada by FITZHENREY & WHITESIDE, LTD.
150 Lesmill Road
Don Mills, Ontario

Cover design by Melissa Martin Goldsmith

PRINTED IN THE UNITED STATES OF AMERICA

Preface

This long labor of love now achieved, I still feel a certain uneasiness in dubbing it, at my publisher's suggestion, *The Essential Plotinus*. Who would dare pretend that he had attained, especially within so small a compass as this brief book, to the essence of any man, much less of that most enigmatic of men, Plotinus?

To allay, then, the reader's likely uneasiness at such a seeming pretense on my part, let me say that here is the "essential" Plotinus as, for Coleridge, there was an "essential" poetry—that to which with the greatest pleasure a reader returns. To the treatises here presented, sixteen centuries of readers have, with the greatest pleasure, in season and out of season, returned.

E.O'B.
December 30, 1962

A Note on This Translation

The advantages today of reading the *Enneads* are not a few. Their particular nature has guided throughout the long labor that went into the making of this small book.

For those like his "born lover with an innate philosophic bent (V, 9 [5], 2)," there is heady instruction in what, existentially, they are. Whatever might be said of the rather gratuitous quality of Plotinus' metaphysics, agreement is general that his introspective analysis is of the best.

For the student of the history of ideas there is to be had at first hand the ideas that, even at second hand, molded Western thinking more than did those of a Plato or an Aristotle. Chiefly this shaping has been in the areas of religious speculation, a fact that—it might reasonably be argued—adds to its interest.

For the increasing number, accordingly, of those sophisticates of the intellect who are properly fascinated by the phenomenon of religious mysticism—its why, its whence, its whither—such treatises of the *Enneads* as are represented here are pretty much required reading. Mainly in accordance with the color of their school ties, scholars laud them as true mysticism or damn them as false mysticism. How talk, how think even, about mysticism true *or* false if one does not know these perduring sources of a centuries-old *cause célèbre?*

It is the editor's belief that the ten treatises provided here in their entirety are the essence of the *Enneads*.

That they should also be, in this new translation, essentially *Plotinus* and not somebody else's (particularly the editor's) idea of Plotinus, various precautionary measures were taken.

The translation itself was made from a conflation of Greek texts. Even the magisterial critical edition of Henry-Schwyzer could not simply be used without further adjustments because the high task of establishing an authentic reading continues apace among Plotinus scholars even since the publication of the first two volumes of their edition; indeed, it has been wonderfully quickened by the rich materials made available by them.

In making the translation, rather more than the text before one and a dictionary beside one was thought sufficient to determine what English word to use. Plotinus is the most difficult of any recognized author to translate. The Greek that he uses is not of the best. His way of using it borders, at times, on the contemptuous. Add to that the facts that he came to composition very late in life and composed with an unreflecting swiftness that was the astonishment of his contemporaries and refused to reread what he had composed with a disinterestedness—or concern for his failing eyesight—that was their admiration, and it will be seen that the translator has more than a fair share of problems on his hands. Therefore much reliance has been placed on the books, monographs, and articles that have appeared especially during the past two decades from the piled desks of that small, wholly admirable, international group of authorities in Plotinian research whose names peep in and out of the pages of this book. A knowledge of Greek is not sufficient if one would translate Plotinus aright. Nor does one's own knowledge of his thought suffice. To have good prospects of success there must be the unblushing pillaging of the work of these men. The present translator has done that. Without a blush.

He has also, to redress the balance somewhat, resisted the temptation of giving the thought of Plotinus a clarity it does not possess.

What clarity it does possess, the cross-references in the text, the references to sources, the related readings, and the Plotinus glossary should help to set in relief. For they serve to set him in relief.

Walt Whitman (after a fashion) comes to mind. "This is no book, cammerade. Who touches this touches a man . . ."

Contents

Introduction   13

BEAUTY (I, 6 [1])   33

THE INTELLIGENCE,
THE IDEAS, AND BEING (V, 9 [5])   45

THE DESCENT
OF THE SOUL (IV, 8 [6])   59

THE GOOD OR THE ONE (VI, 9 [9])   72

THE THREE PRIMAL
HYPOSTASES (V, 1 [10])   90

THE POST PRIMALS (V, 2 [11])   106

VIRTUE (I, 2 [19])   109

DIALECTIC (I, 3 [20])   119

THE SOUL (IV, 3 [27])   125

CONTEMPLATION (III, 8 [30])   162

Appendices:

I RELATED READINGS   176

II A PLOTINUS GLOSSARY   216

III SELECTED ANNOTATED BIBLIOGRAPHY   219

IV GUIDE TO SOURCES   223

THE
ESSENTIAL
PLOTINUS

Introduction

"Mystical classics," William James once said, "have neither birthday nor native land." [1]

He does not seem, strangely enough, to have been thinking at all of the *Enneads* of Plotinus [2] when he said it. Yet of no mystical classic is the observation more alarmingly true and the problem of Plotinus, as a result, is of a sort to introduce a small panic flutter into the hearts of historians. For historians, with a spinsterish instinct that does us little credit, like to have things neat, tabulated, pigeon-holed, and are distressed when this cannot be done. And it cannot be done with the doctrine of the *Enneads*. It has always managed to overleap the usual confinement of time and space in a fashion that would surely have warmed the curious old heart of its creator had he been able to foresee it; the most various of minds down the ages have served

[1] *Varieties of Religious Experience* (New York: New American Library, 1958), p. 321.
[2] Plotinus (204–270) in the last years of his career as philosopher wrote a number of short treatises dealing with particular points as they arose in the discussions of his school. After his death the most famous of his pupils, Porphyry (c. 232–p. 304), with exemplary piety and a rather less exemplary enthusiasm for the Pythagorean theory of numbers, vigorously edited the treatises into six groups of nine (i.e. *enneads*): "I was delighted to find," he tells us, "the product [in the number of treatises] of the perfect number six multiplied by the number nine." His arrangement is the one normally found in all subsequent editions and the convention is to refer to the individual treatises on that basis; thus, for instance, I, 6, 3 would mean the first *Ennead,* sixth treatise, third section. To that mode of reference a further designation is added throughout the present volume. Because of the importance of chronology for the understanding of an author's thought (especially this one), there is indicated, between square brackets, where a particular treatise belongs in the total. Thus I, 6 [1], 3 means the third section of the first treatise Plotinus wrote; V, 5 [31], 7, the seventh section of a treatise from his middle period— the thirty-first.

from time to time as its native land; the most unpropitious of circumstances have seemingly brought about its successive reincarnations in an Augustine, a Hugh of St. Victor, a Meister Eckhart.

Reincarnations. There, really, is the nub of the problem. Many a latter-day mystic has revealed himself as apparently a Plotinus *redivivus*. To determine whether or not he was, it is necessary to know the original, and such knowledge is not easy to come by.

The biographical information, what little of it we possess, is not overly helpful. [3] It is true that German historians of the last century made much of the fact that Plotinus had a bad stomach [4] on the supposition, it would seem, that mystic experience is only a somewhat more poetic expression of an ordinary dyspepsia; but the supposition, despite its inherent fascination, seems never to have been widely held. That the merest of accidents brought him to the shores of the Tiber when he had wanted all along to attain the very different shores of Indus and Ganges [5] is not particularly significant either, unless for the student of history's minor ironies, for Plotinus who had wished thus to become the pupil of Brahmin and Mithraist became instead the teacher, in succeeding generations, of both one and the other. [6] The fact of his long apprenticeship at Alexandria (for almost two decades he studied philosophy there) could be more of a hindrance than a help because Origen, the great Church Father, studied in the same place at almost the same time under the same master, and it is a commonplace how different from that of Plotinus his doctrine was. [7] That his genius—severely oriental—should have germi-

---

[3] The *Life of Plotinus* by Porphyry, which is to be found at the beginning of all complete editions of the *Enneads*, is one's sole source; recent scholarship has shown that the later contributions of Firmicus Maternus or Eunapius or Suidas have no independent value. (See Schwyzer in *Paulys Realencyklopädie der classischen Altertumswissenschaft*, XXI, 475–477.) The opening words of the *Life* indicate ruefully why the information is so meager: "Plotinus seemed ashamed of having a body."

[4] Porphyry, *Life of Plotinus*, Chapter 2.

[5] *op. cit.*, Chapter 3.

[6] Olivier Lacombe, "Note sur Plotin et la pensée indienne," *Annuaire de l'Ecole des Hautes Etudes* (Section science religieuse), 1950–51, pp. 3–17.

[7] For details: Hal Koch, *Pronoia und Paideusis: Studien über Origenes und sein Verhältnis zum Platonismus* (Berlin–Leipzig: De Gruyter, 1932), pp. 163–304.

nated and come to prodigious growth only after he took up residence in Rome in the summer of 244 at the age of forty is worthy of passing notice as an indication of that independence of time and place that characterized himself and his doctrines.

The historical approach, indispensable here, is not impossible for all of that. It is quite possible to ease one's entry into the complexities of Plotinus' mystical doctrine and arrive at a true assessment of it if one initially lays hold of certain of the basic doctrines he seems to have taken over from his predecessors. These basic doctrines first, then what Plotinus did with them: such will be the procedure here.

The first of them and by far the most important—the distinguishing characteristic of Plotinian mysticism and the *clef de voûte* of his entire speculative system—is the doctrine of The One, of a source and term of all being that transcends all being quite as it transcends all knowledge. He derived it, ultimately, from Philo (30 B.C.–40 A.D.). The good case that has been made for its being derivative rather from Plato [8] is not altogether convincing. It was Philo, after all, who effected that minor revolution in Greek thought that established as *point de départ* in philosophy not sense nature, which had hitherto been the accepted procedure, but instead a wholly transcendent and unknowable One.[9] The very unknowableness of the Plotinian One, if nothing else, should alert historians, one would be inclined to think, that it could not be Platonic in origin.

How Plotinus came upon it, since he seems never to have known the writings of Philo at first hand, is a matter about which scholars are happy to conjecture.[10] Albinus (fl. 152) or Numenius (fl. 160) were, very likely, the chief carriers. The doctrine, already elaborated and detached from its Old Testament origin, is discoverable in the writings of both

[8] E. R. Dodds, "The Parmenides of Plato and the Origin of the Neoplatonic One," *Classical Quarterly*, XXII (1928), 129–142.

[9] Régis Jolivet, *Saint Augustin et le néo-platonisme chrétien* (Paris: Denoël et Steele, 1932), pp. 108–9. *Cf.* Henri Guyot, *L'infinité divine* (Paris: Alcan, 1906) and especially Emile Bréhier, *Les idées philosophiques et religieuses de Philon d'Alexandrie*, 2e éd. (Paris: Vrin, 1925), pp. 78–9.

[10] According to Fritz Heinemann (*Plotin*, Leipzig: Meiner, 1921, p. 189, n.1), there is no evidence of direct or indirect contact in Plotinus' "first period"; according to W. R. Inge (*The Philosophy of Plotinus*, 3rd ed. London: Longmans, 1948, I, 97), there is no evidence anywhere of direct contact.

of them;[11] and we know the writings of Numenius at least were utilized by Plotinus, and to such a degree that he was accused in his own lifetime of "parading on the strength of Numenius' ideas." [12] And this Numenius, be it remarked for later reference, was a Pythagorean.

Secondly, there is the notion of the *Ego,* or the self, as a philosophic principle. By some it has been named the great original contribution of Plotinus' philosophy.[13] However, it seems closer to the truth to say that he derived it from the Later Stoics, in whom, in an elementary and unexploited form, it is clearly present.[14] This especially is a dependence that, once adverted to, can make one's progress through the *Enneads* considerably the easier; likely it was the Stoic residue still attaching to this idea that made acute and almost unsolvable the later antinomies of immanence and transcendence within the philosophy of Plotinus.

Thus far two speculative borrowings of some importance. There is, however, a third indebtedness of Plotinus to a predecessor, this time of a more practical sort.

Porphyry again is our informant that it was "by meditation and by the method that Plato teaches in the *Banquet*" that Plotinus "lifted himself . . . to the first and all-transcendent divinity." [15] The reference is to the passage wherein Socrates retails the words of Diotima, the wise woman of Mantinaea.[16] The method taught there is that of a twofold purgation of the mind, one qualitative, the other quantitative. The qualitative consists in a successive transposing of the object of one's thought to a plane progressively more immaterial and spiritual, more completely disengaged from the sense realm, more closely allied to the intelligible; three levels of knowing that correspond to three levels of life: physical beauty, moral beauty, intellectual beauty being the objects respectively of the body, of those parts of the soul ruled by the ethical virtues, and finally of the intelligence, that "eye of the soul," destined to contempla-

---

[11] Eduard Zeller, *Grundriss der Geschichte der Griechischen Philosophie,* 12. Aufl. (Leipzig: Reisland, 1920), pp. 322, 340–1.
[12] See Porphyry, *Life,* Chapter 18.
[13] Julius Stenzel, "Metaphysik des Altertums," *Handbuch der Philosophie,* I. Abt. (München: Oldenbourg, 1934), p. 56.
[14] Thus I. Heinemann, *Poseidonios' metaphysische Schriften* (Breslau: Marcus, 1912), pp. 62–3.
[15] *Life,* Chapter 23.
[16] See pp. 189–91.

tion. The quantitative purgation, in turn, consists in the progressive detachment from the singular, from all the individualities that may characterize this or that object loved; in a separation, that is, from the changing and the incidental in order to attach oneself to an object that is immovable, essential, fixed.

It was Plato who introduced Plotinus to the life of contemplation. He never forgot that lesson nor from whom he learned it.

It is the abiding temptation of the historian of ideas to account for every point of doctrine in a given author as an appropriation, conscious or unconscious, from someone who went before. It is the sort of thing that can lead right back to Adam and provide little or no clarification on the way. It is a temptation that the present author has no intention of giving in to here. The dependencies mentioned thus far, real enough in any case, have been noted merely to provide an entry, an entry three doors wide, into the Plotinian system; to set the stage, if I may change the metaphor, for the consideration of Plotinus' masterly interpreting of philosophical materials that were already widely extant before his time. What he did to them was a thing that seems never to have occurred to Philo, or to the Stoics, or to Plato, so there is no need of going back any further. It was Plotinus and no one else who detected the hidden virtualities of these very diverse doctrines, who separated them out from their context, refurbished them brightly in the large alembic of his mind, brought their latent potentialities to perfection, and expressed them finally in new formulae at once so penetrating and so suasive that it is small wonder so much of subsequent mystical speculation was willing to fall beneath his spell.

It is with the broad lines of that interpretative achievement which is the *Enneads* that we shall now concern ourselves, treating in turn the three themes already mentioned: The One, the dialectic of mystic experience, the self as philosophic principle.

THE ONE

Professor Gilson has remarked somewhere that it is with the historian of ideas as it is with the painter: eventual success or failure depends upon seeing the thing from the proper angle, that it all comes down to something as prosaic as putting one's chair, at the outset, in the right place. Anyone who would succeed in understanding Plotinus must seat himself squarely before the concept of The One.

And it is initially significant both of what he meant by it and of the difficulty of determining *exactly* what he meant by it that Plotinus would be the first to take exception to our referring to it as a concept:

> It would be better not to use the word "one" at all than use it here in the positive sense, for only confusion could come of that. The word is useful solely in getting the inquiry started aright to the extent that it designates absolute simplicity. But then even this designation must be promptly eliminated, for neither it nor any other designation can be applied to what no sound can convey, what cannot be known on any hearing. Only the contemplative knows it; and even he, should he seek to see a form, would know it not (V, 5 [32], 6).

Accordingly, after the initial positive designation (i.e. The One), which serves simply to orient one's efforts in the right direction, the procedure must be negative.

First of all, The One is not a number but the measure of number itself. "It is the measure and not the measured (V, 5 [32], 4)." This, despite the simplicity of expression, is high and complex doctrine. Dean Inge, with characteristic perceptiveness, lays hold of the essential: "We must be careful," he says, "not to give 'The One' a merely numerical sense. In this, the numerical sense, unity and plurality are correlative, so that we cannot have the former without the latter. In this sense the Absolute One would be an impossible abstraction. But for Plotinus the One is the source from which the differentiation of unity and plurality proceeds; it is the transcendence of separability rather than the negation of plurality." [17] Yet not all would go along with Inge's conclusion that had the Greeks a symbol for "zero" Plotinus might well have anticipated Scotus Eriugena who

[17] *The Philosophy of Plotinus*, II, 108.

called it *nihil*.[18] For Plotinus, it so happens, did elsewhere call it *to meden* (III, 8 [30], 10) quite as straightforwardly as Eriugena called it *nihil:* yet he did not mean "zero" any more than Eriugena did. For zero is within the numerical series and is not the measure of it, while according to the text of Plotinus just cited The One transcends the numerical series and is the measure of it. And although Dean Inge seems to have done so with the greatest of ease,[19] most would find it difficult to deny a residual Pythagorean content in the Plotinian notion of The One: for Plotinus as for the Pythagoreans The One is, statically, the unity by which all number is intelligible, and, dynamically, the unity whence and whither all multiplicity moves.[20] Numenius, the Neo-Pythagorean, being one of his informants, such a content is easily understandable.[21] In any case, this much is certain: Plotinus could never have meant "zero"; speculatively, at least, Plotinian mysticism does not end up in a void.[22] Psychologically, it is something else again, but of that later. Not number, then, but the measure of number, The One is not essence either because if it were it would be limited (V, 5 [32], 6); Plotinus seems never to have encompassed the idea of a reality that could be determinate (having, or being, an essence) and yet unterminated (not finite or limited).

Transcending essence it transcends being as well because being implies essence (V, 5 [32], 6). Plotinus, it may be interesting to note, was apparently the first to make the distinction between essence and existence, for although existence in his view implies essence, it is not identical with essence. On the contrary, that is his reason for denying existence to The One, for every existing thing is a determinate thing, its existence circumscribed by essence; thus it is that we can know them.

The One transcends thought, both because thought sup-

---

[18] *op. cit.*, pp. 107–8. Emile Bréhier agrees with Inge's interpretation; see his *La philosophie de Plotin* (Paris: Boivin, 1928), p. 161, n. 1.
[19] *loc. cit.*
[20] Léon Brunschvicq, *Le rôle du pythagorisme dans l'évolution des idées* (Paris: Hermann, 1937), p. 5.
[21] In fact, in the sentence immediately preceding the passage under discussion Plotinus remarks, "The Pythagoreans refer symbolically to The One as 'Apollo' "—that is, as "Not (*a*) Many (*pollon*)." He was obviously thinking in Pythagorean terms.
[22] *See* p. 30.

poses being and essence (I, 7 [54], 1), and because it implies the duality of knower and known (III, 9 [13], 1).

All these are reasons for his view, surely, but not wholly satisfactory ones if taken, as we have taken them thus far, in isolation. But they are founded upon, and have their root justification in, one of Plotinus' most fundamental ideas, that of the nature of causality. The One is not essence nor existence nor intellect nor intelligible because of all of these it is the generative principle and to be thus generative it must be, in this precise regard, "other." To the plaint of either man in the street or professional philosopher that you cannot give what you have not got, his response is regal: "It is not necessary that one have what one gives (VI, 7 [38], 17)."

The One, therefore, transcendent to all differentiation and form, is the source of all.

It is, as well, the term. "The starting point is universally the goal (III, 8 [30], 7)." This is the principle, that in our end is our beginning, which will provide the speculative ingredients of the medieval view of the cosmos that, wittingly or unwittingly, most Christian mystics have made their own.

In that charming view all creation moved in a giant cyclic rhythm, an endless and varied dynamic of process and return. From The One and to The One the multiple eddied and swirled within an ordered pattern that Faith (aided by Plotinus) beheld and that Reason (with his further help) did the best it could to explain. It was the "Thee, God, I come from, to Thee go" of Hopkins centuries later. Yet, to the medieval way of thinking, anything—animate or inanimate—might with equal justice voice that same cry. Such was the pattern on which, as the most faithful reflex of the reality he set himself to discuss, St. Thomas constructed his *Summa Theologica*. It was the schema that many a medieval mystic attempted to reproduce within him, in order to achieve his itinerary to God. It was an idea that came like a flame through the most devious channels of chance phrases, garbled translations, and the rest, to fire the theological genius of such diverse minds as those of Scotus Eriugena, Hugh of St. Victor, Meister Eckhart. The Middle Ages itself performed a masterly exegesis on Plotinian material, an achievement all the more extraordinary when one recalls that apparently it never knew a single word of his at first hand.

According to Plotinus, then, The One is term because it is principle, at the origin of the return because it is the source of participation. Effect is drawn towards cause. Image tends towards prototype. There is at the core of every existing thing an ontic desire for what is lacking to its perfectness, and this perfectness it can find in its fullness solely within that which initially engendered it. Indigence is at the root of this ontic desire. But not merely indigence. There is as well the drive to make up for this indigence. It is a commonplace in Plato that Desire is the child of Penury and Plenitude, and here Plotinus agrees with him. It is what centuries later Pascal has God say to the Christian soul: "You would not seek Me if you had not already found Me."

The source whence came the human soul is the transcendent and unknowable One. The soul's final term, its destiny, its home, is the same transcendent and unknowable One.[23] But it is not only its final term; it is the peak to which in this life the soul should strive to attain however intermittently (III, 8 [30], 5). The manner of its striving is our next concern.

THE DIALECTIC OF THE RETURN

There are three stages of the soul's mystical return to The One with which Plotinus especially concerns himself. His dependence in all this upon the Plato of the *Banquet* is very real, but it is, as we have remarked, not so much a doctrinal as a practical dependence: a method was provided that introduced him into the forecourt of his own eventual complex experience. His own doctrinal exposition supposes it, but is devoted to the later and higher levels of the return to The One.

The first of these stages is attained by separation from the realm of multiplicity, from the "here below" (I, 3 [20], 1). Its term is the intelligible realm (*loc. cit.*). For Plotinus the "intelligible realm" is at once the separate and supreme Intelligence and the World of Forms, made up

[23] V, 4 [7], 1; VI, 9 [9], 3 and 6; V, 2 [11], 1; V, 5 [32], 6; VI, 7 [38], 17 and 32; V, 3 [49], 13; I, 7 [54], 1.

(against Plato) of the forms of individuals that (against the materializations of practically all other ancient philosophers) are not a measurable area of that World nor pieces of The Intelligence. For Plotinus one is what—even on the intellectual level—one does.[24] As a result, these stages, even including the first, are levels of transformation into an otherness that is yet one's most interior selfhood.[25]

The second stage is attained by separation from a more lofty multiplicity, from reasoning itself: "It leaves to another art the so-called logical inquiry that treats of propositions and syllogisms (I, 3 [20], 4)." Its term is the highest point in the intelligible realm: "The second [stage is] for those who have already reached [the intelligible realm] and taken root there and who must proceed from there till they have reached the summit, the highest point in the realm of intelligence, which is the goal of their journeying (I, 3 [20], 1)."

The second stage completes the first and is never achieved without it. The first—propaideutic—is the *via negativa*, apophatic as the later mystical writers will say; it is the area of the rejection of images. The second, an interim stage, is, despite its purgative effects, positive and cataphatic.

These first two stages of the way lead "towards" rather than "to" The One. They are only successive despoilments, indispensable yet only preparatory, their highest achievement being still enveloped within the intelligible. And beyond the intelligible is The One. How attain it? How know the unknowable? How can intellect grasp what is beyond intellect?

There are, according to Plotinus, two capacities of the intellect: *to noein*—the ability to act as intellect, by which in "possession of its faculties" it beholds what is within it; and *to me noein*—the ability not to act as intellect, by which "inebriated" and outside itself it attains to what is beyond it (VI, 7 [38], 35).

The intellect's penchant for getting drunk, for being ren-

---

[24] *See* VI, 7 [38], 6, on the three men—intelligible, sensible, and intermediary—that are potentially in us.
[25] Here is evident the difficulty in which his borrowings from the Stoics left him when attempting to resolve the immanence-transcendence antinomy. *Cf.* Joseph Maréchal, *Etudes sur la psychologie des mystiques* (Paris: Desclée De Brouwer, 1937), II, 426–7.

dered tipsy by deep draughts of, one might suppose, intellectual day has always been highly regarded in the Neoplatonic tradition. Recall the jibes leveled at Aristotle by the Neoplatonists as though he were official philosopher of an intellectual temperance league. The sneer of Proclus is famous: "Aristotle leads one up to acts of understanding with never a hint that there is anything beyond them." [26] And, like Plotinus, Proclus distinguishes between a knowledge wherein man acts as intellect, proceeding by the way of affirmation, and one wherein man acts as not being intellect, and in which "he sees The One, or rather does not see it" because "what one sees is still intelligible" and not supra-intelligible.[27] Thus for Proclus this capacity of attaining directly to the transcendent and unknowable is above intellect.[28] But for Plotinus it is not. It is the capacity of intellect itself, which it always has, although it uses it rarely (VI, 7 [38], 35). He characterizes it in these words: "Because it is intellect, it contemplates what it contemplates [The One] by reason of that in it which is not intellect (V, 5 [32], 8)." Intellect has in its most profound reality the capacity for going beyond itself into the nonintelligible. There is little doubt where his preference lies between intellect which behaves as intellect, that calm and reasonable intellect (*nous emphrôn*), and intellect which does not (*nous erôn*), which is drunk with love (VI, 7 [38], 35).

He would appear from all this to have put within nature a tendency to its own destruction: intellect has an ontic drive to nonintellect. But such a disastrous consequence is deducible only if one persist in reading somebody else's philosophy into that of Plotinus. According to his own system everything is dominated by, proceeds from, and is drawn to a transcendent and unknowable One. To The One the soul must return: it is the law embedded in its ontological structure. It cannot wholly return by knowledge, because knowledge implies duality, not merely the duality of discursive thought (which is excluded early) but the duality of intuitive thought as well, and so long as it abides

---

[26] "De Providentia et Fato," *Opera,* V. Cousin, ed. (Paris: Eberhart, 1820–7), III, 171.

[27] *op. cit.,* 172.

[28] "In Parmenidem Platonis," *op. cit.,* VI, 1045, 1047, 1074–5.

in knowledge the soul has not fulfilled its destiny. It can return completely to The One only by the elimination of these ordinary intellectual processes. Then the unfettered deploying of that which is basic to them, desire, becomes possible. This, then, is not destruction but fulfillment. It is, in his own vigorous language, a blow, a capture, a sort of ravishment, fulfillment, and of course inebriation.[29]

Just as every other act is meaningful only in the dynamic of process from and return to The One, so also that of intellect. The intellect's ordinary cognitive acts are both intermediate manifestations and progressive releases of that desire and, at the last stage of inner purgation, they must be silenced and stilled so that nothing remains except root desire unencumbered now and wholly released.

That is the reason why the most appropriate term to describe the experience is ecstasy, not merely in the conventional sense that the exercise of the faculties, internal and external, is suspended, nor that the mystic is beyond the realm of conceptual thought, but that, in the primal sense of the word *ekstasis,* the mystic "stands outside" himself.[30] He has gone beyond the contingency of the ego and is fixed, established upon, something immovable that intimately penetrates the ego while infinitely transcending it. His efforts have been a grasping aloft, if you will, not into a void but into plenitude, the plenitude in which all the fumbling potentialities of the ego are luminously fulfilled, because these potentialities were never anything more than shadows of this substance, partial sharings in this plenitude.

THE EGO

Plotinus provides a number of variations on the philosophical theme of the ego, the self. The variations, all of them, will mysteriously reappear in mystical writings of later centuries.

Man as Microcosm

The idea that man is somehow a world in little, a complex and obscurely explanatory summary of the universe, is one that, however bizarre and seemingly ill-adapted to

[29] VI, 7 [38], 31; V, 8 [31], 10 and 11; VI, 8 [39], 11; VI, 9 [9], 7; V, 8 [31], 10.
[30] VI, 9 [9], 11; VI, 7 [38], 17; V, 3 [49], 7.

the modern mind, has nevertheless played a long and frequently significant role in the most varied sort of speculation, and it is not indeed fully unknown to modern thought: there is much of it in Fechner and in the social theory of Spencer, and, of course, the nineteenth century had as well the entire *Mikrokosmos* of Hermann Lotze.

Although only with Plotinus, who, as we said, was the first clearly to establish self as a philosophical principle, would it have a speculative atmosphere wholly congenial to its development, it makes brief appearances in previous systems that are extremely dissimilar and not, one would think, congenial to it at all. Anaximander, Anaximenes, Heracleitus, Democritus, the Plato of the *Philebus*, the Aristotle of the *Physics* might be cited as instances. But all extensive treatment is discoverable, as one might likely expect, in authors more directly tributary to Plotinus, as for instance the Stoics, Poseidonius, and especially Philo. Philo, in particular, is an interesting source, and the orientation he gave the notion is the more remarkable in that at one time he considered it to be only an aberrant metaphor.[31] He it was who made the connection between man-as-microcosm and the extremely important mystical concept of man-as-image (of which we will treat later)[32] and situated the whole in a context of process and return.[33]

The eventual restatement of the doctrine by Plotinus, although it might at first seem a retrogression after Philo, contains all the ingredients that later ages will variously exploit and contains them, further, arranged in such a pattern that subsequent exploitation for all its variety will always be essentially in terms of mystic experience: "The soul is many things, linked to the realm of sense by what is lowest in us, linked to the intelligible realm by what is highest. For each of us is an intelligible cosmos. By what is intellective, we are permanently in the higher realm; by our lower part, we are prisoners of sense." [34]

If one but recall what has been said about his dialectic of the return, Plotinus' doctrine of man-the-microcosm

---

[31] "Quis Rerum Divinarum Heres Sit," *Opera Quae Supersunt*, L. Cohn and P. Wendland, edd. (Berlin: Reimer, 1896ff.), III, 502 c.
[32] *See* p. 28.
[33] "De Opificio," *op. cit.*, I, 69, on which see Bréhier, *Les idées philosophiques et religieuses de Philon*, p. 169.
[34] III, 4 [15], 3; *cf.* III, 9 [13], 2; IV, 4 [28], 11.

comes pretty much to this: Within this world-in-little, man, the cyclic rhythm perceptible throughout the universe-at-large, the macrocosm, is to be recurrently portrayed. Mediate term of the return is the intellect within us, that which is most properly self (I, 1 [53], 10) and which is linked to the intelligible; the mode of return is by withdrawal from the multiple and lowest in us, which we share with material and sentient nature, to that which is approximative to The One and highest in us and which we share with The Intelligence and where is encountered the mysterious upsurge to The One.

This affinity he establishes between mystic and cosmos, rooted as it is in the notion of man-the-microcosm, explanatory—as it at least pretends to be—of both mystic and cosmos, economical accordingly in a manner appealing to the most various minds (for everyone prefers one apparently fundamental and cohesive reason to a scattered plurality), will be exploited for all it is worth (and for perhaps considerably more than it is worth) until the Middle Ages and beyond.[35]

Introspection

To be the correlative of the cyclic rhythm of the macrocosm, the inner rhythm of the microcosm must somehow tend towards a oneness.

Plotinus, as we have already noted, speaks of an inner movement of the soul preparatory to union, which is at least a flight from multiplicity. It is an aspect of his doctrine that must be considered here in somewhat greater detail since it is particularly pertinent to the matter at hand.

Plato, in a passage that has been called, with considerable justice, "the Magna Charta of Western mysticism," [36] wrote as follows:

[35] See Rudolph Allers, "Microcosmos from Anaximandros to Paracelsus," Traditio, II (1944), 319–407.
[36] Rufus M. Jones, "Liberalism in the Mystical Tradition," in David E. Roberts and Henry Pitney Van Dusen, Liberal Theology: An Appraisal (New York: Scribner's, 1942), p. 124.

When the mind returns into itself from the confusion
of sense [that is, of cave life], as it does when it reflects,
it passes into another region of that which is pure and
everlasting, immortal and unchanging, and feels itself
kindred thereto, and its welfare under its own control
and at rest from its wanderings, being in communion
with the unchanging (Phaedo 79 c).

One might well prefer that a "Magna Charta" be less
vague, less imaginative, more positive than this. Plotinus
made it so. He clarified the point of origin, defined the intermediary and final terms, described the mode of movement, and afforded finally the justification of introspection
as a practice that is liberative rather than inhibiting.

The introspection that leads towards The One is initially
directed at sensation as inherently multiple (I, 3 [20], 1-2)
and subsequently at the self as engaged in discursive thinking (I, 3 [20], 4; cf. V, 5 [32], 4). Its final term, of course,
is the transcendent One (V, 5 [32], 4, etc.). The intermediate term is what he calls the "center of the soul (VI, 9
[9], 8)." The mode of movement is a deliberate "drawing
inward" of thought, a sort of recessive suction of the intellect into itself.[37]

Such introspection is a liberative process, the much-
desired "flight from here below (I, 2 [19], 1)," because
by it the soul is brought to that point of utmost simplicity
within itself where the last veil of multiplicity is easily
pierced and the soul carried beyond and above even that
slight, residual multiplicity back to its homeland, The One,
which is

present only to those who are prepared and are able to
receive it, to enter into harmony with it, to grasp
and to touch it by virtue of their likeness to it, by
virtue of that inner power similar to and stemming
from The One when it is in that state in which it was
when it originated from The One. Thus will The One

---

[37] VI, 9 [9], 8. In this, the key passage, Plotinus speaks of a "circling,"
not a "drawing inward." Neither expression is wholly happy because
there is no question of spatial motion, but the second has the advantage
of being rather more in conformity with the general tenor of his thought.
The movement seems not unlike the *encogimiento* of St. Teresa (*Interior
Castle*, IV, 3).

be "seen" as far as it can become an object of contemplation. . . . [For] all discourse of reason left behind, established now in its own beauty, the contemplative is suddenly swept by the wave of The Intelligence beneath and carried on high and sees, never knowing how; vision floods the eyes with light but it is not light that shows some other thing; the light is itself the vision.[38]

Man the Image

The inscription above the cave of the Delphic Oracle, *Know Thyself,* has had a long and varied history in Christian religious thought. During the last several centuries it has managed to become the capsule expression of what may be termed a circumspect voluntarism, inculcating under classic auspices the necessity of an unbiased appraisal of the girth, firmness, and lifting capacities of one's spiritual biceps. But in earlier times it had for the most part a loftier, if less helpful, connotation. It is that connotation that provides a vast clarification of the stages of the mystic return to The One.

It will be recalled that, for Plotinus, man is essentially intellect (I, 4 [46], 4) and that human intelligence in turn is the closest approximation to The Intelligence (VI, 2 [43], 22); that in withdrawing into his intelligence, man withdraws into The Intelligence of which his is the emanated effulgence (VI, 7 [38], 13). This preliminary withdrawal is by way of knowledge, by that capacity of intellect insofar as it is intellect, so that, in other words, in thus knowing himself man knows the "divine," sees (in seeing his own inner beauty) "the radiance of The Intelligence" (I, 6 [1], 5).[39]

This doctrine became characteristic of almost all subsequent Christian speculation on mystical experience for, given the teaching of the book of Genesis (1: 26-27) that man was created in the image of God, it was inevitable that the biblical data be thought to confirm the insight of

---

[38] VI, 9 [9], 4, and VI, 7 [38], 36. *Cf.* VI, 7 [38], 35.
[39] Basic to all this is the Neoplatonic (and un-Aristotelian) principle that like is known by like.

Plotinus. For Platonic thinkers, such as Gregory of Nyssa
and Augustine, it became a basic motif. The soul knows
God, they said, not by concluding from external things nor
yet by a deduction from a series of attributes to a concept,
but by a return to its own proper interior, a return that is at
the same time a willed separation from exteriority. True
knowledge of self and true knowledge of God are so intimately linked within the soul that, if the soul is purified
of all that is not itself, it knows at one and the same time
itself, and in itself, God.[40]

The Center of the Soul

No other theme is more widely met with in the writings
of the mystics than that of the soul's center being somehow
the area of mystic experience.

Plotinus called the mediate term of the return "the center
of the soul (VI, 9 [9], 8)." That phrase, Rufus Jones has
said,

> went across the world like a winged seed to spring up
> and bear fruit wherever there was suitable soil for
> it. . . . It is obvious what Plotinus meant by it in the
> context where it occurs, the "soul-center" which at-
> taches—is "bound by gold chains"—to its eternal
> source. But *kentron* in biblical Greek, and very often
> too, in classical Greek, means a sharp point, or a
> goad or an apex. There naturally sprang from it the
> idea of the "apex of the soul" as its point of contact
> with the divine. . . . From Plotinus there came into
> circulation, then, the two phrases, "the apex of the
> soul" and "the soul-center," and both terms meant
> that essential Divine bestowal which links the Soul
> with God.[41]

Various names will be given it later: the *centro del alma*
by St. Teresa, *la fine pointe de l'âme* by St. Francis of

---

[40] *Cf.* Endre von Ivanka, "Die unmittelbare Gotteserkenntnis als Grund-
lage des natürlichen Erkennens und als Ziel des übernatürlichen Streb-
ens bei Augustin," *Scholastik*, XIII (1938), 522.
[41] "Liberalism in the Mystical Tradition," p. 130.

Sales, the *burgelin* by Eckhart. But it will always be present, the variation of the term chosen depending, it would seem, upon the variety of mystic experience that is had, *i.e.*, whether it is an experience of divine immanence or of divine transcendence.

MYSTICAL EXPERIENCE ACCORDING TO PLOTINUS

The clearest thing Plotinus says of mystical experience itself is to be found in the comparison he makes of it to the condition of a person absorbed in his reading to the point of being unaware that he is reading (I, 4 [46], 10). Such a one has broken through the barrier that ordinarily stands between himself, as knowing subject, and the object of his knowledge; there is no longer consciousness of himself as subject because he is situated now at the interior of the object. He is not reasoning, evaluating, judging. He is not reflecting upon himself nor is he reflecting upon his reactions; as soon as he does, the absorption is destroyed and he is once more placed at a remove from the object of his knowledge. His absorbed state is a *pathema*, he is "acted upon."

With this comparison in mind, it is rather easier to understand what Plotinus means by saying that it is a presence that is felt rather than a knowledge that is had (VI, 9 [9], 4), for in the act of knowledge there is always the aspect of "otherness," which, at least upon subsequent reflection, can be detected as one of the components in all cognition. More intelligible as well becomes what he says of its being the presence of a light (V, 3 [49], 17) that is not joined to the form of an object but is light by itself and in itself (V, 5 [32], 7). And his saying that it is an unconsciousness that is not a vacuity (VI, 7 [38], 34) also makes quite good sense since the areas of normal consciousness are filled by the total "action upon" one (III, 8 [30], 6).

Any attempt to disengage the ontological suppositions of the experience Plotinus describes necessarily leads one to a level more basic still. The ontology of Plotinus reposes upon the psychology of introspection. Introspectively, he found the twin consciousnesses, the empirical and the metaphysical, of which Kristeller has justifiably made so much.[42] Both spoke to him of incompleteness, desire—the empirical in terms of the fluctuations and recurrent inadequacies of one's daily living, which to the reflex understanding implies the stable and the perfect (for how else experience them as inadequate?); the metaphysical in terms of the transcendency of mind over matter, of its capacity to disengage itself from the drag of matter and the confusion of the multiple by unitive intuitions which, however, always have at their interior the seeds of disillusion that in turn imply once again the stable, the perfect, the finally unitive.

Therefore, he *postulates* the stable, the perfect, the finally unitive. The wish is father to the thought; it is sentiment, overlaid with speculation, that founds the synthesis.

No exception is being taken here to the operative presence of sentiment in the construction of a philosophic system, nor to Plotinus' long odyssey of the mind having been, really, a sentimental journey: sentiment has been an accepted human commodity for rather too long a time for one to begin quarreling with it now.

The point is rather this: the nature of the ultimately real, what it is and why it must be what it is, is determined by felt need; it is what desire, in search of rest, wants it to be. Therefore, it is not an essence, for every essence, every "Whatness," attained, becomes—because limited—just another "Why?". Still less is it an existent, because every existent implies essence. It is not an intelligence, because every intelligence—as intelligence—implies the duality of knowing, a genuine multiplicity however rarefied and minimal. And multiplicity, the experienced occasion of one's unrest, cannot be the cause of one's rest. Stable, perfective, unitive, it is called The One because there is no better name for it. Indeed, it is the best of names for it because it is the term of the escape from the multiple.

Man, the soul, is essentially desire. Means to the fulfillment of desire are accorded the soul by what is highest in it, the intellect. By progressive eliminations of what is multiple in the operations of intellect one ascends to the point where there remains nothing but the assimilative

[42] P. O. Kristeller, *Der Begriff der Seele in der Ethik des Plotin* (Tübingen: Mohr, 1929).

capacity of intellect, the being able to be absorbed into the center of the soul, where the soul as desire becomes wholly unfettered and is caught out of itself. Ecstasy, it is not knowledge, for the faculty of knowledge is stilled. It is union of soul with The One. It is, Plotinus hoped, desire fulfilled.

BEAUTY

(I, 6 [1])

This, the earliest of the treatises, is an admirable introduction to all the rest. There is here a simplicity of presentation that Plotinus was to find impossible to maintain in discussing other subjects, and his method—the same from the beginning to the end of his productive life—can therefore be the more easily grasped. Here, too, there is a noble care for language and even for the occasional polished phrase that haste of composition or failing eyesight would later preclude. And here, finally, are all the basic themes of the total Plotinian synthesis. For centuries *Beauty* was the sole treatise by which Plotinus was known. But, such is its quality, succeeding generations knew their Plotinus well in knowing only it.

The entire discussion in the treatise is situated deliberately within a Platonic framework, where alone Plotinus felt himself completely at home. But here, as often later, the framework is less what Plato himself erected than what Plotinus believed he would have liked to erect, so that there are often subtle and unannounced corrections of Plato's thought even while he is using Plato's words. It is, one must admit, a most disarming instance of the *Amicus Plato, sed magis amica veritas.*

1. Chiefly beauty is visual. Yet in word patterns and in music (for cadences and rhythms are beautiful) it addresses itself to the hearing as well. Dedicated living, achievement, character, intellectual pursuits are beautiful to those who rise above the realm of the senses; to such ones the virtues, too, are beautiful. Whether the range of beauty goes beyond these will become clear in the course of this exposition.

What makes bodily forms beautiful to behold and has one give ear to sounds because they are "beautiful"? Why is it that whatever takes its rise directly from the soul is, in each instance, beautiful? Is everything beautiful with the one same beauty, or is there a beauty proper to the bodily and another to the bodiless? What, one or many, is beauty? [1]

Some things, as the virtues, are themselves beautiful. Others, as bodily forms, are not themselves beautiful but are beautiful because of something added to them: the same bodies are seen to be at times beautiful, at other times not, so that to be body is one thing and to be beautiful is something else again.

Now what this something is that is manifest in some bodily forms we must inquire into first. Could we discover what this is—what it is that lures the eyes of onlookers, bends them to itself, and makes them pleased with what they see—we could "mount this ladder" for a wider view.

On every side [2] it is said that visual beauty is constituted by symmetry of parts one with another and with the whole (and, in addition, "goodly coloration" [3]); that in things seen (as, generally speaking, in all things else) the beautiful simply is the symmetrical and proportioned. Of necessity, say those who hold this theory, only a composite is beautiful, something without parts will never be beautiful; and then, they say, it is only the whole that is beautiful, the parts having no beauty except as constituting the whole.

However, that the whole be beautiful, its parts must be

---

[1] The close dependence of these introductory queries and observations upon the Platonic *Greater Hippias* 297 c–298 b is beyond question.
[2] A slight exaggeration. However, the symmetry theory of beauty professed by the Stoics was, in Plotinus' day, the prevailing one.
[3] A small philosophic sneer at the requirement demanded by Cicero (*Tusculan Disputations*, IV, 31) before him and Augustine (*The City of God*, XXII, 19) after him.

so, too; as beautiful, it cannot be the sum of ugliness:
beauty must pervade it wholly. Further: colors, beautiful
hues as those of the sun, this theory would rule out; no
parts, therefore no symmetry, therefore no beauty. But is
not gold beautiful? And a single star by night? [4] It is the
same with sound: the simple tone would be proscribed,
yet how often each of the sounds that contribute to a
beautiful ensemble is, all by itself, beautiful. When one
sees the same face, constant in its symmetry, now beautiful
and now not, is it not obvious that beauty is other than
symmetry, that symmetry draws its beauty from something
else?

And what of the beauty of dedicated lives, of thought
expressed? Is symmetry here the cause? Who would suggest there is symmetry in such lives, or in laws, or in intellectual pursuits?

What symmetry is there in points of abstract thought?
That of being accordant with one another? There may be
accord, even complete agreement, where there is nothing
particularly estimable: the idea that "temperance is folly"
fits in with the idea that "justice is naïve generosity"; the
accord is perfect.

Then again, every virtue is a beauty of The Soul—more
authentically beautiful than anything mentioned so far.
The Soul, it is true, is not a simple unity. Yet neither does
it have quantitative numerical symmetry. What yardstick
could preside over the balancing and interplay of The
Soul's potencies and purposes?

Finally, in what would the beauty of that solitary, The
Intelligence, consist?

2.   Let us, then, go back to the beginning and determine what beauty is in bodily forms.

Clearly it is something detected at a first glance,
something that the soul—remembering—names, recognizes, gives welcome to, and, in a way, fuses with. When
the soul falls in with ugliness, it shrinks back, repulses it,
turns away from it as disagreeable and alien. We therefore
suggest that the soul, being what it is and related to the
reality above it, is delighted when it sees any signs of

---

[4] We accept here the argumentation of Harder and his textual emenda-
tion (*Plotins Schriften*, I, 369–70).

kinship or anything that is akin to itself, takes its own to itself, and is stirred to new awareness of whence and what it really is.

But is there any similarity between loveliness here below and that of the intelligible realm? If there is, then the two orders will be—in this—alike. What can they have in common, beauty here and beauty there? They have, we suggest, this in common: they are sharers of the same Idea.

As long as any shapelessness that admits of being patterned and shaped does not share in reason or in Idea, it continues to be ugly and foreign to that above it. It is utter ugliness since all ugliness comes from an insufficient mastery by form and reason, matter not yielding at every point to formation in accord with Idea. When Idea enters in, it groups and arranges what, from a manifold of parts, is to become a unit; contention it transforms into collaboration, making the totality one coherent harmoniousness, because Idea is one and one as well (to the degree possible to a composite of many parts) must be the being it informs.

In what is thus compacted to unity, beauty resides, present to the parts and to the whole. In what is naturally unified, its parts being all alike, beauty is present to the whole. Thus there is the beauty craftsmanship confers upon a house, let us say, and all its parts, and there is the beauty some natural quality may give to a single stone.

3. The beauty, then, of bodily forms comes about in this way—from communion with the intelligible realm. Either the soul has a faculty that is peculiarly sensitive to this beauty—one incomparably sure in recognizing what is kin to it, while the entire soul concurs— or the soul itself reacts without intermediary, affirms a thing to be beautiful if it finds it accordant with its own inner Idea, which it uses as canon of accuracy.

What accordance can there be between the bodily and the prior to the bodily? That is like asking on what grounds an architect, who has built a house in keeping with his own idea of a house, says that it is beautiful. Is it not that the house, aside from the stones, is inner idea stamped upon outer material, unity manifest in diversity? When one discerns in the bodily the Idea that binds and masters matter of itself formless and indeed recalcitrant to formation, and when one also detects an uncommon form stamped upon those that are common, then at a stroke one grasps the scattered multiplicity, gathers it together, and draws it within oneself to present it there to one's interior and indivisible oneness as concordant, congenial, a friend. The procedure is not unlike that of a virtuous man recognizing in a youth tokens of a virtue that is in accord with his own achieved goodness.

The beauty of a simple color is from form: reason and Idea, an invasion of incorporeal light, overwhelm the darkness inherent in matter. That is why fire glows with a beauty beyond all other bodies, for fire holds the rank of Idea in their regard. Always struggling aloft, this subtlest of elements is at the last limits of the bodily. It admits no other into itself, while all bodies else give it entry; it is not cooled by them, they are warmed by it; it has color primally, they receive color from it. It sparkles and glows like an Idea. Bodies unable to sustain its light cease being beautiful because they thus cease sharing the very form of color in its fullness.

In the realm of sound, unheard harmonies create harmonies we hear because they stir to an awareness of beauty by showing it to be the single essence in diversity. The measures in music, you see, are not arbitrary, but fixed by the Idea whose office is the mastering of matter.

This will suffice for the beauties of the realm of sense, which—images, shadow pictures, fugitives—have invaded matter, there to adorn and to ravish wherever they are perceived.

4. But there are beauties more lofty than these, imperceptible to sense, that the soul without aid of sense perceives and proclaims. To perceive them we must go higher, leaving sensation behind on its own low level.

It is impossible to talk about bodily beauty if one, like one born blind, has never seen and known bodily beauty. In the same way, it is impossible to talk about the "luster" of right living and of learning and of the like if one has never cared for such things, never beheld "the face of justice" and temperance and seen it to be "beyond the beauty of evening or morning star." Seeing of this sort is done only with the eye of the soul. And, seeing thus, one undergoes a joy, a wonder, and a distress more deep than any other because here one touches truth.

Such emotion all beauty must induce—an astonishment, a delicious wonderment, a longing, a love, a trembling that is all delight. It may be felt for things invisible quite as for things you see, and indeed the soul does feel it. All souls, we can say, feel it, but souls that are apt for love feel it especially. It is the same here as with bodily beauty. All perceive it. Not all are stung sharply by it. Only they whom we call lovers ever are.

5. These lovers of beauty beyond the realm of sense must be made to declare themselves.

What is your experience in beholding beauty in actions, manners, temperate behavior, in all the acts and intents of virtue? Or the beauty in souls? What do you feel when you see that you are yourselves all beautiful within? What is this intoxication, this exultation, this longing to break away from the body and live sunken within yourselves? All true lovers experience it. But what awakens so much passion? It is not shape, or color, or size. It is the soul, itself "colorless," and the soul's temperance and the hueless "luster" of its virtues. In yourselves or others you see largeness of spirit, goodness of life, chasteness, the courage behind a majestic countenance, gravity, the self-respect that pervades a temperament that is calm and at peace and without passion; and above them all you see the radiance of The Intelligence diffusing itself throughout them all. They are attractive, they are lovable. Why are they said to be beautiful? "Because clearly they are beautiful and anyone that sees them must admit that they are true realities." What sort of realities? "Beautiful ones." But reason wants to know why they make the soul lovable, wants to know what it is that, like a light, shines through all the virtues.

Let us take the contrary, the soul's varied ugliness, and contrast it with beauty; for us to know what ugliness is and why it puts in its appearance may help us attain our purpose here.

Take, then, an ugly soul. It is dissolute, unjust, teeming with lusts, torn by inner discord, beset by craven fears and petty envies. It thinks indeed. But it thinks only of the perishable and the base. In everything perverse, friend to filthy pleasures, it lives a life abandoned to bodily sensation and enjoys its depravity. Ought we not say that this ugliness has come to it as an evil from without, soiling it, rendering it filthy, "encumbering it" with turpitude of every sort, so that it no longer has an activity or a sensation that is clean? For the life it leads is dark with evil, sunk in manifold death. It sees no longer what the soul should see. It can no longer rest within itself but is forever being dragged towards the external, the lower, the dark. It is a filthy thing, I say, borne every which way by the allurement of objects of sense, branded by the bodily, always immersed in matter and sucking matter into itself. In its trafficking with the unworthy it has bartered its Idea for a nature foreign to itself.

If someone is immersed in mire or daubed with mud, his native comeliness disappears; all one sees is the mire and mud with which he is covered. Ugliness is due to the alien matter that encrusts him. If he would be attractive once more, he has to wash himself, get clean again, make himself what he was before. Thus we would be right in saying that ugliness of soul comes from its mingling with, fusion with, collapse into the bodily and material: the soul is ugly when it is not purely itself. It is the same as with gold that is mixed with earthy particles. If they are worked out, the gold is left and it is beautiful; separated from all that is foreign to it, it is gold with gold alone. So also the soul. Separated from the desires that come to it from the body with which it has all too close a union, cleansed of the passions, washed clean of all that embodiment has daubed it with, withdrawn into itself again—at that moment the ugliness, which is foreign to the soul, vanishes.[5]

6. For it is as was said of old: "Temperance, courage, every virtue—even prudence itself—are purifications." That is why in initiation into the mystery religions the idea is adumbrated that the unpurified soul, even in Hades, will still be immersed in filth because the unpurified loves filth for filth's sake quite as swine, foul of body, find their joy in foulness. For what is temperance, rightly so called, but to abstain from the pleasures of the body, to reject them rather as unclean and unworthy of the clean? What else is courage but being

[5] This theory of ugliness is a constant in Plotinian thought, expressed here in what apparently is the first of his treatises and as well in the treatise, *On the Origin of Evil* (I, 8 [51]), which is one of his last.

unafraid of death, that mere parting of soul from body, an event no one can fear whose happiness lies in being his own unmingled self? What is magnanimity except scorn of earthly things? What is prudence but the kind of thinking that bends the soul away from earthly things and draws it on high?

Purified, the soul is wholly Idea and reason. It becomes wholly free of the body, intellective, entirely of that intelligible realm whence comes beauty and all things beautiful. The more intellective it is, the more beautiful it is. Intellection, and all that comes from intellection, is for the soul a beauty that is its own and not another's because then it is that the soul is truly soul. That is why one is right in saying that the good and the beauty of the soul consist in its becoming godlike because from the divinity all beauty comes and all the constituents of reality. Beauty is genuine reality; ugliness, its counter. Ugliness and evil are basically one. Goodness and beauty are also one (or, if you prefer, the Good and Beauty). Therefore the one same method will reveal to us the beauty-good and the ugliness-evil.

First off, beauty is the Good. From the Good, The Intelligence draws its beauty directly. The Soul is, because of The Intelligence, beautiful. Other beauties, those of action or of behavior, come from the imprint upon them of The Soul, which is author, too, of bodily beauty. A divine entity and a part, as it were, of Beauty, The Soul renders beautiful to the fullness of their capacity all things it touches or controls.

7. Therefore must we ascend once more towards the Good, towards there where tend all souls.

Anyone who has seen it knows what I mean, in what sense it is beautiful. As good, it is desired and towards it desire advances. But only those reach it who rise to the intelligible realm, face it fully, stripped of the muddy vesture with which they were clothed in their descent (just as those who mount to the temple sanctuaries must purify themselves and leave aside their old clothing), and enter in nakedness, having cast off in the ascent all that is alien to the divine. There one, in the solitude of self, beholds simplicity and purity, the existent upon which all depends, towards which all look, by which reality is, life is, thought is. For the Good is the cause of life, of thought, of being.

Seeing, with what love and desire for union one is seized
—what wondering delight! If a person who has never seen
this hungers for it as for his all, one that has seen it must
love and reverence it as authentic beauty, must be flooded
with an awesome happiness, stricken by a salutary terror.
Such a one loves with a true love, with desires that flame.
All other loves than this he must despise and all that once
seemed fair he must disdain.

Those who have witnessed the manifestation of divine or
supernal realities can never again feel the old delight in
bodily beauty. What then are we to think of those who see
beauty in itself, in all its purity, unencumbered by flesh
and body, so perfect is its purity that it transcends by far
such things of earth and heaven? All other beauties are
imports, are alloys. They are not primal. They come, all of
them, from it. If then one sees it, the provider of beauty
to all things beautiful while remaining solely itself and receiving nothing from them, what beauty can still be lacking? This is true and primal beauty that graces its lovers
and makes them worthy of love. This is the point at which
is imposed upon the soul the sternest and uttermost combat,
the struggle to which it gives its total strength in order not
to be denied its portion in this best of visions, which to
attain is blessedness. The one who does not attain to it is
life's unfortunate, not the one who has never seen beautiful colors or beautiful bodies or has failed of power and
of honors and of kingdoms. He is the true unfortunate who
has not seen this beauty and he alone. It were well to cast
kingdoms aside and the domination of the entire earth
and sea and sky if, by this spurning, one might attain this
vision.

8. What is this vision like? How is it attained? How
will one see this immense beauty that dwells, as
it were, in inner sanctuaries and comes not forward
to be seen by the profane?

Let him who can arise, withdraw into himself, forego all
that is known by the eyes, turn aside forever from the
bodily beauty that was once his joy. He must not hanker
after the graceful shapes that appear in bodies, but know
them for copies, for traceries, for shadows, and hasten
away towards that which they bespeak. For if one pursue
what is like a beautiful shape moving over water— Is there

not a myth about just such a dupe, how he sank into the depths of the current and was swept away to nothingness? Well, so too, one that is caught by material beauty and will not cut himself free will be precipitated, not in body but in soul, down into the dark depths loathed by The Intelligence where, blind even there in Hades, he will traffic only with shadows, there as he did here.

"Let us flee then to the beloved Fatherland." Here is sound counsel. But what is this flight? How are we to "gain the open sea"? For surely Odysseus is a parable for us here when he commends flight from the sorceries of a Circe or a Calypso, being unwilling to linger on for all the pleasure offered to his eyes and all the delight of sense that filled his days. The Fatherland for us is there whence we have come. There is the Father. What is our course? What is to be the manner of our flight? Here is no journeying for the feet; feet bring us only from land to land. Nor is it for coach or ship to bear us off. We must close our eyes and invoke a new manner of seeing, a wakefulness that is the birthright of us all, though few put it to use.

What, then, is this inner vision?

9. Like anyone just awakened, the soul cannot look at bright objects. It must be persuaded to look first at beautiful habits, then the works of beauty produced not by craftsman's skill but by the virtue of men known for their goodness, then the souls of those who achieve beautiful deeds. "How can one see the beauty of a good soul?" Withdraw into yourself and look. If you do not as yet see beauty within you, do as does the sculptor of a statue that is to be beautified: he cuts away here, he smooths it there, he makes this line lighter, this other one purer, until he disengages beautiful lineaments in the marble. Do you this, too. Cut away all that is excessive, straighten all that is crooked, bring light to all that is overcast, labor to make all one radiance of beauty. Never cease "working at the statue" until there shines out upon you from it the divine sheen of virtue, until you see perfect "goodness firmly established in stainless shrine." Have you become like this? Do you see yourself, abiding within yourself, in pure solitude? Does nothing now remain to shatter that interior unity, nor anything external cling to your authentic self? Are you entirely that sole true light which is not contained by space, not confined to any circumscribed form, not diffused as something without term, but ever unmeasurable as something greater than all measure and something more than all quantity? Do you see yourself in this state? Then you have become vision itself. Be of good heart. Remaining here you have ascended aloft. You need a guide no longer. Strain and see.

Only the mind's eye can contemplate this mighty beauty. But if it comes to contemplation purblind with vice, impure, weak, without the strength to look upon brilliant objects, it then sees nothing even if it is placed in the presence of an object that can be seen. For the eye must be adapted to what is to be seen, have some likeness to it, if it would give itself to contemplation. No eye that has not become like unto the sun will ever look upon the sun; nor will any that is not beautiful look upon the beautiful. Let each one therefore become godlike and beautiful who would contemplate the divine and beautiful.

So ascending, the soul will come first to The Intelligence and will survey all the beautiful Ideas therein and will avow their beauty, for it is by these Ideas that there comes all beauty else, by the offspring and the essence of The Intelligence. What is beyond The Intelligence we affirm to be the nature of good, radiating beauty before it.

Thus, in sum, one would say that the first hypostasis is Beauty. But, if one would divide up the intelligibles, one would distinguish Beauty, which is the place of the Ideas, from the Good that lies beyond the beautiful and is its "source and principle." Otherwise one would begin by making the Good and Beauty one and the same principle. In any case it is in the intelligible realm that Beauty dwells.

SOURCES

For the key to abbreviations see *Guide to Sources,* page 223.

1 ¶4   "mount this ladder": Plato, *Banquet* 211 c 3.
   ¶5   On every side it is said: *cf.* Stoic., III, n. 278-9, 472.
   ¶8   "temperance . . . generosity": Plato, *Republic* 560 d 2-3, 348
          c 11-12; *cf.* Plato, *Gorgias* 491 e 2.

2 ¶2   it shrinks back: Plato, *Banquet* 206 d 6.

4 ¶2 "luster": Plato, *Phaedrus* 250 b 3.
"the face . . . morning star": Euripides, *Melanippe* in *Trag.*, fr. 486.

5 ¶2 What is . . . in souls?: *cf.* Plato, *Banquet* 210 b-c.
What do you . . . within?; *cf.* Plato, *Phaedrus* 279 b 9.
"colorless": Plato, *Phaedrus* 247 c 6.
"luster": Plato, *Phaedrus* 250 b 3.
the courage . . . countenance: *cf.* Homer, *Iliad*, V, 212.

¶4 It is dissolute . . . filthy pleasures: *cf.* Plato, *Gorgias* 525 a.
"encumbering it": Plato, *Phaedo* 66 b 5.

6 ¶1 "Temperance . . . purifications.": Plato, *Phaedo* 69 c 1-6.
find their joy in foulness: *cf.* Heracleitus in *Vorsokrat.*, fr. B 13.
that mere parting: *cf.* Plato, *Phaedo* 64 c 5-7.

¶2 beauty of the soul . . . godlike: *cf.* Plato, *Theaetetus* 176 b 1.

7 ¶2 simplicity and purity: Plato, *Banquet* 211 e 1.

¶4 What then . . . heaven: *cf. op. cit.* 211 a 8, d 8 - e 2.
This is the point . . . blessedness: *cf.* Plato, *Phaedrus* 247 b 5-6, 250 b 6.

8 ¶1 immense beauty: Plato, *Banquet* 218 e 2.

¶3 "Let us . . . Fatherland.": Homer, *Iliad*, II, 140.
For surely: *cf.* Homer, *Odyssey*, IX, 29 ff. and X, 483-484.

9 ¶2 "working at the statue": Plato, *Phaedrus* 252 d 7.
"goodness . . . shrine": Plato, *Phaedrus* 254 b 7.

¶5 place of the Ideas: *cf.* Aristotle, *On the Soul*, III, 4; 429 a 28.
(See p. 212.)
"source and principle": Plato, *Phaedrus* 245 c 9.

THE INTELLIGENCE,
THE IDEAS, AND BEING

(V, 9 [5])

Plotinus the academician is much to the fore in this treatise
in both senses of that ambiguous label: his thought, basically,
is that of the Academy of Plato, and its expression has about
it a classroom clarity. It is well that this is so. After the
virtuoso flourish of *Beauty,* the strong thought here could take
one off one's guard and there would be little understanding of
what in the Plotinian system it is supremely important to
understand.

Following an introduction (§§1–2) that links the present
question—"What is The Intelligence?"—with what has gone
before in *Beauty,* he proceeds to the consideration of the three
further questions he feels it implies: whether it is a "separate"
intelligence in the Aristotelian sense, whether it is the same as
Being, and whether it contains the (Platonic) Ideas.

It is, he answers (§§3–4), a "separate" intelligence, be-
traying an unaccustomed fidelity to Aristotle as he does so.
The vocabulary is Aristotelian and the argumentation—in the
beginning at least—is Aristotelian as well. It is a situation that
could lead the unwary to miss both his sly insertion of this
Aristotelianism into the Platonic and un-Aristotelian (last
paragraph of §3) and the authentic Plotinianism that promptly
sprouts from the grafting: Aristotle's analysis of the soul
Plotinus transfers to the universe—psychology is joined to cosmology—and the doctrine of The Intelligence as creative artist,
of The Soul as the giver of the cosmic pattern, of the seminal
reasons as the givers of individual sense forms comes into
existence.

45

The Intelligence is Being (§§5–6). Again the language and logic is Aristotelian, but the doctrine is Platonic. Aristotle had balked at giving his god a knowledge of sense forms and had thus introduced a large embarrassing lacuna into his system. Plotinus, good Platonist, who sees bright shoots of everlastingness in all creation, lets the Aristotelian logic run its course so that The Intelligence does know the sensate in its archetypes, does know all beings, does know them not as other but as itself, and is therefore Being.

Finally (§§7–10), The Intelligence contains the Ideas. The Ideas of which Plotinus speaks are apparently those of Plato, but the reader should not be put off by appearances. In their ancestry Plato figures—but so do the Stoics and Philo. And in the thick air of Middle Platonism they took on a robustiousness of which Plato himself would hardly have approved. They are now living beings leading genuine lives, now active, now contemplative. It is only with difficulty that one can count this somewhat uncouth adulthood of the Ideas a gain. The loss of philosophic precision is balanced solely by the gain of other postulated existents in the Plotinian cosmos whose presence serves to clarify what Plotinus says of the mystic ascent.

Almost as though what we had here were the transcript of an actual class, the treatise concludes (§§10–14) with Plotinus answering (somewhat) related questions.

1.   All men, from birth onward, live more by sensation than by thought, forced as they are by necessity to give heed to sense impressions.

Some stay in the sensate their whole life long.[1] For them, sense is the beginning and end of everything. Good and evil are the pleasures of sense and the pains of sense; it is enough to chase the one and flee the other. Those of them who philosophize say that therein wisdom lies. Like big earthy birds are they, prevented by their bulk from rising off the ground even though they have wings.

[1] The Epicureans.

Others do lift themselves, a little, above the earth.[2] Their higher part transports them out of the pleasurable into the honorable. But, unable to perceive anything higher and with nowhere to set themselves, they fall back—in virtue's name—on the activities and "options" of that lower realm they had thought to escape.

But there is another, a third, class of men—men godlike in the greatness of their strength and the acuity of their perceptions.[3] They see clearly the splendors that shine out from on high. Thither, out of the mist and fogs of earth, they lift themselves. There they stay, seeing from above what is here below, taking their pleasure in truth, like a man at home once again in his well-governed country after a far journeying.[4]

Where is this country? How does one get there?

2.   If one is a born lover with an innate philosophic bent, one will get there. Such a one labors to realize beauty. Bodily beauty contents him not. To the beauty of the soul he turns his attention—to virtue, knowledge, noble deeds, law. He then goes higher still to the source of this loveliness of the soul and to what is beyond it, the uttermost limit, Beauty itself. At this point, and not before, all sufferings cease.

But how does one start this ascent? Where does one get the needed strength?

In what thought is love to find its guide?

This is the guiding thought: beauty perceived in material things is beauty borrowed. It is there as is form in matter. It can pass and leave ugliness in its place. Reason tells us it is a share of beauty only.

What gives a body its beauty? A twofold cause in varying degrees: Beauty, of which they partake, and the soul, by which they are what they are.

Is the soul, then, of itself beautiful? No, it is not. One soul may be wise and lovely and another one foolish and ugly; a soul's beauty is constituted by wisdom.

---

[2] The Stoics are envisaged here. See the references in "Sources."
[3] The Platonists.
[4] Here Plotinus is thinking of Ulysses, the hero's return to Ithaca being for him as for many another at that time the symbol of the soul's ascent. *Cf.* Homer, *Odyssey,* V, 37, and *Enneads,* I, 6 [1], 8.

Well, what gives the wisdom that constitutes the beauty? Is it The Intelligence? Is it that authentic intellect, wise without intermission and therefore beautiful of itself? Can one be content that it is this principle, or must one look further? One must look further. One must go beyond The Intelligence that, from our point of approach, stands before the supreme principle, providing the mind free access to the knowledge of all because all that can be known is there. It is a vestibule introducing one into the presence of the Good. Vestibule? Yes, and vestige, too, the trace in the multiple of the Good which itself remains in absolute unity.

3. We must inquire more closely into the nature of The Intelligence.

It is not unreasonable to identify it simply with authentic essence and existence. Ours, however, must be a more circuitous route: we must decide whether it really exists.

There is something ridiculous, surely, about questioning the existence of The Intelligence, but there are people who do it. So let us inquire whether it really is as we say, whether it is "separate," [5] whether it is identical with existents,[6] and whether it is the seat of the Ideas.[7] We shall do this right now.

Clearly, everything we call "being" is composite, whether man made it or nature. The man-made, with its metal or stone or wood, is not achieved until skill, by the induction of a form, has turned it into statue or house or bed. The natural, however, is even more complicated—I mean what we call a "compound," the sort of thing that can be analyzed into constituent elements and form, as man, for example, into soul and body, and the human body into the four elements.

Now, finding everything to be made up of materials and a shaping form (of itself the matter of the elements is formless), one naturally asks whence comes the shaping form.

[5] *Choristos,* Aristotle's technical expression (*On the Soul,* III, 5, 430a17). *See* §4.
[6] *See* §5.
[7] *See* §9.

And one has questions of a similar sort about the soul. Is it partless? Is it, on the contrary, composite? Has it something representing matter and something else representing form? Is the intelligence within it the equivalent of the shape of the statue and the sculptor giving it shape? [8]

Adopting the same method in regard to the cosmos, one will once more end up with an intelligence and think it the true maker and demiurge. The matter, then, is fire, water, earth, and air. Formation comes from yet another being, The Soul. The Soul it is that gives them their cosmic pattern. But The Intelligence provides them the seminal reasons much as skill gives the soul of the artist norms of performance. For there is an intelligence that is the form of The Soul. And there is The Intelligence that gives the form to The Soul, like the sculptor who gives shape to the statue, still possessing the while all that is given. What it gives to The Soul is neighbor to the true real; what body receives is image and imitation.[9]

4. But why must one go beyond The Soul? Why not make it the supreme? [10]

First off, The Intelligence is different from The Soul and is its prior; there is no truth in the belief that The Soul begets The Intelligence. How could potentiality become actuality unless cause brought it about? Could chance effect it? Then it might never become actuality. What has to be admitted is that the primal beings are in act, sufficient unto themselves, and perfect. Those that are sequent to them are imperfect and receive what perfection they have from their begetters—as children, imperfect when born, are brought to adulthood by their parents. Produced is to producing principle as matter is to form and it is brought to perfection by its informing principle. If, further, The Soul is thus changeable while there must be somehow something unchangeable—else time would wear all away—this something must be prior to The Soul. Again, there must be something prior to The Soul since The Soul is in the world; there has to be something outside a world that, all body and matter, has nothing enduring about it. Were there not,

[8] In other words, is it immanent and transcendent?
[9] *Cf.* III, 8 [30].
[10] As did the Stoics.

neither mankind nor the seminal reasons would know
either survival or identity.

Arguments such as these make clear that The Intelligence must be prior to The Soul.

5. If words are going to mean anything, "The Intelligence" must be understood not as intelligence in
potency or intelligence evolving (which would, in
any case, require another and prior intelligence) but as
intelligence in actuality and for all eternity. It does not
acquire thoughts; it has thoughts of itself. It thinks of itself
and by itself; it is its thoughts. Were its thoughts a reality
other than itself, its own reality would not be the object
of its thinking and it would be in potency and not in act.
We should not separate these realities from one another
even though we are so inclined, in thinking, to do so.

What, then, is this that is both the knower and the
known?

It is, without doubt, authentically The Intelligence: it
thinks beings and they are. It is these beings, for it will
perceive them either as being somewhere else or as in itself
and as itself. The "somewhere else" is out of the question.
Where could it be? So they are itself and the content of
itself. They are not things of sense, although that has been
suggested.[11] Sense existence is primal in no being. Form
inherent in things of sense is imitation of authentic form.
Every form that is in anything has come from another
form and is its imitation.

What is more, if The Intelligence is "maker of this all,"
it cannot think these things in order to produce them in
this cosmos, for the cosmos would not yet exist. Such beings must exist before the cosmos, must not be typical of
other beings, but must themselves be archetypal. They are
the very essence of The Intelligence.

The suggestion might be made that the seminal reasons
would suffice here. But then they must be eternal. If eternal,
if immune to change, they must exist in The Intelligence
such as we have described it—a principle prior to condition,
to nature, to soul, for they are contingent existents.[12]

[11] By the Stoics. *See* "Sources."
[12] "Condition, nature, soul" are the three degrees of being in Stoicism:
the cohesion of the mineral, the vegetation of the plant, the life of the
animal.

The Intelligence, accordingly, is itself the authentic exist-ents. It is not a knower that knows them as somewhere else. They are not prior to it. They are not after it. Of being it is rather the lawgiver, or—better still—the law. Thus is it true to say that "to be and to think are the same thing," and "in beings that involve no matter, thinker and thought are identical," and "I sought myself" as a being. The theory of reminiscence bears on this as well.

None of the beings is off in space, outside The Intelli-gence. They all subsist in themselves without end, under-going no change or decay. It is for this reason that they are real. Things that come and go have only borrowed being; not they, but they on whom they draw are real. Only by such borrowing are sense objects the things we say they are, their substrate having received formation from else-where, as bronze from the sculptor's skill or wood from the carpenter's. The skill penetrates them with form and yet remains integrally apart from them, continuing to carry within it the reality of statue or bed. So it is with all cor-poreal things.

This cosmos of ours, characteristically a participant in images itself, shows how copies differ from authentic beings. Against the variability of the first there is the unchanging quality of the second—reposing in themselves, not needing space because not having magnitude, possessing an exist-ence intellective and self-sufficing. Bodies seek their suffi-ciency in others than their own kind. The Intelligence, sustaining by its wondrous power all that would of them-selves fail, seeks no stay anywhere.

6. Let it be said, then, that The Intelligence is identi-cal with these beings and contains them all, not locally but as containing itself and being one with its content.

"All, in it, are one" and yet distinct. It is rather like the way the mind contains many items and branches of knowl-edge at the same time without any one of them merging into any other; at a given moment each does what is expected of it without involving any of the others, every concept active singly. In this way, but with even greater unity, The Intelligence is every one of the beings and not every one of the beings at the same time because each of the beings is a distinct power. As the genus contains all the species or as the whole contains all the parts, The Intelligence contains all the beings.

The seminal reasons provide an illustration of this. All the properties of a being are, in an undivided state, there as in one kernel—the form of eye and the form of hand, for instance, whose difference is manifest only in the bodily organs they subsequently bring into being. Each of the seminal reasons is, with its content, an intelligence which has something spatial (as a liquid) for its matter while it is itself the form complete and is identical with generative soul—the generative soul, for its part, being the image of a higher soul.

Sometimes the name "Nature" is given to this seminal power. Partner to its prior as light is to flame, it both transforms and informs matter, not by push and pull and a working of levers—of which we hear so much[13]—but by bestowal of reasons.

7.   In the rational soul there is knowledge of sense objects (if one must call it "knowledge"; "opinion" would be the better word); it is of later origin than the objects since it is a reflection of them. There is also knowledge—truly knowledge this—of intelligible objects. It comes from The Intelligence and traffics not with things of sense. Truly knowledge, it actually is everything it takes cognizance of. It is its own object and the thought of the object, because The Intelligence is the primals themselves, ever self-present, never compelled to seek or acquire (it is no journeyman as is The Soul), but immobile, the whole of all, not given to thought that beings should be. It is not by its thinking "god" that a god exists. It is not by its thinking "movement" that movement arises. That is why it is not correct to say that "each of these forms is a thought," if one means by it that a thing exists or is made to exist because The Intelligence has thought it. The object of intellection must exist before there is the act of intellection. If it did not, how would The Intelligence come to know it? Certainly not by luck and haphazard.

8.   If, then, thought here is thought of an object interior to The Intelligence, that interior object is form and form is Idea.

[13] Plotinus always took Aristotelian mechanism ill.

What is Idea? An intelligence or intellective essence. No Idea is different from The Intelligence but is itself an intelligence. The Intelligence in its totality is made up of the Ideas and each of the Ideas is each of the intelligences. In the same way, a science in its totality is made up of theories and each of the theories is a part of the total science, a part that is not spatially separate from its fellows but, in the totality, having its distinctive qualities for all of that.

The Intelligence is in itself. It possesses itself, is itself ever-unchanging abundance. If prior to being, it would be, by its thought and action, the begetter of being. But we are unable to conceive of existence not preceding what knows it. So it were better to say that the beings are the content of its thought, that its actual thought is as proximate to the beings as the act of fire is to fire so that they, in their inmost, are as proximate to The Intelligence as they are to their own proper act.

But being also is an act. Hence the act of The Intelligence and the act of being are one sole act—or, better, The Intelligence and Being are one. They are the same nature. The same nature, too, are the beings as the act of The Intelligence and the act of Being. And in this sense the Ideas, too, are the same nature as the idea of Being, its form, and its act. It is only our way of thinking that splits them up. Quite different is The Intelligence that, itself undivided, does not divide up either Being or beings.

What, in The Intelligence, do we thus split up?

9.   There is no escape; we must list them all, as they are, much as one would catalog the various constituents of some one science.

The cosmos is a living organism capable of containing every form of life within it. From another realm it draws its existence and its modes of existing. That realm has as source The Intelligence. The Intelligence, therefore, contains the archetype of the cosmos and is itself the intelligible realm—what Plato in the *Timaeus* calls "the ideal animal." Given the seminal reason of "animal" and matter that is receptive to it, inevitably an animal comes into existence. Similarly, given The Intelligence—all-powerful—inevitably there is formation and formed since no obstacle intervenes between giver and receiver. All is held by the cosmic recipient in division—here man, there sun—while in the giver all remains one.

All form in the sense realm comes from above.
10.   What is not form does not.

Above, there is nothing that is in conflict with nature any more than in art there can be anything inartistic or—in a seed—lameness, for a lame leg is the result of a thwarting of the seminal reason or a marring of the achieved form by some accident.

In that intellectual realm all is in accord with nature globally and in detail—qualities and quantities, numbers and magnitudes, origins and conditions, actions and passions. Instead of time, there is eternity; instead of space, mutual inclusiveness. Since all there is "all at once," the perceptible is always an intellective essence and a sharer in life; it is identity and difference, motion and rest, mobile and immobile, essence and quality. All is essence there, for every real being must actually be and not just possible to be; quality therefore is never separated from essence.

"Are there in the intelligible realm only the forms of the things of sense, or are there other forms as well?"

We must first examine the question of the man-made, for in the intelligible realm there is no evil. Evil is of this lower realm, brought into being by need, privation, defect; it is the condition of matter or of the assimilative of matter that is incapable of attaining to form.[14]

The imitative arts—painting, sculpture, dancing,
11.   pantomime—are products of this lower realm. The models they mimic are found in the sensate for it is visible shape or motion or symmetry that is copied. It would be false to ascribe them to the intelligible realm except in the sense that they are contained within the mind of man. On the other hand, to proceed from the observing of the symmetry of living things to the symmetry of all life is to exercise a part of that faculty which, even here below, knows and contemplates the perfect symmetry of the intelligible realm. The same must be said for music; since its thought is on rhythm and harmony, it is not unlike heavenly harmony.

[14] *See* I, 8 [51], *The Nature and Source of Evil,* where Plotinus studies the relation of matter to evil.

Skills such as those of architect and carpenter, exercised though they are upon sense objects, draw their principles and patterns from the intelligible realm to the extent that symmetry is their goal. But, to the extent that they bring them down into contact with the realm of sense, the principles and patterns are not wholly of the intelligible except, again, as contained in the mind of man.

So it is with agriculture, whose concern is material growth. So also with medicine, whose concern is bodily health. So also gymnastics, which aims at bodily strength and fitness, for in the intelligible realm strength and fitness have another meaning—the fearlessness and self-sufficiency of what is alive.

Oratory and generalship, administration and sovereignty, by contributing beauty to action, introduce in their exercise an element from the intelligible and from such knowledge as is there.

Geometry, as the science of intelligible entities, has a place in the intelligible realm. So also—and much more—has that philosophy whose high concern is being.

On arts and artifacts, let these observations suffice.

12.   I might add, however, that if the Idea of man exists in the intelligible realm, there must exist there as well the Idea of reasoning man and of artistic man. And the arts themselves, as products of intelligence, must be there, too.

This, too, must be remarked: The Ideas will be of universals, not of "Socrates" but of "man." And à propos of man, the Idea of individual man might well bear investigation. Individuality consists in this: the traits of all are not all the same; one has a nose that is flat and another a nose that is hooked; the two shapes of noses should be considered differentiations in the human species quite as are the differentiations in the animal kingdom. Differences in complexion are to appreciated in the same fashion, determinations as they are of seminal reason on the one hand and matter and environment on the other.

Now to return to the question.

13.   Are there in the intelligible realm models only of the things of sense or are there (as man-as-such differing from individual man) a soul-as-such different from

the soul and an intelligence-as-such different from intelligence?

First off, there is no reason for thinking that everything here below is the image of a model. The soul is not the image of soul-as-such. Soul differs from soul in nobility and is, even here on earth, a soul-as-such—although perhaps not in the same sense as when it is in the intelligible realm. Each authentic soul is temperate and just. There is, even in our souls, authentic knowledge compounded not of images and reflections of the rational amid the sensate but of the same things that are there above; they are here below merely in another manner. The Ideas are not spatially estranged from us. Wherever there is a soul that has risen from its body, the Ideas are there. The realm of sense is localized; the intelligible realm is not. So whatever the freed soul attains to here is also there. If by the content of the realm of sense we mean what is visible, then the intelligible realm contains all of it and more. If we mean to include in the content of this lower realm soul and the things of soul, then all that is there above is here.

14. One must admit, then, the existence of such a primal as this, which embraces all that is in the intelligible realm.

"But how is this possible if this primal is really one and partless and the beings are multiple?" "How is multiplicity to be added to unity? How do they all exist?" "Why is The Intelligence all existing things?" "Whence comes The Intelligence?"

These questions can be answered only from a different approach than ours here at this time.

"Are there in the intelligible realm ideas of the products of putrefaction and of filth and of mud?"

The Intelligence derives from The One only what is of the noblest; in its Ideas the base is not; such repulsive things point not to The Intelligence but to The Soul, which, drawing upon The Intelligence, takes from matter certain other things—these included. But it will be easier to handle this question when we come back to the difficulty of how the multiple can come from The One.[15]

---

[15] See V, 4 [7], *How the Secondaries Arise from The One,* and V, 2 [11], *The Origin and Order of Beings.*

Compounds that owe their existence to chance and not to
The Intelligence are not to be included under the Ideas.
The products of putrefaction stem from The Soul's inability
to bring some other thing into existence. Otherwise it would
produce in strict accord with nature. As it is, it does what it
can.

As to the arts and crafts, all that are to be traced to
human need are contained in man-as-such.

As to the soul, there is—anterior to The Soul—soul-as-
such, which is either universal life or that life which is in
The Intelligence and before The Soul in order that The
Soul should be.

SOURCES

For the key to abbreviations see *Guide to Sources,* page 223.

1 ¶2 Some stay: This paragraph and the one following are a version, even more acerbic than the original, of Plato,
Phaedo 81 b-c.
¶3 Others . . . escape: *cf. Stoic.,* III, n. 23.
"options": *op. cit.,* n. 64, 118.
¶4 But there is another: *cf.* Plato, *Phaedo* 82 b 10.
in his . . . far journeying: *cf.* Homer, *Odyssey,* V, 37.

2 ¶2 If one is a born lover: *cf.* Plato, *Phaedrus* 248 d 3-4.
Bodily beauty . . . law: The dependence on Plato here includes large verbal citations. *Cf. Banquet* 210 b 3 - c 6.
¶5 beauty perceived . . . borrowed: *cf. ibid.* 210 e 3.
¶8 wise without intermission: *cf.* Aristotle, *On the Soul,* III,
5; 430 a 22.
vestibule . . . of the Good: Plato, *Philebus* 64 c 1.
remains in absolute unity: *cf.* Plato, *Timaeus* 37 d 6.

3 ¶3 "separate": *cf.* Aristotle, *On the Soul,* III, 5; 430 a 17.
¶7 image and imitation: *cf.* Plato, *Timaeus* 50 c 5.

4 ¶2 The Intelligence . . . its prior: *cf.* Aristotle, *On the
Heavens,* I, 2; 269 a 19-20.
belief . . . begets The Intelligence; *cf. Stoic.,* I, nn. 374, 377;
II, nn. 835-7, 839.

5 ¶3 although that . . . suggested: *cf. op. cit.,* II, n. 88.
¶4 "maker of this all": Plato, *Timaeus* 28 c 3-4.
¶5 to condition, to nature, to soul: *cf. Stoic.,* II, n. 1013.

¶6   "to be . . . same thing": Parmenides in *Vorsokrat.*, fr. B3.
"in beings . . . are identical": Aristotle, *On the Soul*, III,
4; 430 a 3-4.
"I sought myself": Heracleitus in *Vorsokrat.*, fr. B 101.
The theory of reminiscence: *cf.* Plato, *Phaedo* 72 e 3.

¶7   bronze from . . . skill: *cf.* Aristotle, *Metaphysics*, V, 2;
1013 b 6-9.
the reality . . . bed: *cf.* Plato, *Republic* 597 c 3.

¶8   Bodies seek . . . in others: *cf.* Plato, *Cratylus* 400 c 7.

6   ¶2   "All, in it, are one": Anaxagoras in *Vorsokrat.*, fr. B 1.

¶4   Sometimes . . . seminal power: *cf. Stoic.*, III, n. 743.
of which . . . so much: *cf.* Aristotle, *Physics*, VII, 6; 259 b
20.

7   "opinion" would . . . word: *cf.* Plato, *Republic* 533 e 8 -
534 a 2.
It is its . . . acquire: Aristotle, *Metaphysics*, XII, 7; 1072
b 21-23.
"each of . . . a thought": Plato, *Parmenides* 132 b 5.

8   ¶3   is . . . abundance: *cf.* Plato, *Cratylus* 396 b 6-7.

9   ¶3   a living . . . of life: Plato, *Timaeus* 33 b 2-3.
"the ideal animal": *op. cit.* 39 e 8.

10   ¶3   qualities . . . passions: Plato, *Sophist* 254 d 5; 254 e 5 -
255 a 1.

12   ¶2   The Ideas . . . universals: *cf.* Aristotle, *Metaphysics*, VIII,
1; 1042 a 15.

14   ¶4   of filth and of mud: *cf.* Plato, *Parmenides* 130 c 6.

THE DESCENT
OF THE SOUL

(IV, 8 [6])

It had become traditional in Plotinus' day to interpret the myths of Plato's *Phaedrus* and *Republic* pretty much according to the letter. The descent of the soul was represented as a tumble through the spheres to the earth where the soul took on, one after another, various irrational faculties.

To refute this, Plotinus steps out of his usual anonymity to appeal to his own experience.

The appeal, for us, has a double worth. It shows most graphically the noble opinion that Plotinus always entertained of the human soul, an opinion already to the forefront in his discussion of beauty. But it is also a valuable indication of the nature of his mystical experience—its ecstatic quality, its relative brevity, its character of fulfillment rather than negation.

As the treatise progresses it becomes clear that the appeal to personal experience was not thought sufficient to solve wholly the problem of the soul's relationship to a cosmos animated by soul. Dismissing Heracleitus for the moment with words that some may feel excellently applicable to himself ("he engages in metaphor and is little concerned with explaining") and Empedocles, along with him ("he speaks as a poet"), he turns to Plato, of whom he remarks, this unusual saturnine mood still upon him, that "consistency is not his strong point." He continues, however, to see himself as faithful to Plato in his fashion, and there is an undercurrent of protest throughout his discussion of the doctrine of the *Phaedo* and that of the *Timaeus* against those who would find any lack of harmony between them.

59

According to the *Phaedo* and its moral perspective, all commerce of soul with body is evil. According to the *Timaeus*, where the concern is cosmological, the demiurge dispatched both The Soul and individual souls for the good of the whole. So Plotinus starts by showing that The Soul's governance of body does not involve its penetration of body or its uniting with body or its loss of its contemplative capacity. His authority is the *Phaedrus* (240b-e) and the picture it provides of Soul and souls that rule the cosmos and yet contemplate not one whit the less. (This theme from the *Phaedrus* will reappear, magisterially orchestrated, in the late treatise *On Contemplation.*) There is no disagreement, therefore, between the *Phaedo* and the *Timaeus;* the second does not so much as consider the union of soul with body.

But why, co-regent of the cosmos with The Soul, did the human soul abandon its lofty status and take on flesh and all the ills that flesh is heir to? Why, even if joined to a body, did it not continue immune as do the souls of the stars?

Here the impatience of the modern reader, disinclined as he is to star-souls and the like, must be kept severely in tether. Demythologized, these pages of the *Enneads* portray the coming into existence of the Neoplatonic theory of the soul, born—it would seem—of the laudable desire to have Plato agree with himself.

The way is prepared by §3: as The Intelligence has within it many intelligences, so The Soul has within itself many souls; from The Soul must come souls differing in the degrees of their rationality for only thus can there be a graded hierarchy of animate beings; each of these souls must influence the reality beneath, for such is their *raison d'être,* and yet remain all the while in the intelligible realm, for such is their nature.

As preparation, this seems less than adequate. If the souls rule bodies while still remaining in the intelligible realm, why is it necessary that they "fall" from there in order to rule them? Clearly, nothing said so far would indicate any such necessity in the order of things. But then, to cap it, we are told the souls "are tired of living with someone else" and so come down into their own individuality; the "fall" is a Fall, an Original Sin, freely committed. And, with that, we are certain that something very important has been left out.

It puts in its appearance in §5: the descent of the soul is the result of "an eternal law of nature."

Inexorable law is the unvarying pattern in the Platonism of Plotinus. If he did not mention it earlier, in providing the materials preparatory to his solution, it was only because—to his mind—it would be to belabor the obvious. He mentions it now only to show how the soul's free fault is necessary fault. The demonstration consists in the simple assertion that there is no contradiction between necessity and free choice because "necessity includes free choice." We have here, as commentators are pleased to point out, a doctrine of pre-established harmony long before Leibniz—and as little convincing.

One would be right in saying that Plotinus has not thought the question through. He is seeking, at the moment, to show that no contradiction exists between the doctrine of the *Phaedo* and that of the *Timaeus*. He would be the last to say that because they are not in contradiction they are therefore true; one need only recall his rejection of that sort of reasoning in *Beauty*, §1. His chief purpose throughout this treatise is to protect his conviction of the nobility of the human soul. And that he succeeds in doing. He receives for his trouble a theory of the soul that will be his to the end. Despite its inadequacies from the metaphysical point of view, it is a theory that squares with what one learns of the soul's nature in introspection. And that, for him, suffices.

So, the final section (§8). Union with body is not an insurmountable obstacle to contemplation. He knows that from his own experience. The human soul never wholly departs the intelligible realm; of the same nature as The Soul, by its higher part it is always there. One may become unaware of its continuing residence there but that is only because of the clamor of the lower part, which is in body.

Through this treatise there moves a note of nostalgia. Plotinus remembers there where, in contemplation, he has often been—"outside everything else and inside myself." The treatises that follow it in this small volume show him plotting out the pattern of all reality in terms of the necessary return of the soul after the descent. Nothing less than a total cosmos, wholly new, could satisfy this man's need.

It has happened often.

1.   Roused into myself from my body—outside everything else and inside myself—my gaze has met a
beauty wondrous and great. At such moments I have been
certain that mine was the better part, mine the best of lives
lived to the fullest, mine identity with the divine. Fixed
there firmly, poised above everything in the intellectual that
is less than the highest, utter actuality was mine.

But then there has come the descent, down from intellection to the discourse of reason. And it leaves me puzzled.
Why this descent?

Indeed, why did my soul ever enter my body since even
when in the body it remains what it has shown itself to be
when by itself?[1]

Heracleitus, who urges the study of this matter, says
that "contraries necessarily change into each other." But
talking of "the way up and the way down," asserting that
"change is repose," that "to make the same efforts and to
obey is a wearisome business," he engages in metaphor
and is little concerned with explaining himself, feeling perhaps that we should seek out the answers for ourselves as
he did for himself.

Empedocles, for his part, says it is ordained that souls
at fault descend into this world, that he himself was "fugitive from the divine, to mad discord enslaved." But he is,
I fear, no more revealing than Pythagoras; his interpreters,
here as elsewhere, find allegory; what is more, he speaks
as a poet, and that adds to the obscurity.

But then there is the divine Plato who has had so much
that is beautiful to say of the soul.

In the *Dialogues* he frequently treats of the soul's arrival
in this world and awakens hope that here will be clarity.
Unfortunately, consistency is not his strong point, so it is
not easy to catch his meaning. However, everywhere he
holds the bodily in low esteem; he deplores the association
of soul with body; he says that the soul is enchained and
entombed by the body; he considers "high doctrine with
challenging implications" the assertion of the mystery religions that the soul when here below is in a prison. What
he calls "the cave" seems to me, like the "grotto" of Em-

---

[1] The rarity of such personal references in a philosophy so personal as
that of Plotinus is remarkable. There are only two others (I, 6 [1], 7 and
VI, 9 [9], 4), both of them in the third person.

pedocles, to signify the realm of sense, because for the
soul "to break its chains and ascend" from its cave is, he
says, to rise "to the intelligible realm." In the *Phaedrus*
"the loss of its wings" is cause of the soul's descent;
periodically recurring cycles bring the soul back down here
after it has gone aloft. Judgments, loss, chance, and necessity drive other souls down into this world. In all these
instances Plato deplores the association of soul with body.

Yet, treating of the sense world in the *Timaeus,* he praises
it and calls it a "blessed god" and contends The Soul was
given it by the goodness of the demiurge so that the sum
of things might be possessed of intelligence, which, without The Soul, it could not be. The soul of each of us is
dispatched hither for the same reason: if the realm of
sense is to be complete, it is necessary that it contain as
many kinds of living beings as does the intelligible realm.

2. So seeking in Plato an answer to questions about
one's own soul, one is driven to questions about
soul in general: How has soul been brought into
association with body? Of what sort is this world in which
soul (freely or necessarily or in any other way) lives? Did
the demiurge do right in making this world? Or as our
souls do? [2]

It would seem that our souls, charged with the managing
of bodies less perfect than they, had to penetrate into them
if they were to manage them truly. For such bodies have
a tendency to come apart, their parts struggling to return
to their natural places (since everything in the cosmos has
its natural place).[3] More than that, such bodies require a
knowing management that is both extensive and detailed
because they are forever exposed to the assaults of alien
bodies, are forever oppressed by wants; they need help,
unremittingly, in the multiple adversities that beset them.

The body of The Soul, on the other hand, is perfect. It
is complete. It is self-sufficient. It is not subject to influences
that prevent its expressing its own nature. It requires, accordingly, only a light control. That is why The Soul re-

[2] This passage has long been a subject of wide disagreement among
scholars. For discussion, see Cilento, *Enneadi,* II, 575–9. Here the
reading of Henry-Schwyzer, *Plotini Opera,* II, 230, is followed. The
meaning: "Did the demiurge do right [*i.e.,* act freely] in making this
world? Or as our souls do [*i.e.,* act out of necessity]?"
[3] Paradoxically, the Aristotelian theory of "natural places" is here used
in favor of the Platonic theory of the soul.

mains free of care and molestations, its native disposition
intact—"nothing going out, nothing coming in." Hence
Plato says that the human soul, when it is with this perfect
one, becomes perfect itself and "journeys on high and controls the whole world," and, so long as it does not withdraw (to enter a body, to be attached to something individual), exercises a control as effortless as that of The
Soul. That it gives body existence is not necessarily to the
soul's hurt: providing for a lower nature does not necessarily prevent the agency that exercises it from remaining
itself in a state of perfection. Providence is of two kinds:
it is directed to the whole and regulates everything after
the fashion of kings, giving orders to be executed by others,
or it is involved with detail and operates directly, adapting
agent and acted upon one to the other. The Soul, divine,
administers the heavens in the first way: transcending them
in its highest phases and immanent to them solely in its
lowest. One cannot accordingly accuse divinity of having
assigned an inferior place to The Soul; it has never been
deprived of its native status; this operation, which is not
counter to its nature, it always possessed and always will.

In saying that the relation of the souls of the stars to
their bodies is the same as that of The Soul of the world
to the world (since these starry bodies are encompassed
in the circuit of The Soul), Plato also accords the stars
their appropriate happiness. Of the two objections against
the interaction of soul and body—that it "hinders" the
soul's intellective act and that it "fills" the soul with pleasure, "lust," fear—neither holds here. The soul has not
penetrated deeply into body and is not dependent on the
particular. Body is for it and not it for body. Its body
lacks nothing, wants nothing. Hence the soul is free from
both desires and fears. Since the starry body is what it is,
the soul has no cause for disturbance on its account.
Nothing intrudes upon its repose and makes it incline downward, robbing it of the high happiness of contemplation. It
is always with the things in the realm above and, empow-
ered and undisturbed, governs the realm of sense.

3.   Let us now consider the human soul, which while
in the body is subject to ills and suffering, a prey
to griefs, lusts, fears, and evils of every kind, whose

body is a "chain" or a "tomb" and the realm of sense a "cave" or a "grotto."[4] That it should be thus does not go counter to the preceding; it is simply that the causes of its descent are different.

To begin with, The Intelligence dwells entire within that region of thought we call the intelligible realm, yet it comprises within itself a variety of intellective powers and particular intelligences. The Intelligence is not merely one: it is one and many. In the same way is there both Soul and many souls. From the one Soul proceeds a multiplicity of different souls, as from one and the same genus proceed species of various ranks, some of which are more rational and others (at least in their actual existence) less rational in form.

Again, in the intelligible realm there is The Intelligence, which like some huge organism contains potentially all other intelligences, and there are the individual intelligences, each of them an actuality. Think of a city as having a soul. It would include inhabitants, each of whom would have a soul. The soul of the city would be the more perfect and more powerful. What would prevent the souls of the inhabitants from being of the same nature as the soul of the city? Or, again, take fire, the universal, from which proceed large and small particular fires; all of them have a common essence, that of universal fire—or, rather, all partake of that essence whence proceeds universal fire. The function of The Soul, as intellective, is intellection. But it is not limited to intellection. If it were, there would be no distinction between it and The Intelligence. It has functions besides the intellectual and these, by which it is not simply intelligence, determine its distinctive existence. In directing itself to what is above itself, it thinks. In directing itself to itself, it preserves itself. In directing itself to what is lower than itself, it orders, administers, and governs. The reason for such an existent as The Soul is that the totality of things cannot continue limited to the intelligible so long as a succession of further existents is possible; although less perfect, they necessarily are because the prior existent necessarily is.

4. Thus individual souls are possessed by a desire for the intelligible that would have them return there whence they came, and they possess, too, a power

[4] *Cf.* §1 above.

over the realm of sense much in the way that sunshine, although attached to the sun above, does not deny its rays to what is below. If the souls remain in the intelligible realm with The Soul, they are beyond harm and share in The Soul's governance. They are like kings who live with the high king and govern with him and, like him, do not come down from the palace.

Thus far all are in the one same place.

But there comes a point at which they come down from this state, cosmic in its dimensions, to one of individuality. They wish to be independent. They are tired, you might say, of living with someone else. Each steps down into its own individuality.

When a soul remains for long in this withdrawal and estrangement from the whole, with never a glance towards the intelligible, it becomes a thing fragmented, isolated, and weak. Activity lacks concentration. Attention is tied to particulars. Severed from the whole, the soul clings to the part; to this one sole thing, buffeted about by a whole worldful of things, has it turned and given itself. Adrift now from the whole, it manages even this particular thing with difficulty, its care of it compelling attention to externals, presence to the body, the deep penetration of the body.

Thus comes about what is called "loss of wings" or the "chaining" of the soul.[5] Its no longer are the ways of innocence in which, with The Soul, it presided over the higher realms. Life above was better by far than this. A thing fallen, chained, at first barred off from intelligence and living only by sensation, the soul is, as they say, in tomb or cavern pent.

Yet its higher part remains. Let the soul, taking its lead from memory, merely "think on essential being" and its shackles are loosed and it soars.

Souls of necessity lead a double life, partly in the intelligible realm and partly in that of sense, the higher life dominant in those able to commune more continuously with The Intelligence, the lower dominant where character or circumstance are the less favorable. This is pretty much what Plato indicates in distinguishing those of the second mixing bowl: after they have been divided in this way they must, he says, be born. When he speaks of divinity "sow-

---

[5] Cf. §1 above.

ing" souls, he is to be understood as when he has divinity
giving orations and speeches; he describes the things contained in the universe as begotten and created and presents
as successive what in truth exist in an eternal state of becoming or of being.

5.
There is no contradiction between the sowing to
birth and the willing descent for the perfection of
the whole, between justice and the cave, between
necessity and free choice (necessity includes free choice),
being in the body being an evil; nor, in the teaching of
Empedocles: the flight from God and the wandering and
the sin that is justly punished; nor, in that of Heracleitus:
the repose that is flight; in general, willing descent that is
also unwilling.[6] Everything that becomes worse does so un-
willingly, yet when it becomes so through inherent tendency, that submission to the lower can be regarded as a
penalty. Then, too, these experiences and acts are determined by an eternal law of nature, so that it may be
said, without being either inconsistent or untruthful, that
a soul that descends from the world above to some lower
being is sent by the divinity; for final effects, however far
removed by intermediate effects, are always to be referred
back to the starting point.

There are two wrongs the soul commits. The first is its
descent; the second, the evil done after arrival here below.
The first is punished by the very conditions of its descent.
Punishment for the second is passage once more into other
bodies, there to remain at greater or less length according
to the judgment of its deserts. (The word "judgment" indicates that this takes place as a result of divine law.) If,
however, its perversity goes beyond all measure, the soul
incurs an even more severe penalty administered by aveng-
ing daimons.

Thus, too, The Soul enters body—although its nature is
divine and its realm the intelligible. A lesser divinity, it is
impelled by the stress of its powers and the attraction of
governing the next below it. By voluntary inclination it
plunges into this sphere. If it returns quickly, it will have
suffered no harm in thus learning of evil and of what sin
is, in bringing its powers into manifest play, in exhibiting
activities and achievements that, remaining merely po-

[6] *Cf.* §1 above.

tentialities in the intelligible realm, might as well never have been if they were never meant to be actualized: The Soul itself would never really know these suppressed, inhibited potencies. Potencies are revealed by acts, for potencies in themselves are hidden and undetectable and, for all practical purposes, nonexistent. As it is, all now marvel at the inner greatness of The Soul exteriorly revealed in the richness of its acts.

6.

The One must not be solely the solitary. If it were, reality would remain buried and shapeless since in The One there is no differentiation of forms. No beings would exist if The One remained shut up in itself. More than that, the multiplicity of beings issued from The One would not exist as they do if there did not issue from The One those beings that are in the rank of souls. Likewise, souls must not play the solitaries, their issue stifled. Every nature must produce its next, for each thing must unfold, seedlike, from indivisible principle into a visible effect. Principle continues unaltered in its proper place; what unfolds from it is the product of the inexpressible power that resides in it. It must not stay this power and, as though jealous, limit its effects. It must proceed continuously until all things, to the very last, have within the limits of possibility come forth. All is the result of this immense power giving its gifts to the universe, unable to let any part remain without its share.

Nothing hinders anything from sharing in the Good to the extent it is able. That statement holds true even for matter. If, on the one hand, matter is assumed to have existed from all eternity, it is impossible that, having existence, it should not have a share in that which, in accord with each receptivity, communicates the Good to all. If, on the other hand, matter is held to be the necessary consequence of anterior causes, it will not be separated from this principle either as though, having graciously given it existence, it was powerless to reach it.

The excellence, the power, and the goodness of the intelligible realm is revealed in what is most excellent in the realm of sense, for the realms are linked together. From the one, self-existent, the other eternally draws its existence by participation and, to the extent it reproduces the intelligible, by imitation.

7. As there are these two realms, the intelligible and that of sense, it is better for the soul to dwell in the intelligible. But, such is its nature, it is necessary that it live also in the realm of sense. Accordingly it occupies only an intermediate rank. Yet there is no cause for complaint that it is not in all respects the highest. By nature divine, it is located at the nethermost limit of the intelligible realm, bordering on the realm of sense, and there gives to the realm of sense something of its own. In turn it is itself affected when, instead of controlling the body without endangering its own security, it lets itself be carried away by an excessive zeal and plunges deep into the body and ceases to be wholly united to The Soul. Yet the soul can rise above this condition again and, turning to account the experience of what it has seen and suffered here below, can better appreciate the life that is above and can know more clearly what is the better by contrast with its opposite. Indeed, knowledge of good is sharpened by experience of evil in those incapable of any sure knowledge of evil unless they have experienced it.

For The Intelligence, to reason discursively is to descend to its lowest level rather than to rise to the level of the existence beyond. But it cannot remain within itself. Of necessity it produces. Of necessity, then, by the very law of its nature, it proceeds to the level of The Soul. It goes no further. Entrusting the later stages of being to The Soul, it returns once more to the intelligible realm.

For The Soul it is much the same. Its lowest act is the realm of sense; its highest, contemplation of the supernal beings.

For individual souls this contemplation is fragmentary and divided by time, so their conversion begins on a lower level. But The Soul never becomes involved in the activities of the lower world. Immune to evil, it comprehends intellectually what is below it while always cleaving to what is above it. Therefore is it able, at one and the same time, to be debtor to what is above and, since as soul it cannot escape touching this sphere, benefactor to what is below.

8. This, now, goes counter to current belief. But let us take our courage in our hands and say it: No soul, not even our own, enters into the body completely. Soul always remains united by its higher part to the intelligible realm. But if the part that is in the realm of sense dominates, or rather becomes dominated and disturbed, it keeps us unaware of what the higher part of the soul contemplates. Indeed we are aware of what the soul contemplates only if the content descends to the level of sensation. We do not know what happens in any part of the soul until it becomes present to the entire soul. (For instance, an appetite does not become known to us as long as it remains in the faculty of desire. We detect it only when we perceive it by interior sense or by the act of judgment, or by both.)[7]

Every soul has a lower part directed towards the bodily and a higher part directed towards the intelligible. The Soul, effortlessly, manages the universe by that part directed towards the bodily. For The Soul governs the bodily not by discursive reasoning, as we do, but by intuition (much as is done in the arts). Individual souls, each of which manages a part of the universe, also have a higher phase. But they are preoccupied with sensation and its impressions. Much they perceive is contrary to nature and troubles and confuses them. This is so because the body in their care is deficient, hedged about with alien influences, filled with desires, deceived in its very pleasures. Yet there is a part of the soul insensitive to the lure of these passing pleasures, whose living is correspondent to its reality.

[7] For more of Plotinus' theory of the unconscious, see I, 4 [46], 10, and the excellent study of H. R. Schwyzer, " 'Bewusst' und 'unbewusst' bei Plotin," in *Les sources de Plotin*, pp. 341–78.

SOURCES

For the key to abbreviations see *Guide to Sources,* page 223.

1 ¶5 "contraries . . . each other": cf. Iamblichus in Stobaeus, *Anthologium* (C. Wachsmuth and O. Hense ed.; Berlin: Weidmann, 1884), I, p. 378, 21-22.
"the way up and the way down": *Vorsokrat.,* fr. B 60.
"change is repose": *op. cit.,* fr. B 84 a.
"to make . . . business": *op. cit.,* fr. B 84 b.
¶6 "fugitive from the divine": *op. cit.,* fr. B 115, 13-14.
¶8 enchained: Plato, *Phaedo* 67 d 1.
entombed by the body: *cf. Cratylus* 400 c 2.
"high doctrine . . . implications": *Phaedo* 62 b 2-5.
"the cave": *Republic* 514 a 5.

"grotto": *Vorsokrat.*, fr. B 120.
"to break . . . intelligible realm": *Republic* 515 c 4, 517 b 4-5.
"the loss of its wings": *Phaedrus* 246 c 2, 247 d 4-5.
bring the soul back down: *cf. op. cit.* 249 a 6.
Judgments . . . world: *cf. Republic* 619 d 7.
¶9 "blessed god": *Timaeus* 34 b 8.
The Soul . . . of the demiurge: *cf.* 29 a 3.
possessed of intelligence: *cf.* 30 b 8.
which . . . it could not be: *cf.* 30 b 3.
if the realm of sense . . . realm: *cf.* 39 e 7-9.

2 ¶3 "nothing . . . coming in": Plato, *Timaeus* 33 c 6-7.
"journeys . . . the whole world": Plato, *Phaedrus* 246 c 1-2.
adapting . . . to the other: *cf.* Plato, *Phaedo* 67 a 5.
¶4 (since these starry . . . Soul): *cf.* Plato, *Timaeus* 38 c 7-8.
"hinders": Plato, *Phaedo* 65 a 10.
"fills" the soul with . . . "lust": *op. cit.* 66 c 2-3.
high happiness of contemplation: *cf.* Plato, *Phaedrus* 247 a 4.

3 ¶1 which while . . . fears: Plato, *Phaedo* 95 d 3.
¶3 like some huge organism: *cf.* Plato, *Timaeus* 30 c - 31 a.

4 ¶6 "think on essential being": Plato, *Phaedrus* 249 e 5.
¶7 what Plato indicates: *cf. Timaeus* 41 d 5-8.
divinity "sowing" souls: *cf. op. cit.* 41 e 1-4.
giving orations: *cf.* Plato, *Timaeus* 41 a - d.

6 ¶1 Principle continues unaltered: *cf.* Plato, *Timaeus* 42 e 5-6.

THE GOOD OR THE ONE

(VI, 9 [9])

In the Introduction the opinion was expressed that Plotinus' ontology reposes upon his psychology of introspection. Some of the grounds for that opinion are discoverable in the treatise that follows, one of the half-dozen or so classics of Neoplatonism.

At the outset a good, pedestrian, academic concern is shown for the question, much debated in the philosophic schools of the day, "Whence comes unity?"—a latter-day refinement of the problem of the one and the many which had so tormented Plotinus' predecessors. And, rather too quickly, the concern is expeditiously satisfied with an answer of which both Pythagoreans and Stoics would approve (§1) and Aristotle is curtly refuted on the basis of that answer (§2) and then the rest of the treatise is given over to an extended analysis of the soul's mode of access to The One (§§3–11). The suspicion accordingly obtrudes that the assertion-denial of §§1–2 rests really upon the psychology of §§3–11.

Throughout, Plotinus reveals an unaccustomed awareness of the difficulties one might have in following his rigorous analyses that is, for all its novelty, quite charming and endearing particularly since he does not allow it to stay his hand in the least.

The human mind dislikes the indeterminate; but indeterminacy must be the burden of one's discoursing on The One; let then the mind rebuff this tendency of its "fallen" nature to flee the indeterminate and take refuge in things of this sure and firm set earth and allow its higher self, still resident in the intelligible realm, to find itself for, in finding itself, it finds The

Intelligence—immediately above which is The One (§3).

That one use words of The One should not be allowed to foster the illusion that The One is, after all, something determinate and that the soul can attain to it in following its usual earthbound way. Such words as one uses are no more than signals providing direction, no more than suggestions of what one's attitude should be. Attitude? Yes. An attitude of faith. Of faith, apparently, in Plotinus himself. Let there at least be confidence if comprehension is out of the question (§4).

Then, with that familiar professorial device of giving back with one hand what one has just taken away with the other, he appeals to comprehension with an argument derived from the admitted existence of The Soul, the intermediary between the soul and The Intelligence, the repository of a multiplicity that is spiritual—and undivided (§5). And the appeals to comprehension continue unabated to the end, as argument follows luminous argument, analysis follows analysis.

It is no great chore to "have faith" in a man as reasonable as this.

It is by The One that all beings are beings.

1. This is equally true of those that are primarily beings and those that in some way are simply classed among beings, for what could exist were it not one? Not a one, a thing is not. No army, no choir, no flock exists except it be one. No house, even, or ship exists except as the unit, house, or the unit, ship; their unity gone, the house is no longer a house, the ship is no longer a ship. Similarly quantitative continua would not exist had they not an inner unity; divided, they forfeit existence along with unity. It is the same with plant and animal bodies; each of them is a unit; with disintegration, they lose their previous nature and are no longer what they were; they become new, different beings that in turn exist only as long as each of them is a unit. Health is contingent upon the body's being coordinated in unity; beauty, upon the mastery of parts by The One; the soul's virtue, upon unification into one sole coherence.[1]

The Soul imparts unity to all things in producing, fashioning, forming, and disposing them. Ought we then to say that The Soul not only gives unity but is unity itself, The One? No. It bestows other qualities upon bodies without being what it bestows (shape, for instance, and Idea, which are different from it); so also this unity; The Soul makes each being one by looking upon The One, just as it makes man by contemplating the Idea, Man, effecting in the man the unity that belongs to Man.

Each thing that is called "one" has a unity proportionate to its nature, sharing in unity, either more or less, according to the degree of its being. The Soul, while distinct from The One, has greater unity because it has a higher degree of being. It is not The One. It is one, but its unity is contingent. Between The Soul and its unity there is the same difference as between body and body's unity. Looser aggregates, such as a choir, are furthest from unity; the more compact are the nearer; The Soul is nearer still, yet—as all the others—is only a participant in unity.

The fact that The Soul could not exist unless it was one should not, really, lead anyone to think it and The One identical. All other things exist only as units, and none of them is The One; body, for instance, and unity are not identical. Besides, The Soul is manifold as well as one even though it is not constituted of parts; it has various faculties—discursive reason, desire, perception—joined together in unity as by a bond. The Soul bestows unity because it has unity, but a unity received from another source.[2]

2. Granted that being is not identical with unity in each particular thing, might not the totality, Being, be identical with unity? Then upon grasping Being, we would hold The One, for they would be the same. Then,

---

[1] *Cf.* VI, 6 [34], 16.
[2] "The One, the first hypostasis, can be confused with the third, The Soul; the Stoics did just that in identifying the supreme god with the soul of the world whence the consequent tension, in their doctrine, throughout the universe because of this oneness of beings. It can also be confused with the second hypostasis, The Intelligence; Aristotle did that; his doing so is examined by Plotinus in §3."—Bréhier, *Plotin: Ennéades*, VI, 2e, p. 172, n. 1.

if Being is The Intelligence, The One would also be The Intelligence; The Intelligence, as Being and as The One, would impart to the rest of things both being and, in proportion, unity.

Is The One identical with Being as "man" and "one man" are identical? Or is it the number of each thing taken individually? (Just as one object and another joined to it are spoken of as "two," so an object taken singly is referred to as "one.") In the second case, if number belongs to the class of being, evidently The One will belong in that way, too, and we shall have to discover what kind of being it is. But if unity is no more than a numbering device of the soul, The One has no real existence; but this possibility is eliminated by our previous observation that each object upon losing unity loses existence as well.

Accordingly, we must determine whether being and unity are identical either in each individual object or in their totality.

As the being of each thing consists in multiplicity and The One cannot be multiplicity, The One must differ from Being. Man is animal, rational, and many things besides; and this multiplicity is held together by a bondlike unity. Thus there is a difference between man and unity: man is divisible, unity indivisible. Being, containing all beings, is still more multiple, thus differing from The One even though it is one by participation. Because being possesses life and intelligence, it is not dead. It must be multiple. If it is The Intelligence, it must be multiple—and the more so if it contains the Ideas, because Ideas, individually and in their totality, are a sort of number and are one only in the way in which the universe is one.

In general, then, The One is the first existent. But The Intelligence, the Ideas, and Being are not the first. Every form is multiple and composite, and consequently something derived because parts precede the composite they constitute.

That The Intelligence cannot be primary should be obvious as well from the following. The activity of The Intelligence consists necessarily in intellection. Intelligence, which does not turn to external objects, contemplates what is superior to it;[3] in turning towards itself it turns towards its

[3] *Cf.* V, 4 [7],10.

origin. Duality is implied if The Intelligence is both thinker and thought; it is not simple, therefore not The One. And if The Intelligence contemplates some object other than itself, then certainly there exists something superior to The Intelligence. Even if The Intelligence contemplate itself and at the same time that which is superior to it, it still is only of secondary rank. We must conceive The Intelligence as enjoying the presence of the Good and The One and contemplating it while it is also present to itself, thinks itself, and thinks itself as being all things. Constituting such a diversity, The Intelligence is far from being The One.

Thus The One is not all things because then it would no longer be one. It is not The Intelligence, because The Intelligence is all things, and The One would then be all things. It is not Being because Being is all things.

What then is The One? What is its nature?

3. It is not surprising that it is difficult to say what it is when it is difficult to say even what being is or what form is, although there knowledge has some sort of approach through the forms. As the soul advances towards the formless, unable to grasp what is without contour or to receive the imprint of reality so diffuse, it fears it will encounter nothingness,[4] and it slips away. Its state is distressing. It seeks solace in retreating down to the sense realm, there to rest as upon a sure and firm-set earth, just as the eye, wearied with looking at small objects, gladly turns to large ones. But when the soul seeks to know in its own way—by coalescence and unification—it is prevented by that very unification from recognizing it has found The One, for it is unable to distinguish knower and known. Nevertheless, a philosophical study of The One must follow this course.

Because what the soul seeks is The One and it would look upon the source of all reality, namely the Good and The One, it must not withdraw from the primal realm and sink down to the lowest realm. Rather must it withdraw from sense objects, of the lowest existence, and turn to those of the highest. It must free itself from all evil since it aspires to rise to the Good. It must rise to the principle possessed within itself; from the multiplicity that it was it

---

[4] *Cf.* VI, 4 [22], 7.

must again become one. Only thus can it contemplate the supreme principle, The One.

Having become The Intelligence, having entrusted itself to it, committed itself to it, having confided and established itself in it so that by alert concentration the soul may grasp all The Intelligence sees, it will, by The Intelligence, contemplate The One without employing the senses, without mingling perception with the activity of The Intelligence. It must contemplate this purest of objects through the purest of The Intelligence, through that which is supreme in The Intelligence.

When, then, the soul applies itself to the contemplation of such an object and has the impression of extension or shape or mass, it is not The Intelligence that guides its seeing, for it is not the nature of The Intelligence to see such things. From sensation, rather, and from opinion, the associate of sensation, comes this activity. From The Intelligence must come the word of what its scope is.[5] It contemplates its priors, its own content, and its issue. Purity and simplicity characterize its issue and, even more, its content and, most of all, its priors or Prior.

The One, then, is not The Intelligence but higher. The Intelligence is still a being, while The One is not a being because it is precedent to all being.[6] Being has, you might say, the form of being; The One is without form, even intelligible form.[7]

As The One begets all things, it cannot be any of them—neither thing, nor quality, nor quantity, nor intelligence, nor soul. Not in motion, nor at rest, not in space, nor in time, it is "the in itself uniform," or rather it is the "without-form" preceding form, movement, and rest, which are characteristics of Being and make Being multiple.

But if The One is not in motion, why is it not at rest? Because rest or motion, or both together, are characteristic of Being. Again, because what is at rest must be so on account of something distinct from it, rest as such. The One at rest would have the contingent attribute, "at rest," and would be simple no longer.

Let no one object that something contingent is attributed

---

[5] *Cf.* II, 9 [33], 14.

[6] Here, refuting Aristotle, Plotinus permits himself the irony of using categories from the previously refuted Stoics.

[7] *Cf.* VI, 7 [38], 34.

to The One when we call it the first cause. It is to ourselves that we are thereby attributing contingency because
it is we who are receiving something from The One while
The One remains self-enclosed. When we wish to speak
with precision, we should not say that The One is this or
that, but revolving, as it were, around it, try to express our
own experience of it, now drawing nigh to it, now falling
back from it as a result of the difficulties involved.

The chief difficulty is this: awareness of The One
4.   comes to us neither by knowing nor by the pure
        thought that discovers the other intelligible things,
but by a presence transcending knowledge. When the soul
knows something, it loses its unity; it cannot remain simply
one because knowledge implies discursive reason and discursive reason implies multiplicity. The soul then misses
The One and falls into number and multiplicity.[8]

Therefore we must go beyond knowledge and hold to
unity. We must renounce knowing and knowable, every
object of thought, even Beauty, because Beauty, too, is
posterior to The One and is derived from it as, from the
sun, the daylight. That is why Plato says of The One, "It
can neither be spoken nor written about." If nevertheless
we speak of it and write about it, we do so only to give
direction, to urge towards that vision beyond discourse,
to point out the road to one desirous of seeing. Instruction
goes only as far as showing the road and the direction.
To obtain the vision is solely the work of him who desires
to obtain it. If he does not arrive at contemplation, if his
soul does not achieve awareness of that life that is beyond,
if the soul does not feel a rapture within it like that of the
lover come to rest in his love, if, because of his closeness
to The One, he receives its true light—his whole soul
made luminous—but is still weighted down and his vision
frustrated, if he does not rise alone but still carries within
him something alien to The One, if he is not yet sufficiently
unified, if he has not yet risen far but is still at a distance
either because of the obstacles of which we have just
spoken or because of the lack of such instruction as would
have given him direction and faith in the existence of things
beyond, he has no one to blame but himself and should

[8] *Cf.* I, 6 [1], 7.

try to become pure by detaching himself from everything. The One is absent from nothing and from everything. It is present only to those who are prepared for it and are able to receive it, to enter into harmony with it, to grasp and to touch it by virtue of their likeness to it, by virtue of that inner power similar to and stemming from The One when it is in that state in which it was when it originated from The One. Thus will The One be "seen" as far as it can become an object of contemplation. Anyone who still lacks faith in these arguments should consider the following:

5. Those who believe that the world of being is governed by luck or by chance and that it depends upon material causes are far removed from the divine and from the notion of The One. It is not such men as these that we address but such as admit the existence of a world other than the corporeal and at least acknowledge the existence of soul. These men should apply themselves to the study of soul, learning among other things that it proceeds from The Intelligence and attains virtue by participating in the reason that proceeds from The Intelligence. Next, they must realize that The Intelligence is different from our faculty of reasoning (the so-called rational principle), that reasoning implies, as it were, separate steps and movements. They must see that knowledge consists in the manifestation of the rational forms that exist in The Soul and come to The Soul from The Intelligence, the source of knowledge. After one has seen The Intelligence, which like a thing of sense is immediately perceived (but which, although it transcends the soul, is its begetter and the author of the intelligible world), one must think of it as quiet, unwavering movement; embracing all things and being all things, in its multiplicity it is both indivisible and divisible. It is not divisible as are the ingredients of discursive reason, conceived item by item. Still its content is not confused either: each element is distinct from the other, just as in science the theories form an indivisible whole and yet each theory has its own separate status. This multitude of coexisting beings, the intelligible realm, is near The One. (Its existence is necessary, as reason demonstrates, if one admits The Soul exists, to which it is superior.) It is nevertheless not the supreme because it is neither one nor simple.

The One, the source of all things, is simple. It is above

even the highest in the world of being because it is above The Intelligence, which itself, not The One but like The One, would become The One. Not sundered from The One, close to The One, but to itself present, it has to a degree dared secession.

The awesome existent above, The One, is not a being for then its unity would repose in another than itself. There is no name that suits it, really. But, since name it we must, it may appropriately be called "one," on the understanding, however, that it is not a substance that possesses unity only as an attribute. So, the strictly nameless, it is difficult to know. The best approach is through its offspring, Being: we know it brings The Intelligence into existence, that it is the source of all that is best, the self-sufficing and unflagging begetter of every being, to be numbered among none of them since it is their prior.

We are necessarily led to call this "The One" in our discussions the better to designate "partlessness" while we strive to bring our minds to "oneness." But when we say that it is one and partless, it is not in the same sense that we speak of geometrical point or numerical unit, where "one" is the quantitative principle which would not exist unless substance, and that which precedes substance and being, were there first. It is not of this kind of unity that we are to think, but simply use such things here below—in their simplicity and the absence of multiplicity and division—as symbols of the higher.

6. In what sense, then, do we call the supreme The One? How can we conceive of it?

We shall have to insist that its unity is much more perfect than that of the numerical unit or the geometrical point. For with regard to these, the soul, abstracting from magnitude and numerical plurality, stops indeed at that which is smallest and comes to rest in something indivisible. This kind of unity is found in something that is divisible and exists in a subject other than itself. But "what is not in another than itself" is not in the divisible. Nor is it indivisible in the same sense in which the smallest is indivisible. On the contrary, The One is the greatest, not physically but dynamically. Hence it is indivisible, not physically but dynamically. So also the beings that proceed from it; they are, not in mass but in might, indivisible and partless. Also, The One is infinite not as extension or a numerical series is infinite, but in its limitless power. Conceive it as intelligence or divinity; it is more than that. Compress unity within your mind, it is still more than that. Here is unity superior to any your thought lays hold of, unity that exists by itself and in itself and is without attributes.[9]

Something of its unity can be understood from its self-sufficiency. It is necessarily the most powerful, the most self-sufficient, the most independent of all. Whatever is not one, but multiple, needs something else. Its being needs unification. But The One is already one. It does not even need itself. A being that is multiple, in order to be what it is, needs the multiplicity of things it contains. And each of the things contained is what it is by its union with the others and not by itself, and so it needs the others. Accordingly, such a being is deficient both with regard to its parts and as a whole. There must be something that is fully self-sufficient. That is The One; it alone, within and without, is without need. It needs nothing outside itself either to exist, to achieve well-being, or to be sustained in existence. As it is the cause of the other things, how could it owe its existence to them? And how could it derive its well-being from outside itself since its well-being is not something contingent but is its very nature? And, since it does not occupy space, how can it need support or foundation? What needs foundation is the material mass which, unfounded, falls. The One is the foundation of all other things and gives them, at one and the same time, existence and location; what needs locating is not self-sufficing.

Again, no principle needs others after it. The principle of all has no need of anything at all. Deficient being is deficient because it aspires to its principle. But if The One were to aspire to anything, it would evidently seek not to be The One, that is, it would aspire to that which destroys it. Everything in need needs well-being and preservation. Hence The One cannot aim at any good or desire anything: it is superior to the Good; it is the Good, not for itself, but for other things to the extent to which they can share in it.

[9] The original text throughout the latter part of the paragraph is grievously defective. The translation attempts, out of the textual materials provided, merely to round off the reasoning begun.

The One is not an intellective existence. If it were, it would constitute a duality. It is motionless because it is prior to motion quite as it is prior to thinking. Anyhow, what would it think? Would it think itself? If it did, it would be in a state of ignorance before thinking, and the self-sufficient would be in need of thought. Neither should one suppose it to be in a state of ignorance on the ground that it does not know itself and does not think itself. Ignorance presupposes a dual relationship: one does not know another. But The One, in its aloneness, can neither know nor be ignorant of anything. Being with itself, it does not need to know itself. Still, we should not even attribute to it this presence with itself if we are to preserve its unity.

Excluded from it are both thinking of itself and thinking of others. It is not like that which thinks but, rather, like the activity of thinking. The activity of thinking does not itself think; it is the cause that has some other being think and cause cannot be identical with effect. This cause, therefore, of all existing things cannot be any one of them. Because it is the cause of good it cannot, then, be called the Good; yet in another sense it is the Good above all.

7.   If the mind reels at this, The One being none of the things we mentioned, a start yet can be made from them to contemplate it.

Do not let yourself be distracted by anything exterior, for The One is not in some one place, depriving all the rest of its presence. It is present to all those who can touch it and absent only to those who cannot. No man can concentrate on one thing by thinking of some other thing; so he should not connect something else with the object he is thinking of if he wishes really to grasp it. Similarly, it is impossible for a soul, impressed with something else, to conceive of The One so long as such an impression occupies its attention, just as it is impossible that a soul, at the moment when it is attentive to other things, should receive the form of what is their contrary. It is said that matter must be void of all qualities in order to be capable of receiving all forms. So must the soul, and for a stronger reason, be stripped of all forms if it would be filled and fired by the supreme without any hindrance from within itself.

Having thus freed itself of all externals, the soul must

turn totally inward; not allowing itself to be wrested back towards the outer, it must forget everything, the subjective first and, finally, the objective. It must not even know that it is itself that is applying itself to contemplation of The One.

After having dwelled with it sufficiently, the soul should, if it can, reveal to others this transcendent communion. (Doubtless it was enjoyment of this communion that was the basis of calling Minos "the confidant of Zeus"; remembering, he made laws that are the image of The One, inspired to legislate by his contact with the divine.) If a man looks down on the life of the city as unworthy of him, he should, if he so wishes, remain in this world above. This does indeed happen to those who have contemplated much.

This divinity, it is said, is not outside any being but, on the contrary, is present to all beings though they may not know it. They are fugitives from the divine, or rather from themselves. What they turn from they cannot reach. Themselves lost, they can find no other. A son distraught and beside himself is not likely to recognize his father. But the man who has learned to know himself will at the same time discover whence he comes.[10]

8. Self-knowledge reveals to the soul that its natural motion is not, if uninterrupted, in a straight line, but circular, as around some inner object, about a center, the point to which it owes its origin. If the soul knows this, it will move around this center from which it came, will cling to it and commune with it as indeed all souls should but only divine souls do. That is the secret of their divinity, for divinity consists in being attached to the center. One who withdraws far from it becomes an ordinary man or an animal.

Is this "center" of our souls, then, the principle we are seeking? No, we must look for some other principle upon which all centers converge and to which, only by analogy to the visible circle, the word "center" is applied. The soul is not a circle as, say, a geometrical figure. Our meaning is that in the soul and around about it exists the "primordial nature," that it derives its existence from the first

[10] On this self-knowledge as divine knowledge, see Arnou, *Le désir de Dieu,* pp. 193–4.

existence especially when entirely separate from the body.
Now, however, as we have a part of our being contained
in the body, we are like a man whose feet are immersed
in water while the rest of his body remains above it. Raising
ourselves above the body by the part of us that is not sub-
merged, we are, by our own center, attaching ourselves to
the center of all. And so we remain, just as the centers of
the great circles coincide with that of the sphere that sur-
rounds them. If these circles were material and not spiritual,
center and circumference would have to occupy definite
places. But since the souls are of the intelligible realm and
The One is still above The Intelligence, we are forced to
say that the union of the intellective thinking being with
its object proceeds by different means. The intellective
thinking being is in the presence of its object by virtue of
its similarity and identity, and it is united with its kindred
with nothing to separate it from them. Bodies are by their
bodies kept from union, but the bodiless are not held by
this bodily limitation. What separates bodiless beings from
one another is not spatial distance but their own differences
and diversities: when there is no difference between them,
they are mutually present.

As The One does not contain any difference, it is always
present and we are present to it when we no longer contain
difference. The One does not aspire to us, to move around
us; we aspire to it, to move around it. Actually, we always
move around it; but we do not always look. We are like
a chorus grouped about a conductor who allow their attention to be distracted by the audience. If, however, they
were to turn towards their conductor, they would sing as
they should and would really be with him. We are always
around The One. If we were not, we would dissolve and
cease to exist. Yet our gaze does not remain fixed upon
The One. When we look at it, we then attain the end of
our desires and find rest. Then it is that, all discord past,
we dance an inspired dance around it.

In this dance the soul looks upon the source of life,
9.   the source of The Intelligence, the origin of Being,
the cause of the Good, the root of The Soul.

All these entities emanate from The One without any
lessening for it is not a material mass. If it were, the ema-
nants would be perishable. But they are eternal because

their originating principle always stays the same; not fragmenting itself in producing them, it remains entire. So they persist as well, just as light persists as long as sun shines.

We are not separated from The One, not distant from it, even though bodily nature has closed about us and drawn us to itself. It is because of The One that we breathe and have our being:[11] it does not bestow its gifts at one moment only to leave us again; its giving is without cessation so long as it remains what it is. As we turn towards The One, we exist to a higher degree, while to withdraw from it is to fall. Our soul is delivered from evil by rising to that place which is free of all evils. There it knows. There it is immune. There it truly lives. Life not united with the divinity is shadow and mimicry of authentic life. Life there is the native act of The Intelligence, which, motionless in its contact with The One, gives birth to gods, beauty, justice, and virtue.

With all of these The Soul, filled with divinity, is pregnant; this is its starting point and its goal. It is its starting point because it is from the world above that it proceeds. It is its goal because in the world above is the Good to which it aspires and by returning to it there its proper nature is regained. Life here below in the midst of sense objects is for the soul a degradation, an exile, a loss of wings.

Further proof that our good is in the realm above is the love innate in our souls; hence the coupling in picture and story of Eros with Psyche. The soul, different from the divinity but sprung from it, must needs love. When it is in the realm above, its love is heavenly; here below, only commonplace. The heavenly Aphrodite dwells in the realm above; here below, the vulgar, harlot Aphrodite.

Every soul is an Aphrodite,[12] as is suggested in the myth of Aphrodite's birth at the same time as that of Eros. As long as soul stays true to itself, it loves the divinity and desires to be at one with it, as a daughter loves with a noble love a noble father. When, however, the soul has come down here to human birth, it exchanges (as if deceived by the false promises of an adulterous lover) its divine love for

[11] *Cf.* the words of St. Paul in Acts 17:27–8. For discussion, Theiler, *Die Vorbereitung des Neuplatonismus*, p. 101.
[12] *Cf.* V, 8 [31], 13.

one that is mortal. And then, far from its begetter, the soul yields to all manner of excess.

But, when the soul begins to hate its shame and puts away evil and makes its return, it finds its peace.

How great, then, is its bliss can be conceived by those who have not tasted it if they but think of earthly unions in love, marking well the joy felt by the lover who succeeds in obtaining his desires. But this is love directed to the mortal and harmful—to shadows—and soon disappears because such is not the authentic object of our love nor the good we really seek. Only in the world beyond does the real object of our love exist, the only one with which we can unite ourselves, of which we can have a part and which we can intimately possess without being separated by the barriers of flesh.

Anyone who has had this experience will know what I am talking about. He will know that the soul lives another life as it advances towards The One, reaches it and shares in it. Thus restored, the soul recognizes the presence of the dispenser of the true life. It needs nothing more. On the contrary, it must renounce everything else and rest in it alone, become it alone, all earthiness gone, eager to be free, impatient of every fetter that binds below in order so to embrace the real object of its love with its entire being that no part of it does not touch The One.

Then of it and of itself the soul has all the vision that may be—of itself luminous now, filled with intellectual light, become pure light, subtle and weightless. It has become divine, is part of the eternal that is beyond becoming. It is like a flame. If later it is weighted down again by the realm of sense, it is like a flame extinguished.

10. Why does a soul that has risen to the realm above not stay there? Because it has not yet entirely detached itself from things here below. Yet a time will come when it will uninterruptedly have vision, when it will no longer be bothered by body. The part of us that sees is not troubled. It is the other part which, even when we cease from our vision, does not cease from its activity of demonstration, proof and dialectic. But the act and faculty of vision is not reason but something greater than, prior and superior to, reason. So also is the object of the vision. When the contemplative looks upon himself in the act of contemplation, he will see himself to be like its object. He feels himself to be united to himself in the way that the object is united to itself; that is to say, he will experience himself as simple, just as it is simple.

Actually, we should not say, "He will see." What he sees (in case it is still possible to distinguish here the seer and the seen, to assert that the two are one would be indeed rash) is not seen, not distinguished, not represented as a thing apart. The man who obtains the vision becomes, as it were, another being. He ceases to be himself, retains nothing of himself. Absorbed in the beyond he is one with it, like a center coincident with another center. While the centers coincide, they are one. They become two only when they separate. It is in this sense that we can speak of The One as something separate.

Therefore is it so very difficult to describe this vision, for how can we represent as different from us what seemed, while we were contemplating it, not other than ourselves but perfect at-oneness with us?

11. This, doubtless, is what is back of the injunction of the mystery religions which prohibit revelation to the uninitiated. The divine is not expressible, so the initiate is forbidden to speak of it to anyone who has not been fortunate enough to have beheld it himself.

The vision, in any case, did not imply duality; the man who saw was identical with what he saw. Hence he did not "see" it but rather was "oned" with it. If only he could preserve the memory of what he was while thus absorbed into The One, he would possess within himself an image of what it was.

In that state he had attained unity, nothing within him or without effecting diversity. When he had made his ascent, there was within him no disturbance, no anger, emotion, desire, reason, or thought. Actually, he was no longer himself; but, swept away and filled with the divine, he was still, solitary, and at rest, not turning to this side or that or even towards himself. He was in utter rest, having, so to say, become rest itself. In this state he busied himself no longer even with the beautiful. He had risen above beauty, had passed beyond even the choir of virtues.

He was like one who, penetrating the innermost sanctuary of a temple, leaves temple images behind. They will be the first objects to strike his view upon coming out of the sanctuary, after his contemplation and communion there not with an image or statue but with what they represent. They are but lesser objects of contemplation.

Such experience is hardly a vision. It is a seeing of a quite different kind, a self-transcendence, a simplification, self-abandonment, a striving for union and a repose, an intentness upon conformation. This is the way one sees in the sanctuary. Anyone who tries to see in any other way will see nothing.

By the use of these images, the wise among the sooth-sayers expressed in riddles how the divinity is seen. A wise priest, reading the riddle, will, once arrived in the realm beyond, achieve the true vision of the sanctuary. One who has not yet arrived there and knows the sanctuary is invisible, is the source and principle of everything, will also know that by hypostasis is hypostasis seen, and that like alone joins like. He will leave aside nothing of the divine the soul is capable of acquiring. If his vision is not yet complete, he will attend to its completion, which, for him who has risen above all, is The One that is above all. It is not the soul's nature to attain to utter nothingness. Falling into evil it falls, in this sense, into nothingness, but still not complete nothingness. And when it reverses direction, it arrives not at something different but at itself. Thus, when it is not in anything else, it is in nothing but itself. Yet, when it is in itself alone and not in being, it is in the supreme.

We as well transcend Being by virtue of The Soul with which we are united.

Now if you look upon yourself in this state, you find yourself an image of The One.

If you rise beyond yourself, an image rising to its model, you have reached the goal of your journey.

When you fall from this vision, you will, by arousing the virtue that is within yourself and by remembering the perfection that you possess, regain your likeness and through virtue rise to The Intelligence and through wisdom to The One.

Such is the life of the divinity and of divine and blessed men: detachment from all things here below, scorn of all earthly pleasures, the flight of the lone to the Alone.

SOURCES

For the key to abbreviations see *Guide to Sources,* page 223.

1   Source of the basic distinctions in the two opening paragraphs is disputed. Harder believes it to be the Stoics (see *Plotins Schriften,* I, 468); Theiler, Poseidonius (see *Die Vorbereitung des Neuplatonismus,* pp. 97-8).

2   ¶2 as "man" . . . identical: *cf.* Aristotle, *Metaphysics,* III, 2; 1003 b 26-29.

3   ¶2 It seeks . . . realm: *cf.* Plato, *Republic* 508 d 5.
    ¶4 without employing the senses: *cf.* Plato, *Banquet* 211 a. without mingling perception: *cf.* Plato, *Theaetetus* 179 c 3; *Timaeus* 28 a 2.
    ¶7 "the in itself uniform": Plato, *Banquet* 211 b 1. "without-form" . . . and rest: *cf.* Plato, *Parmenides* 139 b, 138 b, 141d.

4   ¶2 "It can . . . about.": Plato, *Parmenides* 142 a; *cf. Letter VII* 341 c-d.

6   ¶2 "what is . . . itself": Plato, *Parmenides* 138 a.

7   ¶2 matter . . . all forms: *cf.* Plato, *Timaeus* 50 d ff.
    ¶4 "the confidant of Zeus": Homer, *Odyssey,* XIX, 179. have contemplated much: *cf.* Plato, *Phaedrus* 248 d.

8   The entire first paragraph is a synopsis of Plato, *Timaeus* 43-44.
    ¶1 That . . . their divinity: *cf.* Plato, *Phaedrus* 248 a. or an animal: *cf. op. cit.* 249 b.
    ¶2 "primordial nature": Plato, *Statesman* 273 b 4. whose feet . . . water: *cf.* Plato, *Timaeus* 43 a. by virtue of . . . and identity: *cf. op. cit.* 90 d 4-5.

9   ¶3 gives birth . . . virtue: *cf.* Plato, *Banquet* 209 a; 212 a.
    ¶4 starting point . . . goal: *cf.* Plato, *Laws* 715 e. is for the soul a degradation: *cf.* Plato, *Timaeus* 85 e. loss of wings: *cf.* Plato, *Phaedrus* 246 c; 248 c.
    ¶5 When it is in . . . commonplace: *cf.* Plato, *Banquet* 180 d; 203 b - e.
    ¶6 And then . . . excess: *cf.* Plato, *Phaedrus* 247 d 4.

10 ¶1 its activity . . . and dialectic: *cf.* Plato, *Theaetetus* 189 e; *Sophist* 263 e.

11 ¶11 Such is . . . blessed men: *cf.* Plato, *Theaetetus* 176 a 1. lone to the Alone.: *cf.* Numenius in Eus., XI, 22.

THE THREE PRIMAL
HYPOSTASES

(V, 1 [10])

Aside from its intrinsic interest, which is great, this solid treatise provides graphic witness to the method of Plotinus. Here, with a vengeance, ontology reposes upon personal introspection, cosmology is the extrapolation of psychology. Its very title guaranteed its being a favorite of early Christian theologians involved in the complexities of Trinitarian theory. But its concern is less with the primal hypostases themselves than with acquainting one, by reflection on self, with one's origin, rich endowments, and dignity.

To that end, a reminder is given the soul of that which it tends to forget: where it came from (§1); and a demonstration is accorded as well of one of the chief consequences of such high origin: the soul is of the same nature as The Soul to which must be ascribed all that is vital and beautiful in the cosmos (§2). Intelligence, next, is explored (§§3–4), and its link with The One (§§5–7). After a critical evaluation of the views of ancient philosophers who taught, in whatever rudimentary form, a doctrine of a primal three (§§8–9), the hypostases are described and asserted to exist in the human soul (§§10–11). Because we forget that in them was our beginning, we fail "to attend to tones that come from above" (§12).

For a man speaking of what was so close to his heart, Plotinus' language here is singularly dispassionate and dry. It is not, however, singularly clear; Longinus, writing to Porphyry, complained that this was one of the treatises most corrupted in transmission; Porphyry's observation was that the text was accurate but that Longinus misunderstood its style and

90

language (*Life,* Chapters 19–20). The reader, therefore, is warned.

1. How is it, then, that souls forget the divinity that begot them so that—divine by nature, divine by origin—they now know neither divinity nor self?[1]

This evil that has befallen them has its source in self-will,[2] in being born, in becoming different, in desiring to be independent. Once having tasted the pleasures of independence, they use their freedom to go in a direction that leads away from their origin. And when they have gone a great distance, they even forget that they came from it. Like children separated from their family since birth and educated away from home, they are ignorant now of their parentage and therefore of their identity.

Our souls know neither who nor whence they are, because they hold themselves cheap and accord their admiration and honor to everything except themselves. They bestow esteem, love, and sympathy on anything rather than on themselves. They cut themselves off, as much as may be, from the things above. They forget their worth. Ignorance of origin is caused by excessive valuation of sense objects and disdain of self, for to pursue something and hold it dear implies acknowledgment of inferiority to what is pursued. As soon as a soul thinks it is worth less than things subject to birth and death, considers itself least honorable and enduring of all, it can no longer grasp the nature and power of the divinity.

A soul in such condition can be turned about and led

---

[1] Here a return is made to the matter of *The Descent of the Soul,* especially §4.

[2] By our weak, English "self-will," the Pythagorean *tolma* is meant— the instinct for self-affirmation that is at the origin of the complex universe.

back to the world above and the supreme existent, The One
and first, by a twofold discipline: by showing it the low
value of the things it esteems at present, and by informing
—reminding!—it of its nature and worth. The second
discipline precedes the first and, once made clear, supports
the first (which we shall treat elsewhere rather fully).[3]

The second must occupy us now, particularly as it is a
prerequisite for the study of that supreme object we desire
to know.

It is the soul that desires to know. Therefore the soul
must first examine its own nature in order to know itself
and decide whether it is capable of such an investigation,
has an eye capable of such seeing, and whether such seeking
is its function. If the things it seeks are alien to the soul,
what good will its seeking do? But, if the soul is akin to
them and it seeks them, it can find them.

Each should recall at the outset that soul is the
2. author of all living things, has breathed life into
them all, on earth, in the air, and in the sea—the
divine stars, the sun, the ample heavens. It was soul that
brought order into the heavens and guides now its measured revolving. All this it does while yet remaining transcendent to what it gives form, movement, life. Necessarily,
it is superior by far to them. They are born or they die to
the extent that soul gives or withdraws their life. Soul,
because it can "never abandon itself," exists eternally.

Now to understand how life is imparted to the universe
and to each individual, the soul must rise to the contemplation of The Soul, the soul of the world. The individual soul,
though different from The Soul, is itself no slight thing. Yet
it must become worthy of this contemplation: freed of the
errors and seductions to which other souls are subject, it
must be quiet. Let us assume that quiet too is the body
that wraps it round—quiet the earth, quiet the air and the
sea, quiet the high heavens. Then picture The Soul flowing
into this tranquil mass from all sides, streaming into it,
spreading through it until it is luminous. As the rays of the
sun lighten and gild the blackest cloud, so The Soul by
entering the body of the universe gives it life and immor-

---

[3] II, 4 [12]; III, 4 [15]; VI, 4 [22]; III, 6 [26].

tality; the abject it lifts up. The universe, moved eternally
by an intelligent Soul, becomes blessed and alive. The
Soul's presence gives value to a universe that before was
no more than an inert corpse, water and earth, or rather
darksome matter and nonbeing, an "object of horror to the
gods," as someone has said.

The Soul's nature and power reveal themselves still more
clearly in the way it envelops and rules the world in accordance with its will. It is present in every point of the world's
immense mass, animating all its segments, great and small.
While two bodies cannot be in the same place and are
separated from each other both spatially and otherwise,
The Soul is not thus extended. It need not divide itself to
give life to each particular individual. Although it animates
particular things, it remains whole and is present in its
wholeness, resembling in this indivisibility and omnipres-
ence its begetter, The Intelligence. It is through the power
of The Soul that this world of multiplicity and variety is
held within the bonds of unity. It is through its presence
that this world is divine: divine the sun because ensouled;
so too the stars. And whatever we are, we are on its
account, for "a corpse is viler than a dunghill."

The deities owe their divinity to a cause necessarily their
superior. Our soul is the same as The Soul which animates
the deities: strip it of all things infesting it, consider it in
its original purity, and you will see it to be of equal rank
with The Soul, superior to everything that is body. The
Body, without the soul, is nothing but earth. If one make
fire the basic element, one still needs a principle to give life
to its flame. It is the same even if one combines earth and
fire, or adds to them water and air as well.

If it is soul that makes us lovable, why is it that we seek
it only in others and not in ourselves? You love others
because of it. Love, then, yourself.

So divine and precious is The Soul, be confident
3. that, by its power, you can attain to divinity. Start
your ascent. You will not need to search long. Few
are the steps that separate you from your goal. Take as
your guide the most divine part of The Soul, that which
"borders" upon the superior realm from which it came.

Indeed, in spite of the qualities that we have shown it to

have, The Soul is no more than an image of The Intelligence. Just as the spoken word is the image of the word in the soul, The Soul itself is the image of the word in The Intelligence and is the act of The Intelligence by which a further level of existence is produced,[4] for the act of The Intelligence has this further phase, quite as fire contains heat as part of its essence but also radiates heat. Nevertheless, The Soul does not become completely separated from The Intelligence. Partly it remains in it. Although its nature is distinct because it derives from The Intelligence, The Soul is itself an intellective existent: discursive reason is the manifestation of its intellectual capacity. The Soul derives its perfection from The Intelligence, which nourishes it as a father would. But, in comparison with itself, The Intelligence has not endowed The Soul with complete perfection.

Thus The Soul is the hypostasis that proceeds from The Intelligence. Its reason finds its actualization when it contemplates The Intelligence. So contemplating, it possesses the object of its contemplation within itself, as its own, and it is then wholly active. These intellectual and interior activities are alone characteristic of The Soul. Those of a lower kind are due to an alien principle and they are passive rather than active experiences for The Soul. The Intelligence makes The Soul more divine because it is its begetter and grants its presence to it. Nothing separates the two but the difference of their natures. The Soul is related to The Intelligence as matter is to Idea. But this "matter" of The Intelligence is beautiful: it has an intellectual form and is partless.

How great, then, must The Intelligence be if it is greater than The Soul!

4. Greatness of The Intelligence may also be seen in this: We marvel at the magnitude and beauty of the sense world, the eternal regularity of its movement, the divinities—visible and invisible—that it contains, its daimons, animals, plants. Let us then rise to the model, to the higher reality from which this world derives, and let us there contemplate the whole array of intelligibles that possess eternally an inalienable intelligence and life. Over

[4] *Cf.* I, 2 [19].

them presides pure Intelligence, unapproachable wisdom. That world is the true realm of Cronus, whose very name suggests both abundance (*koros*) and intelligence (*nous*). There is contained all that is immortal, intelligent, divine. There is the place of every soul. There is eternal rest.

Since it is in a state of bliss, why should The Intelligence seek change? Since it contains everything, why should it aspire to anything? Since it is perfect, what need has it of development? All its content is perfect, too, so that it is perfect throughout. It contains nothing that is not of the nature of thought—of thought, however, that is not a search but possession. Its happiness does not depend on something else. It is eternally all things in that eternity of which time, which abandons one moment for the next, is only a fleeting image upon the level of The Soul. The Soul's action is successive, divided by the various objects that draw its attention—now Socrates, now a horse, always some particular.[5] The Intelligence, however, embraces all, possesses all in unchanging identity. It "is" alone. And it always has this character of presentness. Future it has not; already it is all it could ever later become. Past it has not; no intelligible entity ever passes away. All it contains exist in an eternal present because they remain identical with themselves, contented, you might say, with their present condition. Singly they are both intelligence and being. Together they form the totality of intelligence and the totality of being. The Intelligence gives existence to Being in thinking it. Being, by being object of thought, gives to The Intelligence its thinking and its existence.

But there must still exist something else that makes The Intelligence think and Being be—their common cause. It is true that The Intelligence and Being exist simultaneously and together and never part. But their oneness—which is simultaneously intelligence and being, thinking and object of thought—is twofold: The Intelligence inasmuch as it thinks, and Being inasmuch as it is the object of thought. Intellection implies difference as well as identity. Therefore the primary terms are "intelligence," "being," "identity," "difference." And to them must be added "movement" and "rest." Movement is implied in the intellective activity of

---

[5] This doctrine he will slightly modify later. *See* V, 7 [18], 1.

the intelligible realm; rest, in its sameness. Difference is implicit in the distinction between the thinker and the thought because without difference they are reduced to unity and to silence. The objects of thought also require difference in order to be distinguished from one another. Identity is implied in the self-sufficient unity of The Intelligence and in the nature shared in common by all intelligible beings, quite as difference is implied in their being distinguishable. From this multiplicity of these terms come "number" and "quantity," while the proper character of each of them is "quality." From these terms, as from originating principles, everything else proceeds.

5. The Intelligence, manifold and divine, is in The Soul, since The Soul is joined to it, provided The Soul does not will to overstep its bounds and "secede" from it. So close to The Intelligence that it is almost one with it, The Soul is everlastingly vivified.

What established The Intelligence thus?

Its source did, the partless that is prior to plurality, that is the cause both of being and of multiplicity, that is the maker of number.

Number is not the first; one is prior to two and two comes after one. Two, indeterminate in itself, is made determinate by one.[6] When plurality becomes determinate, with a determinacy rather like that of substances, it becomes number. The Soul is number, too, because the primals are not quantitative masses. Masses, the gross in nature, are secondary, for all that sense perception thinks them essences. Nobility of seed or plants consists not in perceptible moisture but in number and seminal reason—both imperceptible.

Number and plurality that are in the intelligible realm are reasons and intelligence. But, in itself, as it were, plurality is indeterminate. The number, however, that comes from it and from The One is form—quite as if all things assumed form in it. The Intelligence is formed differ-

---

[6] From here to the end, this section is a little disconcerting. It seems so out of place and is so confusingly written, one would like to say that it is an extraneous, non-Plotinian fragment that crept in here through some misadventure of manuscripts. Unfortunately, one cannot.

ently by The One than it is formed of itself, that is, like sight made actual, for intellection is the seen as seen—the two are one.

6. Some questions remain: How does The Intelligence see? What does it see? How does it exist and issue from The One in order to see?

The soul accepts what is necessarily so, but now it wishes to resolve the problem so often raised by the ancient philosophers: how multiplicity, duality, and number proceeded from The One. Why did The One not remain by itself? Why did it emanate the multiplicity we find characterizing being and that we strive to trace back to The One?

In approaching this problem let us first invoke the divinity. Let us do so not with words but with a lifting of our souls to it and thus to pray alone to the Alone.

To see The One that remains in itself as if in an inner sanctuary, undisturbed and remote from all things, we must first consider the images in the outer precincts, or rather the first one to appear. This seems to be its message: All that is moved must have a goal towards which it is moved. But The One has no goal towards which it is moved. We must, then, not assume it to be moved. When things proceed from it, it must not cease being turned towards itself. (We have to remove from our minds any idea that this is a process like generation in time because here we are treating of eternal realities. We speak metaphorically, in terms of generation, to indicate the causal relations of things eternal and their systematic order.) What is begotten by The One must be said to be begotten without any motion on the part of The One. If The One were moved, the begotten, because of this movement, would have to be ranked third since the movement would be second. The One therefore produces the second hypostasis without assent, or decree, or movement of any kind. How are we to conceive this sort of generation and its relation to its immovable cause? We are to conceive it as a radiation that, though it proceeds from The One, leaves its selfsameness undisturbed, much in the way the brilliance that encircles and is ceaselessly generated by the sun does not affect its selfsame and unchanging existence. Indeed everything, as existing, necessarily produces of its own substance some further existent dependent on its power and image of its existence. Thus fire radiates heat and snow radiates cold. Perfumes provide an especially striking example: as long as they last they send off exhalations in which everything around them shares. What becomes perfect becomes productive. The eternally perfect is eternally productive, and what it produces is eternal, too, although its inferior.

What, then, are we to say of that which is supremely perfect? It produces only the very greatest of the things that are less than it. What is most perfect after it is the second hypostasis, The Intelligence. The Intelligence contemplates The One and needs nothing but The One. The One, however, has no need of The Intelligence. The One, superior to The Intelligence, produces The Intelligence, the best after The One since it is superior to all the others.[7] The Soul is word and deed of The Intelligence just as The Intelligence is word and deed of The One. But in The Soul the word is obscure, for The Soul is only an image of The Intelligence. Therefore The Soul turns itself to The Intelligence, just as, to be The Intelligence, it must contemplate The One. The Intelligence contemplates The One without being separated from it because there is no other existent between the two of them, just as there is none between The Intelligence and The Soul. Begotten always longs for its begetter and loves it; especially is this so when begetter and begotten are solitaries. But when the begetter is the highest Good, the begotten must be so close to it that its only separateness is its otherness.

7. We call The Intelligence image of The One. This we must explain.

It is its image because what is begotten by The One must possess many of its characteristics, be like it as light is like the sun. But The One is not an intellectual principle. How then can it produce an intellectual principle? In turning towards itself The One sees. It is this seeing that constitutes The Intelligence. For what is seen is different

---

[7] From here to the end of §6 there is a playing about with philosophic and theological terms that involves a small divorce from the traditional meanings. Thus "word" (*logos*) is used to indicate not an existent but a function: each hypostasis is the "word" of the preceding; the "word" is not, as in Christian theology, a unique hypostasis. Again "word"—a notion of Stoic origin—is assimilated to act—an Aristotelian notion. Further, while in both Zeno the Stoic and Aristotle "word" and act are primaries, in Plotinus they become lower than The One. *Cf.* Bréhier, *Ennéades* V, 23, n. 1.

from sensation or intelligence. . . . Sensation as line and so on. . . . But the circle is divisible; The One is not.[8]

In The Intelligence there is unity; The One, however, is the power productive of all things. Thought, apportioning itself in accord with this power, beholds all in the power of The One: did it not, it would not be The Intelligence. The Intelligence is aware of its power to produce and even to limit being through that power derived from The One. It sees that being is a part of what belongs to The One and proceeds from it and owes all its force to it, that it achieves being because of The One. The Intelligence sees that, because it becomes multiple when proceeding from The One, it derives from The One (which is indivisible) all the realities it has, such as life and thought, while The One is not any of these things. The totality of beings must come after The One because The One itself has no determinate form. The One simply is one while The Intelligence is what in the realm of being constitutes the totality of beings. Thus The One is not any of the beings The Intelligence contains but the sole source from which all of them are derived. That is why they are "beings"; they are already determined, each with its specific form; a being cannot be indeterminate, but only definite and stable. For intelligible beings such stability consists in the determination and form to which they owe their existence.

The Intelligence of which we speak deserves to be of this lineage and to derive from no other source than the supreme. Once begotten, it begets with it all beings, all the beauty of the Ideas, all the intelligible deities. Full of the things it has begotten, it "devours" them in the sense that it keeps them all, does not allow them to fall into matter or to come under the rule of Rhea. This the mysteries and myths of the gods obscurely hint at: Cronus, the wisest of the gods, was born before Zeus and devoured his children —quite like The Intelligence, big with its conceptions and in a state of satiety. Then, out of his fullness, Cronus begot Zeus. Thus The Intelligence, out of its fullness, begets The Soul. It begets necessarily because it is perfect and, being so great a power, it cannot remain sterile. Here, again, the begotten had to be inferior, an image, and—since it was indeterminate by itself—be determined and formed by the principle that begot it. What The Intelligence begets is a

[8] The Greek text throughout these last lines is hopelessly corrupt.

word and substantive reasoning, the being that moves about The Intelligence and is the light of The Intelligence, the ray that springs from it. On the one hand, it is bound to The Intelligence, fills itself with it, enjoys its presence, shares in it, and is itself an intellectual existent. On the other hand, it is in contact with lower beings begetting beings lower than itself. Of these we shall treat later.[9] The sphere of the divine stops here at The Soul.

8. This is the reason why Plato establishes three degrees of reality. He says: "It is in relation to the king of all and on his account that everything exists. . . . In relation to a second, the second class of things exists, and in relation to a third, the third class." Further, he speaks of the "father of the cause," by "cause" meaning The Intelligence because for him The Intelligence is the demiurge. He adds that it is this power that forms the soul in the mixing bowl. The Good, he says, the existent that is superior to The Intelligence and "superior to Being," is the father of the cause, *i.e.*, of The Intelligence. Several times he says that Idea is Being and The Intelligence. Therefore, he realized that The Intelligence proceeds from the Good and The Soul proceeds from The Intelligence. These, indeed, are not new doctrines; they have been taught from the most ancient times, without, however, being made fully explicit. Our claim is to be no more than interpreters of these earlier doctrines whose antiquity is attested by Plato's writings.

The first philosopher to teach this was Parmenides. He identified Being and The Intelligence and did not place Being among sense objects. "To think," he said, "is the same as to be," and "Being is immobile." Although he adds thought to Being, he denies that Being (since it must remain always the same) has any bodily motion. He compares it to a "well-rounded sphere"; it contains everything and does not draw thought from without but possesses it within. When in his writings he called Being The One, he was criticized because his unity was found to be multiple.

The Parmenides of Plato speaks with greater accuracy. He distinguishes between the first one, which is one in the

---

[9] Probably II, 4 [12], is meant.

proper sense, and the second one, which is a multiple one, and a third—The-One-and-the-manifold. Therefore this latter Parmenides also distinguished the three degrees here discussed.

9. Anaxagoras, in teaching the simplicity of pure and unmingled Intelligence, also asserted that The One is primary and separate. But, living too long ago, he did not treat the matter in sufficient detail. Heracleitus also knew The One, eternal and intelligible, for he taught that bodies are in a perpetual process of flux and return. According to Empedocles, "Hate" is the principle of division but "Love" is The One, an incorporeal principle, the elements playing the role of matter.

Aristotle says that the first existent is "separate" and intelligible. But in saying that "it thinks itself," he denies it transcendency. He asserts as well the existence of a plurality of other intelligible entities in a number equal to the heavenly spheres so that each of them has its own principle of motion. He therefore advances a doctrine of intelligible entities that is different from that of Plato. And as he has no valid reason for this change, he appeals to necessity. Even if his reasons were valid, one might well object that it seems more reasonable to suppose that the spheres, as they are coordinated in a single system, are directed towards the one ultimate, the supreme existent. We might also ask whether, for him, intelligible beings derive from one first originating principle or whether there are for them several such principles. If intelligible beings proceed from one principle, their condition will be analogous to that of the sense spheres where one envelops another and one alone—the exterior sphere—dominates all of the others. In this case the primal existent will contain all intelligible entities and be the intelligible realm. The spheres in the realm of sense are not empty, for the first is full of stars and the others, too, have theirs. Similarly, the principles of motion in the intelligible realm will contain many entities, beings that are more real than sense objects. On the other hand, if each of these principles is independent, their interrelation will be subject to chance. How, then, will they unite their actions and converge in producing that single effect which is the harmony of the heavens? Further, what is the basis for the assertion that sense objects in the heavens equal in number their intelligible movers? Finally, why is there a plurality of movers since they are incorporeal and are not separated one from another by matter?

Thus the ancient philosophers who faithfully followed the doctrines of Pythagoras, of his disciples, and of Pherecydes have maintained the existence of the intelligible realm. Some of them have recorded their views in their writing; others orally; others have bothered to do neither.

10. That beyond Being there exists The One we have attempted to prove as far as such an assertion admits of proof. In the second place come Being and The Intelligence; in the third, The Soul.

Now it must be admitted that as these three are in the very nature of things, they also are in us.

My meaning is not that they exist in our sense part (they are separate from sense) but in what is external to sense (understanding "external" in the same way that one says they are "external" to the heavens)—the area, that is, that Plato calls "the man within."

Our soul, too, then, is something divine, its nature different from that of sense. It is essentially like The Soul. Possessing intelligence, it is perfect.

It is necessary to distinguish between the intelligence which reasons and that which furnishes the principles of reasoning. The soul's discursive reasoning needs no bodily organ; it keeps its action pure of the bodily in order to reason purely. Separate from the body, it has no admixture of body. It is no mistake to place it in the first degree of the intelligible. We need not seek to locate it in space; it exists outside space. To be within oneself and exterior to all else and immaterial is to be outside body and the bodily. That is why Plato says, speaking of the cosmos, that the demiurge has The Soul envelop the world "from without." His meaning? A part of The Soul remains in the intelligible realm. Thus, in speaking of the human soul, he says that "it dwells at the top of the body." When he counsels separation of soul from body, he does not mean spatial separation, such as is established by Nature, but that soul must not incline towards body even in imagination but must alienate itself from body. Such separation is achieved by raising to the intelligible realm that lower part of the soul which, established in the realm of sense, is the sole agent that builds up and modifies the body and busies itself with its care.

11. Since discursive reason inquires, "Is this just?" or, "Is that beautiful?" and then decides that a particular object is beautiful or that a certain action is just, there must exist a justice that is immutable and a beauty that is immutable according to which the soul deliberates. Otherwise, how could it reason? Moreover, since the soul reasons only intermittently about such topics, it cannot be discursive reason that continually possesses the idea, say, of justice. Rather must it be intelligence. We must also possess within us the source and cause of intelligence, the divinity, which is not divisible and exists not in a place but in itself. Not in a place, it is found in that multitude of beings capable of receiving it just as if it were divisible—quite as the center of the circle remains in itself while each of the points of the circle contains it and each of the radii touches it. Thus we ourselves, by one of our parts, touch the supreme, unite ourselves to it, and are suspended from it. We establish ourselves in it when we turn towards it.

12. How is it that we who possess in ourselves such great things are not aware of them, that some of us often, and some of us always, fail to actualize these capacities? The realities themselves, The Intelligence and the self-sufficient above it, are "always active." The Soul, too, is always active. As to our own souls, we are not aware of all that goes on in them. Such activities are known only when perceptible by sensation. Unless they attain to sense they are not communicated to the entire soul and thus we are not conscious of them. Yet the faculty of sense perception is only part of man; it is the whole soul with all of its parts that constitutes the man. Each part of the soul is always alert and always engaging in its appropriate function, but we are aware only when there is communication as well as perception.

To grasp what is within us we must turn our perceptive faculties inward, focusing their whole attention there. Just as the person who wants to hear a cherished sound must neglect all others and keep his ears attuned to the approach of the sound he prefers to those he hears about him, so we too must here close our senses to all the noises that assail us (if they are not necessary) and preserve the perceptive power of the soul pure and ready to attend to tones that come from above.

SOURCES

For the key to abbreviations see *Guide to Sources*, page 223.

2   ¶1   soul is . . . ample heavens: *cf.* Plato, *Phaedrus* 246 b 6-7 and *Laws* 896 e 8-9.
          "never abandon itself": Plato, *Phaedrus* 245 c 9.
   ¶2   quiet too . . . it round: *cf.* Plato, *Timaeus* 43 b 5.
          from all sides: *cf. op. cit.* 36 e 3.
          blessed and alive: *cf. op. cit.* 34 b 8 and 36 e 4.
          "object . . . the gods": Homer, *Iliad*, XXIII, 65.
   ¶3   It is present in every point: *cf.* Plato, *Timaeus* 37 c 7.
          this world is divine: *cf.* Plato, *Timaeus* 92 c 6-7.
          "a corpse . . . a dunghill": Heracleitus in *Vorsokrat.*, fr. B 96.
   ¶4   consider . . . original purity: *cf.* Plato, *Republic* 611 c 3.

3   ¶1   "borders": Plato, *Laws* 705 a 4.
   ¶3   The Soul is . . . to Idea: *cf.* Aristotle, *On the Soul*, III, 5; 430 a 10-15.

4   ¶1   That world . . . (*nous*): Plato, *Cratylus* 396 b 6-7.
   ¶2   Since it . . . change: *cf.* Aristotle, *Metaphysics*, XII, 7; 1072 b 23.
          that eternity . . . image: *cf.* Plato, *Timaeus* 37 d 7.
          It "is" alone.: Plato, *Timaeus* 37 e 6.
   ¶3   "identity" . . . "rest": *cf.* Plato, *Sophist* 254 d 4-5 and 254 e 5 - 255 a 1.

5   ¶1   "secede": Plato, *Parmenides* 144 b 2.
   ¶4   substances, . . . is number: *cf.* Plato in Aristotle, *Topics*, VI, 3; 140 b 2.
   ¶5   Number . . . realm: *cf.* Plato in Aristotle, *Metaphysics*, XIII, 7; 1081 a 14-15.

7   ¶4   of this lineage: Homer, *Iliad*, VI, 211; and Plato, *Republic* 547 a 4-5.
          come under . . . Rhea: *cf.* Hesiod, *Theogony*, 453 ff.
          Cronus . . . his children: *cf.* Plato, *Cratylus* 396 b.

8 ¶1 "It is . . . third class.": *Letter II* 312 e 1-4.
"father of the cause": *Letter VI* 323 d 4.
that forms . . . mixing bowl: *cf.* Plato, *Timaeus* 34 b ff.
and 41 d 4-5.
"superior to Being": Plato, *Republic* 509 b 9.

   ¶2 "To think . . . to be": *Vorsokrat.,* fr. B 3.
"Being is immobile": *Vorsokrat.,* fr. B 8, 26.
"well-rounded sphere": *Vorsokrat.,* fr. B 8, 43.

   ¶3 the first one: *cf.* Plato, *Parmenides* 137 c - 142 a.
second . . . manifold: *cf.* Plato, *Parmenides* 144 e 5 and
155 e 5.

9 ¶1 Anaxagoras . . . separate: *cf. Vorsokrat.,* fr. B 12.
perpetual . . . return: *cf. Vorsokrat.,* fr. A 1; Diog. Laert.,
IX, 8.
"Hate" "Love": *Vorsokrat.,* fr. B 26, 5-6.

   ¶2 "separate": *On the Soul,* III, 5; 430 a 17.
intelligible: *Metaphysics,* XII, 7; 1072 a 26.
"it thinks itself": *Metaphysics,* XII, 7; 1072 b 20.
He asserts . . . motion: *cf.* Aristotle, *Metaphysics,* XII, 8;
1074 a 14-17.

   ¶3 Pherecydes: *cf. Vorsokrat.,* fr. A 7.

10 ¶3 "the man within": *Republic* 589 a 7 - b 1.

   ¶5 "from without": *Timaeus* 36 e 3.
"it dwells . . . body": *Timaeus* 90 a 5.
separation . . . body: *cf.* Plato, *Phaedo* 67 c 6.

12 ¶1 "always active": Plato, *Phaedrus* 245 c 5.

THE POST PRIMALS

(V, 2 [11])

A small bright gem, this, especially after the *longueurs*, however necessary and informative, of the preceding treatise.

Still engaged in plotting out the soul's mystic return to The One, having just shown that the three primals are nobly present in the human soul, Plotinus here shows the cohesion of the intelligible: if he explains how a lower hypostasis "comes from" a higher, it is in order to make clear how they "stay with" one another. There are no crevices or fissures through which the soul might slip on its upward climb.

The reader should find not unprofitable the solving of one sole objection, which takes up the final two-thirds of the treatise. By such indirections often are the directions of this author's thought best discovered.

1. The One is every thing and not every thing. It is not every thing because it is the source of every thing. It is—transcendently [1]—every thing because there every thing is—or, more exactly, is not yet but is to be.

[1] The word here is *ekeinos.* For discussions on how best to translate it that are extremely informative regarding the whole Plotinian perspective, see Henry, *Plotin et l'Occident*, pp. 51–2; Cilento, *Enneadi*, III, 2, pp. 30–1; Harder, *Plotins Schriften*, I, 509–11.

Yet how can every thing come from The One, which is simple and apparently has within it no multiplicity or duality whatsoever? Every thing can come from it precisely because there is no thing in it. In order that being be, The One must be not being but being's begetter.

This, then, it may be said, is the primal begetting: perfect—seeking nothing, having nothing, needing nothing—The One "overflows" and its excess begets an other than itself; begotten turns back towards begetter and is filled and becomes its contemplator, The Intelligence; its abiding with The One constitutes it Being; its contemplating The One constitutes its being Intelligence; because it abides with The One in order to see, it becomes—at one and the same time—Intelligence and Being.

Image of The One, The Intelligence produces as does The One, with—like its prior—a mighty show of strength. This activity is The Soul welling up from Being, The Intelligence the while remaining unchanged quite as its prior, The One, remained unchanged.

But The Soul does not remain unchanged in begetting its image, but is altered. Contemplating its source it is filled and "goes out" (a motion different in kind and in direction) and begets its own image: Sense and, the vegetal principle, Nature.

However, nothing is separated from what is prior.

The Soul's going out seems to extend even to the vegetal level. In one sense it does extend that far for the life of growing things is its province. But it does not go out wholly onto the level of vegetation; it is there solely in the sense that, in going so low by this abasement and desire for what is base, it is the producer of an existent other. Its higher part (its own intelligence, to The Intelligence akin) continues in untroubled self-possession.

2.   Such then is the procession from the first principle to the last with each principle in its own place, begotten positioned below begetter and each, as guided, one with its guide.[2]

When The Soul enters a vegetal form, only a part—the most rebellious and least intellectual—is there since it has gone so far out of itself. When it enters an animal, it is sensation that has taken charge and conducted it there. When it enters a man, its outgoing has been due entirely

[2] *Cf.* IV, 8 [6], 6.

either to its reasoning part or to intelligence insofar as a soul has an intelligence of its own and therefore the desire to know or be moved more generally.

When one clips shoots or branch ends, where does the soul go that was in them? It returns to where it came from; there is no spatial separation; soul abides in its source. But cut a root to pieces, or burn it. Where then is the soul that was in the root? In The Soul; the soul never left The Soul for some place else. In the same place, it must have been some place else since, as we said, it "returns." And, if it does not "return," it is in another plant. Our meaning here is merely that the soul is not compressed into some one place. If the soul returns, it returns within the power of its prior. And where is this power? Within the power of *its* prior. And this last within The Intelligence. Of course, none of this is to be understood spatially, particularly in regard to The Intelligence, but in regard to The Soul as well. The Soul, then, is nowhere. It is in a "where" that is "nowhere" and "everywhere." Still, if it tarry midway in its ascent, it leads a middling existence centered upon the mediocre in its self.

Thus are all these things The One and yet not The One. They are The One because they are from The One. They are not The One because The One abides within itself in giving them existence. All things accordingly are like a life that extends in a straight line: each successive part differs, but the line is of a piece with itself. It has points without end that are different, but previous point is not effaced by subsequent point.

That portion of The Soul that arrives in plants, does it in its turn engender nothing? It engenders the plant in which it resides. But to examine this question, it is necessary to start from another principle.[3]

[3] *See* III, 4 [15], 1–2; IV, 4 [28], 22.

SOURCES

For the key to abbreviations see *Guide to Sources*, page 223.

2 ¶1 each principle . . . place: *cf*. Plato, *Timaeus* 42 e 5–6; *Phaedrus* 246 e.

VIRTUE

(I, 2 [19])

That everything he believes is present in everything he says makes the sorting out of Plotinus' thought into clearly articulated expository stages just about impossible. All, really, that can be done is to emphasize dutifully after him the beliefs he chooses to emphasize in one treatise rather than another. It is what, obviously, is being done in the present book.

Obvious, it is yet deserving of remark, seemingly, here.

The absence so far of any ethical reference in a mystical classic like the *Enneads* should have struck the reader as somewhat strange. The absence in a mystical author like Plotinus, in whom everything everywhere is present that he thinks at all pertinent, must seem stranger still. For there is, after all, the opinion which experience has kept afloat in every age and culture that the mystical is one flowering of the ethical, that mysticism is rooted in morality, that the pure of heart—and they alone—will see God, that vision is for the virtuous.

Only in *Beauty* have virtues been referred to. And there (§6) the ethical puts in no appearance. Nor will it in this treatise. It will not because there simply is no place for it in the Plotinian schema.

No complaint is being voiced here, only a caution. If Plotinus, the better to keep his universe speculatively neat, left morality out, he was perfectly free to do so. But the reader is not free to think, because there is so much talk of virtue in this treatise, that he put it in.

The treatise itself will be found to be a pretty melding of mutually antagonistic doctrines: that of the Stoics, virtue makes one like God, and that of Aristotle, virtue makes one truly oneself and not like anyone else. With recourse as usual to introspection, Plotinus unites by distinguishing: by the civic virtues, which are not in the divine, one becomes truly oneself; become truly oneself, one is closer to the divine, and by the exercise of the higher virtues, which are in the divine, one becomes divine.

Biographers of philosophers had a rather easy time of it in the generations immediately following the composition of this treatise. They felt no need for facts. They merely needed to take its latter part and ascribe what they found there to their hero. Thus Marinos in his *Life of Proclus.* Thus, it is to be feared, Porphyry in his *Life of Plotinus.*

1. Since evils are here "haunting this world by necessary law," and since the soul wishes to flee evils, "it must flee from here."

How is it to flee? Plato says by "becoming like the divinity," that is, by becoming "just, holy, prudent"—virtuous, in other words.

But does not likeness in virtue imply likeness to someone having virtue? Likeness, then, to which divinity? Will it not be to one that seems to have all of them in the highest degree, The Soul in its loftiest part where resides a wondrous wisdom? Because we are in this world, naturally it is to The Soul that we are rendered like by virtue.

And yet it is doubtful that every virtue is present in The Soul—temperance, for example, and courage. Nothing is alien to it, nothing a danger, so how can there be courage? There is nothing alluring whose lack could induce desire of possession, so how can there be temperance? Yet, if it is true that like our own souls The Soul aspires to the intelligible realm, it is clear that the pattern of existence and the virtues as well come to us, as to it, from that realm.

Has The Intelligence, then, these virtues? At the very

least it is unlikely that it has those virtues called "civic," the wisdom that reasons, the courage that is of the heart, the temperance that is the accord and harmony of reason and desire, the rectitude that causes each of these to "fulfill its appropriate function whether in commanding or in obeying."

Is likeness, then, not according to these civic virtues but according to other, higher civic virtues? And, if according to the higher, is it in no wise according to the lower? Would it not be absurd that there would be no resemblance on account of the lower? Those who possess the lower virtues are reputed divine, and, if one must repute them so, is it not because of a likeness, whatever it be? Is it not absurd that the likeness be attained only by the more lofty virtues?

Whichever is true, The Intelligence does possess virtues, different though they may be from ours. If one agrees that we can be like it even by virtues different from its own (even if it is otherwise with other virtues, we do at least have some virtues unlike those of The Intelligence, that is, the properly civic virtues), there is nothing against our going so far as to say that we become like the divinity by our own virtues even though the divinity possesses them not.

How is this possible? Thus: If something is heated by the presence of heat, must the source of the heat be heated itself? Again, if an object is hot because of the presence of fire, is it necessary that the fire itself be hot because of the presence of fire?

Against the first example the retort can be given: There is heat in the source, but it is a heat that is inherent, so that in accord with this analogy virtue would be an acquired characteristic of the soul but inherent in the being the soul imitates and from which it derives it. And this answer can be made to the illustration from fire: The conclusion must be that the being is virtue itself. But did we not judge it superior to virtue?

These refutations would be valid if the virtue in which the soul shares were identical with, and not actually different from, the being that is its source. The house you see is not the same as that which is in the thought (of the architect), although like it. The house you see is orderly and proportioned, while in thought there is neither order, nor proportion, nor any symmetry. In the same fashion we derive from the intelligible realm the order, the proportion, and the harmony that here below make up virtue. But to the intelligible beings, having no need of harmony and order and proportion, virtue is of no use. Nonetheless, a virtue's presence makes us like to them.

Thus much to show that, from the fact that virtue makes us like to an intelligible being, it does not follow necessarily that virtue resides in this being. Now we must go beyond explanation to conviction.

2.　Let us consider first of all the virtues by which, as they say, likeness is to be achieved, seeking out that one element that, an image in us, is virtue and, a reality in the other, is not virtue.

First of all it must be remarked that likeness is of two sorts: that of beings whose likeness is reciprocal, that share an identical element because they spring from the same source; and that of beings which achieve a likeness that is not reciprocal, that do not share an identical element (but there is a different element) because one is the prior of the other.

Now what, both in general and in particular, is virtue? For clarity's sake let us begin with the particular in such a way that the character of all virtues will the more easily become apparent. The civic virtues mentioned above genuinely order our lives for the better. They limit and moderate our desires and all our passions. They deliver us from erroneous opinion, for a being bettered by submission to control escapes beings that control and limit. But, to the extent that they are limits for the soul considered materially, the virtues themselves receive their limits from the image of ideal measure that is in them. They possess a trace of perfection from above. Because what is not wholly submitted to measure is matter, which in no degree can become like the divinity, the more a being shares in form, the more it becomes like the formless divinity. Beings close to divinity share in form the more. The soul, which is closer than is the body, and beings of the same genus as the soul share more than the body to the point that the soul can err in taking itself for the divinity and falsely believe that what is in it is the totality of the divine.

That, then, is the way that men of civic virtue become godlike.

3.   But Plato indicates a likeness to divinity of another sort since it pertains to the higher virtues. Of this we must now treat. Doing so we will see the essence of both civic and higher virtues more clearly and become aware, in a general manner, that there does exist a virtue different from civic virtue.

Plato says first of all that "likeness" consists in "divine flight" from here below. Next he calls the virtues of civil life not virtues simply but "civic" virtues. Finally, he calls all the virtues "purifications." It is evident that he admits two sorts of virtue and that he does not situate divine likeness in civic virtue.

In what sense do we say then that the virtues are purifications and that especially by purification we achieve likeness? In this sense: The soul is evil to the extent that it is "mingled" with body, in sympathy with it and judges in accord with it. And the soul is good and virtuous if this accord no longer has place and if it acts alone (such as thinking and being prudent), if it is no longer in sympathy with the body (this is temperance), if quit of the body it no longer feels fear (this is courage), if reason and intelligence control with ease (this is rectitude). The soul, thus disposed, thinks dispassionately. This disposition can be called likeness to the divinity because the divinity is pure and its act is as well. The being that imitates it possesses prudence then.

Do dispositions such as these exist in divinity?

They certainly do not. They exist only in the soul.

What is more, The Soul thinks in its own way; The Intelligence thinks in a different way; The One thinks not at all. Do the thought of The Intelligence and that of The Soul have then only the name in common? Not at all; but the former is prior and the latter derivative and therefore different. It is an image of the inner word of another being, just as spoken language is an image of the inner language of the soul. As spoken language, compared to the soul's inner language, is fragmented in words, the language of the soul translating the divine word is fragmentary, if compared with that word.

Yes, virtue pertains to The Soul and not to The Intelligence, nor to the hypostasis above The Intelligence.

4. Is purification the same thing as virtue or does purification come first and virtue later? Does virtue consist in being pure or in becoming pure?

Becoming pure is less perfect than being pure for being pure is, as it were, the goal. Being pure is absence of all that is alien; goodness is something else again. If, before being impure, one was good, purification suffices. When purification will suffice, what remains will be the goodness, not the purification.

We must inquire more closely into what this is that remains. Obviously, it is not the Good, which cannot exist with an evil being. The appearance, then, of good? Yes, a nature with two allegiances and unable to abide in the Good. Union with its kin is its good; with the foreign, its evil. Therefore must it purify itself and be united with its kin.

This uniting is a conversion. A conversion after the purification? No. The conversion is accomplished by the purification.

Is virtue, then, conversion? No, virtue is what results in the soul from conversion. And this is . . . ? That it sees, receives the imprint of the intelligible much as the eye does of the visible. But was not the intelligible always there, its presence merely forgotten? Yes, it was always there . . . lying inert in the dark. To drive back the dark and so come to know it was there, light was needed. Further, possessing imprints, not the originals, the soul must conform the imprints to the verities whence the imprints came. But it does possess them. That doubtless means that The Intelligence is not foreign to the soul. It is not foreign when the soul turns its regard towards it otherwise, although present to the soul, it is foreign. It is here as with our scientific knowledge; if we do not ever address ourselves to it, it becomes a stranger to us.

5. Now the scope of purification must be determined. To what divinity does it render us like? With what divinity make us one?

The question chiefly is this: In what sense does virtue purify our being, our desires, and all our other affections, our griefs, and the like? To ask this is to ask how far the soul can separate itself from the body. In separating itself it withdraws into itself, into—as it were—its own place, above passion and affection, the unavoidable pleasures of sense mere medication and assuagement lest it be disturbed. It no longer knows suffering. If that is impossible, it bears suffering without bitterness and eases its sting by refusing assent to it. It suppresses violent feelings. If it cannot do it completely, at least it does not allow such feelings to gain the upper hand and banishes the involuntary to the body where it becomes infrequent and enfeebled. The soul is without fear itself (although there is still sometimes the involuntary shiver) and knows not fear except in the case where fear serves to avert danger. It desires evidently nothing that is shameful. Food and drink it wants, for the satisfying of the body's needs, not for itself. It does not seek erotic delights, or seek only those that nature counsels and that leave it master of itself or, at most, move within the confines of the imagination—and then only fleetingly.

The rational soul would be in itself free of all passion. It wills further to purify the irrational within it in order to avoid the buffeting of external impressions or at least to render it the less violent, the more rare, and wholly and immediately tended to because of the proximity of reason; just as a man who lives next door to a sage profits from his proximity and becomes like the sage or at least capable of shame at doing what the good man would not want him to do.

Hence there is no battling in the soul; it is sufficient that the reason is there. The lower part of the soul respects reason; and, if it is disturbed by violent movement, it is itself that is irritated at not remaining in quiet repose when its master is there, and it reproaches itself with its weakness.

These are not sins, for the man is fully disciplined.
6. His effort is directed not to avoiding evil but to being divine. To the degree that there are these involuntary movements, he is still both god and devil. Or, rather, he has in him a being different from him of a virtue different from his. If these movements are no longer, then there is divinity purely and simply, one of the divine beings that come after The One. He is one of those that have come from on high. If he becomes what he was when first he came, he is on high. But, come here below, he resides

in the here-below and makes it like to himself to the extent that it can be like. And, to the extent that is possible, he is immune to hurt and does none of those things that are displeasing to his overlord.

What form does each of the virtues take in a soul of this sort? Wisdom and prudence consist in the contemplation of all that exists in The Intelligence—what The Intelligence apprehends by presence. They are of two kinds, one in The Intelligence and another in The Soul. In The Intelligence they are not virtues. In The Soul they are virtues. What are they then in The Intelligence? Its act and its essence. But in coming from The Intelligence and taking up residence in a being different from them, they are virtues. Justice in itself, for example, as every virtue in itself, is not a virtue but the exemplar, the source of what, in the soul, becomes virtue. Virtue is predicated of a being. Virtue in itself or the Idea of virtue is predicated of itself and not of a being different from it. Justice, again, consists in this, that each being fulfill its proper function. Does it always presuppose diversity of parts? The justice appropriate to multiplicity does. But not justice in itself; it can function in a unity. True justice, justice in itself, is the relationship of a unity to itself, a unity containing no this, that, or the other. In The Soul this loftier justice is to direct its act towards The Intelligence; temperance, its interior withdrawal towards The Intelligence, its fortitude, an impassiveness that apes the native impassiveness of The Intelligence towards which it directs its gaze. This, through virtue, The Soul must acquire if it would not be the victim of its less noble companion's every passion.

7. Virtues of this sort succeed one another in The Soul as do their exemplars, anterior to the virtues, in The Intelligence.

In The Intelligence knowledge, or wisdom, is thought; temperance is its relation with itself, justice is the achieving of the activity that is proper to it. The analog of courage is The Intelligence's identity with itself and the persistency of its pure state.

In The Soul wisdom and prudence are the vision of The Intelligence. But they are there the virtues of The Soul. The Soul is not its own virtues as is The Intelligence. The same holds true for the entire series of virtues.

All virtues are purifications whose term is perfect purity. The Soul has all virtues by way of purification. If it did not, no one of them would attain perfection.

Whoever has the virtues under this higher form possesses necessarily—in potency—the virtues under their lower form. But one who possesses the second does not necessarily possess the first.

Such is the life of the wise man in its most eminent form. Does he possess as well—in act—the lower virtues, or only the higher ones? He possesses both sorts but in different ways. Each virtue should be examined separately. Take prudence: if he exercises the virtues that are the principles of lower virtues, how could prudence, in its lower form, still subsist when it is no longer used? Take temperance: since the virtues have not the same natural limits, how would it be possible to exercise a temperance that provides bounds only to the desires as well as a temperance that suppresses them completely? It is the same with the other virtues, directly prudence, the first of them, has been put out of court. Yet the wise man will know these lower virtues. He will possess all the qualities that derive from them. Perhaps, even, he will occasionally act in conformity with them. But, once arrived at the higher, he will act in conformity with them, the higher. Henceforth he does not limit temperance to the control of pleasure, but, to the extent that it is possible, he is completely isolated from the body. In a word he does not live the life of one who, according to civic virtue, is a good man. He forsakes that life and chooses another in its place, the life of the gods, for his wish is to become like to the gods and not to good men. Likeness to good men is likeness of one image to another image that comes from the same model. But likeness to God is likeness to the model itself.

SOURCES

For the key to abbreviations see *Guide to Sources,* page 223.

1 ¶1-2 "haunting . . . holy, prudent": Plato, *Theaetetus* 176 a-b.
  ¶5 temperance . . . accord and harmony: *cf.* Plato, *Republic* 431 e 8.
      "fulfill . . . or in obeying": *op. cit.* 434 c 8, 443 b 2.

3 ¶1 Plato indicates: *cf. Theaetetus* 176 b-c.
   ¶2 "likeness" . . . "purifications": *op. cit.* 176 b 1; *Republic* 430 c 3; *Phaedo* 69 c 1.
   ¶3 "mingled": Plato, *Phaedo* 66 b 5.

5 ¶2 Food and drink: *cf.* Plato, *Phaedo* 64 d 3-6.

6 ¶1 then there is divinity purely: *cf.* Plato, *Phaedrus* 246 e 5-6.
   ¶2 In The Intelligence . . . are virtues: *cf.* Aristotle, *Nicomachean Ethics,* VII, 1; 1145 a 26.
       True justice . . . to itself: *cf.* Plato, *Republic* 434 c 8.

7 ¶1 Virtues . . . in The Soul: *cf. Stoic.,* III, nn. 295, 299.

DIALECTIC

(I, 3 [20])

The purpose of *Virtue* was to show the relevance of virtue, in the intellectualist Plotinian sense, in one's mystic way to The One. The purpose of *Dialectic* is to show, in detail, how one makes one's way there.

It is taken for granted that it is by mental discipline. Philosophy, however, is the best of mental disciplines. Does one make one's way best, then, by philosophizing? Yes, but by that which is best in philosophizing—the exercise of dialectic.

Dialectic in Plotinus' day received as bad a press as it does today. Chop-logic, the splitting of hairs 'twixt south and southwest side, sat as ill upon his contemporaries as it does on us. Here, after its long misuse by the Stoics, he restores it to something like its pristine Platonic nobility.

To something like, and something *more* . . . . For Plato, the object of dialectic is not terminology but reality. So also for Plotinus. But with §4 Plotinus ennobles dialectic beyond the dreams of Plato. That he does so with the aid of his chief adversaries, the Stoics, makes his achievement all the more remarkable and, for himself, all the more vengefully sweet.

The exposition is of the clearest: There is only one way to The One, but it has two stages—from "here below" to the intelligible realm, and from a first firm foothold in that realm to its peak (§1). The manner of initially making one's way is explained with regard to each of the three types of men (§§2–3). The later progress aloft within the intelligible realm is the sole concern of the latter part of the treatise where, in turn, the nature of Plotinian dialectic is shown (§§4–5, first paragraph) and its relation to philosophy set in relief (§5, second paragraph–§6).

119

1. What is the skill, the method, the discipline that will bring us there where we must go?

We may take it as agreed that our goal is the Good, the first hypostasis; this has already been demonstrated in many different ways, the demonstrations themselves being initiations of a sort.

What kind of being can make this journey? Will it be a soul "that has seen everything or most things at least, who in its first birth entered the seed from which is to come a philosopher, a musician, or a born lover," as Plato says? Yes, the philosopher taking to the path instinctively, the musician and the lover needing guidance.

What is the course to be followed? Is it one and the same for all, or different for each? For all there is one way with two stages: the first for those who are rising to the intelligible realm from here below and the second for those who have already reached it and taken root there and who must proceed from there till they have reached the summit, the highest point in the realm of intelligence, which is "the goal of their journeying." For the moment we will set aside the second of these ways and try to say something about the ascent of the soul to the intelligible realm.

From the beginning one must distinguish the three types of men we have mentioned.

Let us take the musician first. What is he like? He is easily moved and charmed by beauty. Of himself somewhat sluggish, he spontaneously responds to outer stimuli. As nervous people are sensitive to noise, he is sensitive to tones and the beauty they convey. The unharmonious and unrhythmic repel him; he yearns for measure and melody. This is the starting point for such a man. Having experienced these purely sensuous tones, rhythms, and patterns, he must come to separate the beauty residing in the proportion and symmetry from the matter in which they exist.[1] He will have to be taught that what in these things quickens his pulse is their intelligible harmony, the beauty contained in this harmony—briefly, Beauty itself and not something beautiful. He will have to be introduced to philosophy by arguments that will lead him to the conviction of truths he possessed in himself without knowing it. What these arguments are will be indicated later.[2]

[1] *Cf.* I, 6 [1], 3.
[2] §4.

2. The musician can rise to the rank of the lover and either remain there or rise higher still.

The born lover has some remembrance of Beauty. But as he is here below separated from it, he is unable to know clearly what it is. Beautiful objects that meet his gaze arouse his enthusiasm. He must therefore be taught not to find his happiness in some one embodied form but with the grasp of reason to take unto himself the whole of corporeal nature: he must be told that what is identical in each of the bodies comprising the whole is something different from the bodies themselves and that it comes from elsewhere, that it exists in an even higher degree in other things such as dedicated living and the beautiful order of law. Because he is now used to seeking the objects of his love in bodiless things, he will further be shown the beauty that is found in the arts, the sciences, the virtues. Then he will be made to perceive their oneness and the source whence they come. From the virtues he must progress to The Intelligence and Being and from there to the highest goal.

3. The philosopher, by nature, is disposed to rise to the intelligible realm. Being, you might say, "endowed with wings," he flies to it without the need of disengaging himself from sense objects as do the men we have just spoken of. His sole uncertainty will be in what direction to go; his sole need, a guide. Therefore he must be shown the way, having as he does the desire by his very nature and being already detached. For this purpose he will be asked to study mathematics to acquire a notion of and a belief in the bodiless. Eager for instruction, he will learn easily. As he is virtuous by nature, he should be led to the perfection of his virtues. After mathematics he should be taught dialectic until he is adept in it.

4. This training in dialectic is to be imparted to all three types of men. What, then, is it?

It is the art of reasoning that enables us to say what each thing is, in what it differs from other things, in what it resembles them, in what category it is and where it stands therein, whether or not it is a true existent, how many existents there are and, again, how many nonexistents to be distinguished from existents. It also treats of what is good and what is not, what is subordinate to the good and what is subordinate to its opposite, of the nature of the eternal and of that which is not, with sure knowledge about everything and not mere opinion. It puts an end to error in sense knowledge by establishing itself in the intelligible realm. It concentrates its whole attention there, and after having left deception behind it allows the soul, as Plato says, to feed in the "meadows of truth." It uses his method of division in order to distinguish ideas, to define each object, to separate the supreme kinds of being. It alternates between synthesis and analysis until it has gone through the entire domain of the intelligible and has arrived at the principle. Stopping there, for it is only there that it can stop, no longer busying itself with a multitude of objects since it has arrived at unity, it contemplates.

Dialectic leaves to another art the so-called logical inquiry that treats of propositions and syllogisms, just as it does the art of writing. It recognizes that some of these ways of reasoning are determined by necessity and precede all art. It subjects them, along with others, to its examination, judges some of them useful and some of no use to it but to be inquired into by those who are interested in that sort of thing.

Where does this science get its principles?

5. The Intelligence furnishes clear principles if there is a soul able to receive them. Then dialectic resorts to synthesis, combination, division, until it has arrived at perfect understanding because, according to Plato, dialectic is "the purest part of intelligence and wisdom." Therefore since dialectic is our most valuable mental discipline, it must be directed to being and to the existence that is of most value, which is to say, as wisdom it is concerned with being and as intelligence it is concerned with what is beyond being.

But is not philosophy the most valuable mental discipline? Is dialectic the same as philosophy?

Dialectic is the most valuable part of philosophy. Dialectic is not merely the tool of philosophy. It is not just abstract theories and rules. It works with things as they are—existents are, as it were, its material—following a method by which it possesses, together with the statements about them, the objects themselves. Dialectic knows error and sophism only indirectly: discerning another's error to be alien to the truths within itself, thus recognizing what is advanced as counter to the canon of truth.

Dialectic, accordingly, has no knowledge of propositions as such (they are to it as letters are to words); but it knows the propositions in knowing the truth. In general it knows the operations of the soul, affirmation and denial, whether denial is of affirmation or of something else; it knows identity and difference. These it grasps as immediately as sensation grasps its objects. The task of treating them in detail it leaves to those who have a taste for it.

6. Dialectic therefore is the most valuable, but philosophy has other parts. It studies nature, using dialectic as other sciences use arithmetic, but drawing a much greater benefit from dialectic because they are so closely allied. Again, aided by dialectic, philosophy treats of conduct, the study of habits and the exercises productive of good habits. The rational habits derive their characteristics from dialectic and preserve much of it even in their interaction with material things.

If other virtues imply as well the application of reason to their respective experiences and actions, prudence, being concerned with the universal, applies reason in a still higher fashion and considers whether actions are consistent; whether an action should be engaged in now or be deferred, or whether there is a better action to take its place. Dialectic and wisdom, in a universal and immaterial form, provide prudence with all the principles it needs.

Without dialectic and wisdom, could the lower virtues exist? Exist they could, but they would remain imperfect and deficient. On the other hand, is it possible to be a wise man and a dialectician without these lower virtues? No, that could not happen. The virtues must either precede or accompany the progress made in dialectic. The natural virtues one possesses will with the assistance of wisdom become perfect virtues: wisdom comes after the natural virtues to perfect the habitual. The natural virtues either grow and are perfected along with wisdom, or wisdom enters in at one point and perfects them.

In general, natural virtue implies only imperfect vision

and conduct. Our perfection we owe primarily to both natural virtue and wisdom.

Sources

For the key to abbreviations see *Guide to Sources,* page 223.

1 ¶3 "that has seen . . . lover": *Phaedrus* 248 d 1-4.
  ¶4 "the goal of their journeying": Plato, *Republic* 532 e 3.

2 ¶2 take unto himself . . . nature: *cf.* Plato, *Banquet* 210 b 3.
  dedicated living . . . law: *cf.* Plato, *Banquet* 210 c 3-4.
  the sciences: *cf.* Plato, *Banquet* 210 c 6.

3 ¶1 "endowed with wings": Plato, *Phaedrus* 246 c 1.

4 ¶2 how many existents there are: *cf.* Plato, *Sophist* 242 c 5-6.
  sure knowledge . . . opinion: *cf.* Plato, *Republic* 534 c 6.
  "meadows of truth": Plato, *Phaedrus* 248 b 6.
  his method of division: *op. cit.* 265 e - 266 b.

5 ¶2 "the purest . . . wisdom": Plato, *Philebus* 58 d 6-7.

6 ¶1 as other sciences use arithmetic: *cf.* Plato, *Republic* 522 c 1-6.

THE SOUL

(IV, 3 [27])

The goal of the mystic's ascent was established early and at length. The way of the ascent was spelled out in the two treatises immediately preceding. What makes the ascent—the soul—is now analyzed in terms of the ascent.

The title, actually, that Porphyry gave to this treatise and the two following in his edition was "Problems of the Soul," and he was right in doing so. Advertence by the reader to the particular problematic under which the analyses are conducted can be a large help to understanding, especially since they are not the sort of problems that would normally occur to one today.

The relationship of the individual soul to The Soul is the first of the two problems taken up here (§§1–9).

In an earlier treatise, *Are All Souls One?* (IV, 9 [8]), Plotinus proves the unity of origin of all souls. Here he is concerned with the manner in which they originate: Does The Soul share itself with individual souls so that they, in fact, are parts of it? Or does The Soul remain intact and undivided? To the first alternative he says, "No"; to the second, "Yes."

That his answer has become a traditional one in the Platonism of his day seems clear from the reasons he reports as being against it (§1); it is an established position that his adversaries attack as they point out what appear to be inner illogicalities or flagrant infidelities to Plato. The defense of his position, however, far transcends in the subtlety of the analyses involved any mere antiquarian interest. They (§§2–3), and the hardy presentation of the consequences of his position (§§4–8), make singularly good reading today and are compact with insights into the basic essentials of his psychology.

The second problem, the body-soul relationship (§§9–32), is one that will engage the wits of philosophers up to the Middle Ages and, occasionally, beyond.

Although it is the relationship of The Soul to its (cosmic) body that is first discussed (§§9–11), much light is surreptitiously cast on the human body-soul relationship that is to be considered next: *e.g.,* matter informed as a net is by the sea (§9), The Soul the more effective the more despoiled it is of matter (§11). After this, what he has to say explicitly of the human soul (especially §§12–24) may not seem particularly enlightening. But if the reader, forewarned, will submit this section to a severe de-mythologizing, he will find, behind the myths, the most exigent and reliable sort of introspective analysis.

The treatise ends with a pleasant catalog of the consequences for memory of the body-soul relationship just advanced (§§25–32). One aware of the role of memory in both the aesthetical and mystical theories of Plotinus will give them their due.

1. Whether one here will end in solving problems relative to soul or, because they prove insoluble, have only the small satisfaction of bringing them— in their true colors—into the clear, this is a worthwhile enterprise. What subject of inquiry, analysis, or discussion could be preferable to this? Aside from everything else, one's attention is directed both to those realities of which soul is the source and to those others of which it is the product. Obedience, too, is shown the deity that bade us know ourselves. Desirous as we are to explore all things knowable (and thus achieve contemplation, that object of our love) we should surely explore that which makes the exploration.

The Intelligence itself contains a duality. All the more, then, should there be in individual intelligence a subject that receives and an object received. We will take up the question of how our intelligence receives the divinities, but only when we consider how the soul comes into the body.[1] Now we return once more to those who hold that our souls come from The Soul.[2]

They say that it is not sufficient to contend that our souls are not parts of The Soul on the basis that our Souls can attain to what The Soul attains to and in a similar way (if one admits this similarity). Their objection is that parts are always homogeneous with the whole.

More than that, they invoke the authority of Plato, who expressed the following opinion in the passage where he proves that the universe is animated: As our body is a part of the universe, so also our soul is a part of The Soul of the universe.

Besides, they contend, Plato states and proves to a nicety that we follow the circular movement of the universe, that we receive from it both our character and our condition, and that, come to birth at the interior of the universe, we receive our soul from this universe which wraps us round in the same way that each part within us receives a part of our soul: so also, and by analogy, we are ourselves parts in relation to the universe and we receive, as parts, a part of The Soul.

The statement of Plato, "The Soul in its totality has the care of all that is inanimate," has the same meaning; he does not admit, after The Soul, any other soul foreign to it, since The Soul is concerned with the totality of inanimate things.

2. Here is the first answer that must be given to this thesis. Our opponents admit the homogeneity of individual souls with The Soul since they admit they attain to the same objects as it does. Therefore they must admit that individual souls are of the same genus as The Soul. But to do that is to deny by implication that individual souls are parts of The Soul. It would be more logical to say that one same soul is both the unique Soul

[1] §§9–23.
[2] *Cf.* IV, 9 [8], *Are All Souls One?*—especially §1.

and each of the individual souls. But even then, admission of such a soul would make it depend upon a principle that is no longer the soul of this or that, not of the cosmos nor of anything else, yet fathers forth whatever is soul to the cosmos or to any animated being. Actually, The Soul cannot be the soul of any one given thing because it exists essentially; souls that are the souls of particular things exist only incidentally.

Doubtless it is necessary to explain more clearly in what sense one understands here the word "part."

In one sense "part" is a part of body, whether the body be homogeneous or heterogeneous—a sense excluded here; we merely note in passing that in a body whose parts are homogeneous they differ quantitatively rather than specifically (for example, the whiteness of this body is not a part; the whiteness that is in a portion of milk is not a part of the whiteness that is in all milk: it is the whiteness of this portion, not a part of the whiteness of milk, for whiteness, absolutely speaking, has neither size nor measure).

In another sense the word "part" is applied to the incorporeal, or to numbers (for example, two is a part of ten, where it is question of abstract numbers alone); or it is used in the sense that one speaks of the part of a circle or of a line, or again in the sense that one speaks of the part of a science. With units of reckoning and geometrical figures, as well as in bodies, the whole necessarily is lessened by the division into parts and each part is smaller than the whole because they are quantities, and, their existence being essentially quantitative yet not being quantity in itself, they necessarily are susceptible to "more and less."

But the word "part" cannot be taken in this sense when it is a question of the soul for the soul is not a quantity. One cannot say that The Soul would be "ten" and another soul "one." Among many other absurd consequences, it would follow, since The Soul would not be a unity, that either each of its components would be a soul or The Soul would be made up of inanimate things. And we should also recall that our adversaries hold that the parts of The Soul are homogeneous with the whole. Further, in the case of quantitative continua, it is no more necessary that the parts be as the whole than, for example, the parts of a circle and of a square be circles and squares or, in the case where the

parts can be taken as similar to the whole, is it necessary
that the parts be all of them alike; for example, in a triangle
the parts are not each of them triangles but different figures.
Yet they assert that The Soul is homogeneous with its
parts. In a line, doubtless, the part is certainly a line; however, it differs from the entire line by its size. But if one
were to say that there is a difference in size between the
soul, which is a part, and The Soul, which is the whole, one
would then make a quantity and a body of The Soul, since,
as soul, it would have the distinctive properties of quantity.
Let it be supposed that souls are all alike and complete. Then it is evident that The Soul is not divided as
quantity is divided. Our adversaries themselves would
admit that The Soul is not broken up into parts; this would
be to lose The Soul; it would become no more than a piece
of terminology, something to be thought of as wine separated into many portions, and each portion in its jar being
described as a portion of the total thing, wine.

Is the individual soul a "part" in the sense that a theorem
of a science is called a "part" of this science taken in its
totality, since the science continues to exist despite this
division into theorems? This division consists only in the
enunciation and actualization of each of its parts. Each
theorem contains accordingly the total science in potency
and the total science does not exist one whit the less. But
if this were true of The Soul and of particular souls, The
Soul, which has parts, would not be the soul of this or that
but it would exist in itself. It would not be The Soul but a
partial soul. Then all souls, including The Soul, being of
the same species and therefore partial, would be parts of
some other soul. But how then would one among them be
The Soul and the others parts of it?

3.   Are souls parts of The Soul in the same sense that
in an organism the soul that is in the finger would
be called a part of the total soul that is in the
entire body? This theory would admit either that no soul
is outside a body or that every soul is not in a body and
that The Soul is outside the body of the world. This is
a point that will be examined later.[3] For the moment let us

---

[3] IV, 9 [8].

examine, following the comparison taken up, what meaning
it might have.

If The Soul is accorded to all particular organisms, as
the individual soul is to each part of the organism, and if
each soul is in this sense a part of the Soul, it should be
noted that, divided, it would not be itself that The Soul
would give to the individual organism. It ought to be
everywhere the same, everywhere entire, one, and present
in many beings at one and the same time.

There is no longer question of a soul that is a part against
a soul that is an all, especially when an identical power
is present; because, if the function of one part is different
from that of another—that of seeing from that of hearing,
for example—it cannot be said that the part of the soul
that is concerned with seeing is different from that concerned with hearing. Such distinctions we can leave to
others.[4] It is the same soul, although a different faculty
acts in each of the two cases. But in each of these two
faculties are all the others implicitly. Difference of perception comes only from the difference of the organs. All
perception is perception of forms. This fact proves that all
impressions must reach a unique center. If each of the
organs is unable to receive all the impressions, each organ
has its distinct impressions, but the judgment of these impressions depends upon the one same principle that, like a
judge, comprehends what has been said and done.

The Soul is, accordingly, as will be seen,[5] a unity everywhere present but with differing functions. If it were present
as sensation, then the individual organism would be unable
to think—only The Soul would be able to. If each organism
had its own thought, it would exist in itself. But The Soul
is rational and as universal as it is rational. If identical with
an individual organism, it could not be party to the whole.

4. If The Soul is one in this way, what are we to
say in answer to queries about the consequences?
The first difficulty to be raised will be this: Is a
unity possible that is simultaneously present in all things?
Again, what happens when The Soul is in body but a
particular soul is not? Perhaps the consequence will be

---

[4] The reference, not necessarily sarcastic, is to the Stoics.
[5] §9. And cf. VI, 4 [22], 4; IV, 9 [8], 1.

that every soul is always in a body and The Soul especially
because it is not said to abandon the body as ours is.
(Some people say that our soul will leave this particular
body but will never be completely unembodied.) But,
assuming that it is going to be completely out of the body,
how will the soul leave the body and not The Soul when
they are the same?

No such difficulty stands in our way where The Intelligence is concerned because it is differentiated into distinct
parts that nevertheless remain together because its substance is undivided. But for The Soul, of which we speak
as being "distributed among bodies," this unity of all souls
presents many difficulties.

Perhaps one might establish the unity as something
existing independently, which does not fall into body, and
all the others, The Soul and the rest, as depending upon it.
They would be, to a certain extent, altogether one single
soul because they are not souls of particular organisms,
connected with the higher unity by their fringes, united in
their upper parts and striking out in different directions
like the light on the earth spreading itself among the houses
without being split up, all the while remaining one. The
Soul would always remain transcendent because it would
have nothing to do with descent to the lower or any tendency towards the things here below. Our souls would come
down because their place would be marked off for them
in this sphere and because they turn to those things that
need their care. The Soul in its lowest part would be like
the soul in a great and growing plant that directs the plant
effortlessly and in silence. The individual soul in its lowest
part would be like maggots in a rotting part of the plant
because that is what the ensouled body is like in the totality
of existence. The rest of the soul, which is of the same
nature as the higher parts of The Soul, would be like a
gardener concerned about the maggots in the plant and
carefully caring for it. Or it would be like a healthy man
living with other healthy men and aiding them with his
action or contemplation, and a sick man, concerned with
the care of his body, at the service of his body and absorbed
with it.

5.   But, on this supposition, how can there be one
soul that is yours, a second soul that is another
man's, and a third that is yet another's? In the

lower order are they the souls of particular individuals yet in the higher order the souls of that higher unity? This would mean that Socrates would exist as long as Socrates' soul is in the body and would cease to exist when he attains perfection. Now no real being ever ceases to exist. In the intelligible realm the intelligences, because they are not divided among bodies, do not cease to exist; each continues to exist, complete, distinct in its common being.

Souls depend upon the intelligences, are the "expressions" of the intelligences, their further unfolding. They come from the intelligences as a large number comes from a small. They are linked to their sources as to what are less manifold than they. They desire manifoldness but do not achieve it. They preserve both identity and difference. Each is subsistent being. But all are one together.

Our argument is summarized thus: all souls come from one Soul as intelligences come from The Intelligence, separated and yet not separated; The Soul, which remains, is the unique "expression" of The Intelligence and from it come the partial "expressions" of the intelligible realm.

6.   But how is it that while The Soul has produced a cosmos, the soul has not, although it is of the one same sort and contains, it too, all things in itself? We have already said that one and the same thing can enter and exist in many things at the same time. Now it is necessary to say how this comes about. Then perhaps one will know how the same thing, inserted in different things, accomplishes a particular action and is subject to a particular passion, or acts and reacts at the same time.

First, however, it is necessary to examine the question in itself: How has The Soul made the world and why, while individual souls govern each part of the world?

Well, we are not surprised that, among men who possess the same knowledge, some govern a large number and others a small number of people.

But why, one might ask, is this?

The answer might be that there is great difference between souls; some, never having fallen away from The Soul, dwell within it and assume body within it, while others received their allotted spheres when the body was already in existence, when The Soul, their kin, was already in control and, as it were, had already prepared habitations for them.

It is also possible that there is a soul that contemplates The Intelligence while other souls see only the partial intelligences upon which they depend. Perhaps they might still be able to produce the world, but as The Soul has already done so, they are no longer able to: they have been anticipated. This same difficulty would remain if any other soul, of whatever sort, had been the first.

But it were better to say that The Soul has made the cosmos. Its position is firmer in the superior realm. Souls that tend towards the intelligible realm have the greater strength; they husband it in security and they act with ease. For great strength takes the sting out of action. This strength on high remains on high. The Soul remains in itself and acts upon things that draw nigh to it. On the contrary, the other souls "go forth," which can mean only that they have deserted towards the abyss. The multiplicity in these souls is drawn downward and draws along with it the souls themselves and their thinking.

The "secondary and tertiary" souls, of which we hear, must be understood in the sense of a closer or a more remote position in regard to the intelligible realm. Quite as among us, all souls have not the same relation to intellectual things. Some make them their own. Others have an impression of them and desire them. Still others are much less apt. The reason is that they do not act with the same faculties. Some use the highest faculty, others that which is lower, still others the third, although all souls possess all the faculties.

7. So far, so good. But what of the passage in the *Philebus* that implies that other souls are parts of The Soul?

This statement of Plato has not the meaning that some people believe to see in it. It signifies, as it was useful for Plato to have it signify in this instance, that the heavens are animated. He proves it in saying that it is absurd to think that the heavens are without a soul since we, who possess a part of the body of the universe, have a soul, for how could there be a soul in the part and none in the whole?

Further, his thought is particularly clear in the *Timaeus:*

once The Soul is begotten, the demiurge makes other souls but "compounded from the same mixing bowl." He makes them accordingly of the same species as The Soul and makes them different only by their ranking second or third.

As to the phrase from the *Phaedrus,* "The Soul in its totality has the care of all that is inanimate," it is true. What is it that controls bodily nature, sets it in order and builds it up, except The Soul? It is not true that there is power in the nature of one soul and none in the nature of others. The perfect soul, The Soul, "going its lofty journey," as we read, operates upon the cosmos not by sinking into it, but, as it were, by brooding over it; and "every perfect soul exercises this governance." Plato distinguishes the other, the soul in this sphere, as "the soul that has shed its wings."

As for our souls being entrained in the cosmic circuit and taking character and condition from it: this is no indication that they are part of The Soul. The Soul is able to receive many impressions of the nature of places, water and air. Residence in this city or in that, and the varying makeup of the body, may have their influence upon our souls and yet are not parts of place or of body. We have always admitted that as citizens of the universe we take something from The Soul of the universe. We also admit the influence of the cosmic circuit. But against all this we oppose another soul in us which shows that it is another precisely because of the resistance it offers. The fact remains that we were engendered at the interior of the universe. But the infant in its mother's womb has a distinct soul; the soul that enters its body is not its mother's soul.

Thus are these difficulties resolved.

8.   That sympathy exists between souls offers no obstacle to my thesis. Souls are responsive one to another because they all come from the same soul—The Soul.

We have already explained that there is The Soul, unique, and souls, multiple, and how there is a different relationship of parts to the whole as well as a diversity in general of souls among themselves. Now we may add briefly that differences may be induced also by the bodies with which the soul has to do and, even more, by the character and mental operations carried over from the living of previous lives. We read, in fact, that souls choose a life conformable to their previous lives.

As regards the nature of soul in general, the differences have been pointed out in the passage [6] in which mention was made of the secondary and tertiary orders and it has been laid down that, while all souls are all-comprehensive, each ranks in conformity to the faculty that, in it, exercises its activity. One is united to the intelligible realm in reality; another is united only in thought; a third in desire. Each, contemplating different things, has become what it contemplates.

Plenitude and perfection are not the same for all souls, but since they form a systematic whole full of variety (for one intellectual principle embraces multiplicity and variety like an animated organism having many shapes at its command), the entities form a system and are not totally scattered. Chance does not rule among them since it does not even rule in the body. The number of entities is consequently a determinate number.

On the other hand, the beings must remain stable. The intelligibles ought to be identical with themselves. Each of them is numerically one. Thus it is that there is a determinate being.

In a body the individual characteristics develop naturally because it has received a specific form and there is never reality except in imitation of authentic realities. Authentic realities do not rise out of any such conjunction as that of form and matter since they have their being in what is numerically one, was from the beginning, and neither becomes what it has not been nor can cease to be what it is.

Let us suppose for a moment there were an agent that brings them into existence. They would not be produced from matter since they would not be composites. The productive principle then would infuse into them, from within itself, something of its own substances. Then there would be in it a change depending upon whether at any given moment it produced more or less. But what would be the reason that it should produce at one moment and not produce always in the same fashion? Further, the produced total, variable from more to less, could not be eternal, and everyone agrees that the soul is eternal.

But how can a thing be infinite if it is determinate? [7] It

[6] §6.
[7] There seems a jump in the argumentation here. Logically it would go like this: Everyone agrees that the soul is eternal. But, if it is eternal, it must be infinite. But how can a thing be infinite, etc.

is question here of an infinity of power, and a power can be infinite without being divided infinitely. For example, the divinity is not a finite being.

Souls, then, are what they are and do not receive their determinations from elsewhere. Each has the quantity it itself chooses. Without ever going beyond itself it penetrates everywhere throughout the body whither it is its nature to penetrate. It is never separated from itself whether it is in foot or finger. It penetrates body entire. This it does, for example, in each several part of a plant and even in the part cut off from the stem. It is at the same time in the plant and in the part cut off. For the body of the whole is a body that is one, and it is everywhere in it as in a one.

When an animal rots and from it come many beings, the animal soul is no longer in the body. The body has ceased to be receptive of the soul. Had it not ceased to be thus receptive, it would not now be dead. If the bodily parts, disposed by corruption to the engendering of animals, still have a soul, it is because there is no being from which The Soul alienates itself, yet one being is able to receive it and another is not. However, animated beings born of putrefaction do not increase the number of souls. All of them depend upon The Soul, which continues in its unity. Just as with ourselves, some elements are shed, others grow in their places. The Soul abandons the discarded and flows into the newcomer as long as soul subsists in body. But in the cosmos The Soul subsists eternally; although, among the things contained in this cosmos, some possess and others reject a soul, the powers of The Soul themselves abide.

9.   Now we must ask how soul comes to be in body —what is the manner, what the process. This is well worth pondering and inquiring into.

There are two ways in which soul may enter body. The first is for a soul already embodied to change bodies (for instance, to pass from a body of air or fire to one of earth; if people do not call this a simple change of bodies, it is because the body from which it comes to enter into the earthly body remains invisible). The second way is for a soul, after an existence in which it was never embodied, to pass into some body or other: for the first time the soul forms a relationship with body. In this second case it is advisable to examine what happens when a soul that is completely pure and free from body takes a bodily nature unto itself.

We may, or rather we must, begin with The Soul and in talking about it we must realize that we use the terms "entry" and "ensoulment" only for clarity. Never has this cosmos been without a soul, nor was there a time when body existed in the absence of soul or when matter was without form. But in discussion we can consider them separately: it is always legitimate, when reasoning about any kind of composite, to break it down, in thought, into its parts, soul and body, matter and form.

Here is the truth of the matter. Were there no body, soul would not "go forth" since there is no other place where it can exist according to its nature. If it would "go forth," it must make a place for itself, thus a body. But The Soul is at rest: its rest is in repose itself. It is like an enormous light whose radiance, extending out to its term, becomes obscure. The Soul sees this obscurity and gives it form since the obscurity is there as a substrate form. It were hardly fitting for what borders upon soul to be without reason; to the degree that it is capable of receiving, "dimly in dimness" [8] as has been said, it receives it.

It is as if a fair and richly varied house were built which is not cut off wholly from its architect yet to which he has not given a share of himself. He has considered it all, everywhere, as deserving of care expended in making it exist and in making it as beautiful as possible. His doing this occasions him no inconvenience because he manages everything with detachment.

In this sort of way the cosmos is ensouled. It has a soul that does not belong to it yet is present to it. It is not master but mastered; not possessor but possessed. It is in The Soul, which bears it up, and shares in it wholly.

The cosmos is like a net thrown into the sea, unable to make that in which it is its own. Already the sea is spread out and the net spreads with it as far as it can, for no one of its parts can be anywhere else than where it is. But because it has no size The Soul's nature is sufficiently ample to contain the whole cosmic body in one and the same grasp.

[8] VI, 5 [23], 9.

Wherever body extends, there is soul. If body did not exist, it would make no difference to The Soul's "size" because The Soul is what it is.

The cosmos extends as far as The Soul goes. The boundaries of its extension are the point to which in going forth it has The Soul to keep it in being. The shadow projected by The Soul is coterminous with its "expression," and this "expression" is of that grandeur intended by its form.

10.
Now we must return to the master idea, that the universe is eternally what it is, and grasp it in its entirety.

In the groups "air-light-sun" and "moon-light-sun" the members exist simultaneously, although having the degrees of primal, secondary, and tertiary. So let us also imagine The Soul as eternally subsisting and then the things that first come from it and then those that come next. They are like the last weak flames of a fire, flickerings of the ultimate intelligible fire that is The Soul. Then the darkness is lightened and there is an Idea, as it were, hovering over depth that is complete and ultimate darkness. This black shadowy depth is brought under the scheme of reason by The Soul.

The Soul possesses within itself this rationalizing power. It is the same as with the seminal reasons that fashion and inform animals, which are thus like little worlds: what is in contact with The Soul is fashioned in conformity with the characters that the substance of The Soul naturally possesses.

The Soul acts without reflection and without pause for deliberation and examination. An action that was deliberate would not be a natural action but would imply artifice: but art is subsequent to nature; it imitates nature and produces only imitations that are dim and evil—toys they are, and worthless things, despite all the mechanisms involved in their production.

The Soul, by the power of its being, is master of bodies. It brings them into existence and leads them to what condition it pleases; and they have not, at the beginning, the power to oppose its will. Later, doubtless, they do hinder one another and thus fail to attain the shape proper to each that is intended by the seminal reason in each of them. But at first the shape of the cosmos in its totality is the product of soul. All things come to be together effortlessly and with order. And the result, clashing with nothing else, is beautiful.

There The Soul has constructed sanctuaries for divinities, domiciles for men, and other objects for other beings. What else should come from The Soul except things it has the power to make? Fire's power is to heat, that of another body is to chill. But the power of The Soul is twofold depending upon whether it exercises it upon something other or upon itself.

The action of lifeless beings is in a way dormant when it remains enclosed within them. But when it is exercised upon something other, it renders that other, if amenable, like unto itself. It is a common characteristic of all active entities to draw others to a likeness of themselves. But The Soul's action, even that which remains interior to it, is as alert as that which it exercises upon something other. Hence it gives life to things that of themselves do not possess life and it makes them live a life like its own. Living in reason, it accords the body a reasonableness that is a reflection of that which it possesses. Everything it gives to body is an image of its life. It gives to bodies all the shapes of which it possesses the forms. It possesses the forms of the divinities as of everything else. Hence it is that the cosmos contains all things.

11. Therefore those ancient sages who sought to obtain the presence of divine beings by erecting shrines and statues seem to me to have showed insight into the nature of the universe. They have understood that it is always easy to attract The Soul but that it is especially easy to keep it by constructing an object disposed to undergo its influence and to receive from it a sharing. But the imaginative representation of a thing is always disposed to undergo the influence of its model, like a mirror capable of catching the appearance. Nature, with admirable skill, makes things after the image of beings whose forms it possesses. Thus is each thing born, form interior to matter, receiving a shape corresponding to a form that is superior to matter. Thus every particular entity is linked to that divine being in whose likeness it is made, the divine principle which The Soul contemplated and contained in each productive act. Accordingly it is impossible that there should be anything that does not participate in this divine being. But it is equally impossible that the divine being descend here below.

The sun of that sphere (we return to our example [9]) is The Intelligence, and The Soul immediately follows upon it and depends upon it, remaining in the intelligible realm quite as The Intelligence itself. It accords the sun of the realm of sense its appropriate limits. By The Soul's mediation it effects the union between our sun and The Intelligence. It is like an interpreter who conveys to the sun the wishes of The Intelligence and to it the aspirations of the sun to the extent that it can attain to The Intelligence by the mediation of its soul.

For nothing is far away from anything else. To be far away is to be different and to be mingled with something different. There is union in this their separation. These beings are divine because never separated from the intelligible. They are linked to The Soul, to that which in some fashion proceeds from The Intelligence. And by The Soul, which makes them what they are truly called, they contemplate The Intelligence towards which The Soul exclusively directs its gaze.

And the souls of men? They see their images as if
12.   in the mirror of Dionysus and come down to their
level with a leap from above. They do not cut themselves off from their principles, which are the intelligences. And they do not descend with their intelligence. They descend to the earth, and their head remains fixed above the heavens. They have had to come down so low because their middle part is compelled to care for that to which—as needing their care—they have gone. But their father "Zeus has pity" on their fatigue. He makes the bonds in which they labor soluble by death and he gives them a temporary rest in freeing them from their bodies in order that they may, they themselves, come into the intelligible

<hr>

[9] Most scholars are of the opinion that this is rather more than an example for Plotinus. The solar cult was widespread in his day and the Emperor Aurelian was to make it official throughout the Roman Empire.

realm where eternally abides The Soul without any turning towards the things of here below.

The cosmos possesses all that it needs to be self-sufficient and always will. The limits of its duration are determined by unchanging forms. At the end of a given time, it always returns to the same state in the measured alternation of its cyclic lives. It leads the things of this realm to be of one voice and one plan with the intelligible realm. All is determined by subjection to one single form. All is thereby regulated, as well the descent as the ascent of souls and all things else. The proof of this lies in the accord that exists between souls and cosmic order. Their fortunes, their life experiences, their choosing and refusing, are announced by the patterns of stars. From this concordance rises, as it were, one musical utterance.

This could not be so if the universe did not act in conformity with the intelligible realm and had not passions corresponding to the measured cycles of souls, to their ranks and to their lives in the different sorts of careers that they carry out, whether in the intelligible realm, whether in the heavens, or whether they be deflected toward this lower place.

The Intelligence itself remains wholly and always upon high. There is no time when it departs from that to which it belongs. But, although wholly domiciled in the intelligible realm, it influences things here below through the mediation of The Soul.

The Soul, placed most closely to it, is modified according to the form that it receives from it. The Soul communicates this form to things that are its inferiors, sometimes in the same fashion, sometimes in a different fashion, depending upon the season, in an orderly changing course.

The depth of the descent also will differ. Sometimes it is lower, sometimes less low. And this is so even in its entry into any given species. Each descends into a body made to receive it and conformed to its own inner disposition. Each is transported into the body with which it has the greatest resemblance, one into the body of a man, another into the body of a beast, for each one different.

13. The inescapable rule of right consists in a natural principle that compels each soul to go according to its rank towards the image engendered and modeled on its own will and inner dispositions. All souls of this sort are close to that to which they are interiorly disposed. At the appropriate moment there is no need of a being who will send or bring them at such time into particular bodies; the moment arrived, they descend there spontaneously and enter where they ought. To each its own time, and when that moment comes, the soul descends, as at the cry of a herald, and enters the appropriate body—as though stirred and transported by a magic power of irresistible force. The governing of the living thing by the soul works in the same way: at the appropriate time it stirs and brings forth each part, sprouting of beard and horn, new impulses, new flowerings. The soul of a tree governs it, and every incident of its growth is according to a schedule determined in advance.

Souls do not descend freely nor are they sent. At least their willingness is not a free choice. They move towards bodies indeliberately, as if by instinct, as one is drawn without reflection towards marriage or sometimes towards the achieving of great deeds.

Each particular being has its specific destiny and moment, one now and one at another time. The Intelligence, which is prior to the cosmos, has its destiny, too, to abide completely in the intelligible realm and to send forth its light, each ray subject to cosmic law. This cosmic law is innate in each soul and does not draw strength for its accomplishment from without. Given to individuals, each of them uses it and bears it about within itself. When the moment comes, what it wills is done by the beings themselves in which it is. They are able to do so because the law, lodged within them, weighs upon them and gives them a painful longing to go there whither they are bidden from within.

14. Hence it is that our world is brightened by a great number of lights in adorning itself with all these souls. From the moment of its primal organization it accepts unto itself, like multiple worlds, gifts from the intelligences and the deities who confer souls upon it.

Thus it is, likely, that one must interpret the following myth. Prometheus fashioned a woman and the other deities heaped gifts upon her. Aphrodite and the graces brought their gifts and the other divine beings theirs. And they called her Pandora because she had received gifts (*dora*) and because all (*pan*) had given them. All the deities accordingly gave a gift to this being fashioned by Prometheus (who represents providence). And Prometheus' refusal of these gifts, what does it signify except that it is better to choose the intellectual life? But the creator of Pandora himself is bound because he is in some sense the captive of his creation. Such a binding comes from without. His release by Hercules tells us that there is power in Prometheus so that he need not remain in bonds.

Whatever one thinks of this interpretation, the myth certainly signifies the divine gift of souls that introduces them into the world. And it fits in with our thesis.

15. Souls, accordingly, peering out of the intelligible realm, descend first into the heavens and there assume body. Going athwart the heavens they come more or less close to earthly bodies to the extent that they grow more or less in magnitude. Some pass from the heavens to lower bodies. Others go from one base body into another because they have not the strength to raise themselves up from the earth, forever pulled towards it by their weight and by the oblivion that drags upon them. The difference there is among them comes either from the bodies whither they have penetrated, or from their conditions, or from their modes of life, or from the varied character they bring with them, or from all of the reasons, or from certain ones among them.

Some submit their whole life long to the power of earthly destiny. Some at times yield and at times are their own selves. Some, while accepting what must be borne, have the strength of self-mastery in all that is left to their own act. They live according to a law other than that of destiny, according to the law that covers all existing beings, and to it they give themselves wholly.

This law is constituted of seminal reasons that are the causes of all beings, of movements of soul and of their laws, issuing as they do from the intelligible realm. It is conformed to the intelligible realm whence it draws its principles and it joins to it all those things that are in consequence of it. It maintains imperishably all things that can be kept in conformity with their intelligible models. Others it draws whither it is in their nature to go. And, in the descent of souls, that is the reason each has a different position.

The punishment rightly overtaking the wicked must
16.   therefore be ascribed to the cosmic order that leads
all in accordance with justice.

But what of chastisements, poverty, illness, falling outside all justice upon good people? Are they to be charged
to past misdoing? For these events are equally interwoven
into the world order and fall under prediction and take
place conformably to the reasonableness of the cosmos.
Or can one not say that such misfortunes do not respond
to reasons established in the nature of things, that they are
not implied in previous events but are only their accompani-
ments? For example, if a house collapses, the person under
it perishes no matter what sort of man he may be. Or again,
two things move forward (or even one) in an orderly pro-
gression; they crush or destroy what gets in their way. Or
perhaps the undeserved stroke is no evil to the sufferer
if he gives thought to its relation with the beneficent interweaving of things in the cosmos. Perhaps it is even not an
injustice, but has its justification in previous events.

In any case, one must not believe that certain occur-
rences alone are subject to order while others are without
any such link and are purely arbitrary. If everything ought
to happen in accordance with natural cause and effect, in
accordance with a unique reason and a unique order, one
must then believe that this order and this interweaving
extends even to the smallest details. Yes, injustice committed by another is an injustice for the one who has committed it and he is not released from his responsibility. But,
considered within the universal order, it is not an injustice
in the cosmos, not even for the one who has suffered it.
It is a necessary occurrence. If the one who undergoes it
is a good man, it will have for him a happy issue. One must
not believe this cosmic order to be "not of the gods" or
unjust. It distributes exactly to each what is fitting to each.
But we are ignorant of the causes and that accords our
ignorance the occasion for blaming it.

By the following reasoning one can prove that the
17.   soul, in departing the intelligible realm, moves first
into the heavens: If the heavens are that which is
noblest in the realm of sense, they are still the closest to
the intelligible beings. Accordingly the heavenly beings are
the first to receive life from the intelligible realm because

of the greater aptitude they have for sharing it. Earthly
things are the last and, because of their very nature and
their distance from bodiless being, they share less in The
Soul.

All the souls shine down upon the heavens and spend
there the main of themselves and the best. Some souls descend further in order to lighten the lower regions, but it
is not good for them to go so far.

Imagine a center and about this center a luminous circle
that sends off rays; then around this circle another circle
equally luminous, light flowing from light; outside these
two circles a third, which is no longer a circle of light but,
lacking its own light, needs to be lighted by another.
Imagine it like a wheel, or rather like a sphere that receives
its light from the second circle to which it is nigh, and
that is illuminated only to the extent that it receives this
light. The great light remains immobile, therefore, in cast-
ing its light upon things. From it comes naturally a penetrating radiation. Partial lights radiate as does it; some remain immobile; others are drawn by the brilliant reflection produced upon the things they illuminate. More and
more the illuminated demand their care.

It is like a ship buffeted by the tempest: the pilot gives
himself entirely to the safety of the ship and forgets his
own safety and does not think that he is in peril of being
dragged down in the wreck. Similarly the souls go lower
than is needful and lose sight of their own interests. Held
to their bodies, they are fettered in bonds of sorcery, wholly
overcome with their solicitude for bodily nature. Had each
living soul, as has the cosmos, a perfect body, whole and
immune to suffering, the soul that one speaks of as being
present to it would no longer be present but would give
it life while itself remaining entirely upon the heights.

18. Does the soul emerge in reasoning before its entry
into the body and after its exit? At present it uses
reasoning when it is uncertain, when it is full of
distractions, and especially when it is weakened because to
need to reason is the result of a weakening of the intelligence, which no longer is sufficient unto itself. Reasoning
intervenes in craftsmanship when the craftsman encounters
difficulties; when there is no difficulty the craftsmanship
proceeds under its own power.

But if, in the intelligible realm, souls do not use reasoning, how can they be reasonable souls? One might answer that they are able to proceed with a reasoned examination if the occasion is offered them. For the rest, it is necessary to admit this, to take the word "reasoning" in the sense that we have taken it. If one understands by reasoning an interior disposition that always stems from The Intelligence and an act forever stable which is like the reflection of The Intelligence, one must say that the souls use reasoning even in the intelligible realm.

As to language, one should no longer think that the souls use it so long as they are in the intelligible realm or have their bodies in heaven. All the needs and uncertainties that compel us here below to conversation do not exist in the intelligible realm. Acting in a manner both bodily and conformed to nature, the souls have neither orders nor counsels to give. All of them know the others by pure intellection. Even here, below, we know men by sight without their saying a thing. But on high all bodies are pure. Each of them is like an eye. Nothing is hidden nor anything pretended. In seeing someone, one knows what he is thinking before he speaks.

As to daimons and souls which have ethereal bodies, it would be absurd to suggest that they use words, for all such as do are simply animate beings.

19. Are the "indivisible and divisible" in the same place in the soul as if they were mixed together? Or does the indivisible pertain to the soul in another fashion and under a different relationship than the divisible? Does the divisible follow upon the indivisible with their forming two different parts of the soul in the sense that we speak of the rational part as different from the irrational part?

All this one may know if one understands the sense in which we use each of these expressions.

Plato speaks simply of the "indivisible." He does not speak simply of the "divisible" but of "the kind of being that becomes (and not that has become) divisible in bodies." Therefore it is necessary to see what sort of soul the bodily nature needs in order to live and what, in the soul, should be everywhere present to the body.

The sense faculty happens to be divisible because its

exercise is everywhere complete. If it is everywhere, it is (so to speak) because it is in a state of division. Yet, since it is everywhere shown to be complete, one cannot absolutely say that it is divided but only that it becomes divisible in the body.

If one objects that there is certainly a division of this sort in the sense of touch but not in the other senses, it is necessary to answer that it exists also in the others because, since it is the body which takes part in these sensations, it is necessary that they also be divided but with an extension that is less than that in touch.

Vegetation and growth are divided on the same conditions. If desire is in the liver, generosity in the heart, the same contention holds true for them, but perhaps the body does not receive these faculties in this material mixture; it receives them doubtless in a different fashion: they come from one of the things that has previously received from The Soul.

As to reflection and understanding, they have no commerce with the body. Their functions are not achieved through the mediation of a bodily organ. The body is an obstacle, if one wishes to use it in intellectual pursuits.

Hence the indivisible and the divisible are each of them one. Their mingling does not consist in forming one single being. They form a whole of two distinct parts of which each remains pure and separated from the other in its operation.

Yet, if the part that becomes divisible in the body receives from a higher power the character of indivisibility, it is the same being that is able at the same time to be indivisible and divisible as if a mixture were made between it and the power from on high that has come to it.

20. Are the faculties of the soul and all that which one still calls the "parts" of the soul in a place? Or can one say that the first are not in a place and that the others are? Or is neither of them in a place? That is what we must find out.

If we do not establish a determinate place for each part of the soul, and if we do not put them more within than without, we will make of the body an inanimate being and the question will arise about how the operations of the soul that are effected by bodily organs are produced. And if we assign a place only to certain parts of the soul, it seems that we will not situate in us those to whom no such attribution has been made. Hence it follows that we will not have within us a complete soul.

Speaking generally, one must say that neither the parts of the soul nor the complete soul are in the body as in a place. Place is a container and it contains a body. The body is where each of its parts is and it is unable to be completely in some one point of this place. The soul is not body and it contains rather than is contained. It is no more in the body than it is in a vase. For the body to contain the soul as a vase or as a place the body would be soulless. The soul, gathered into itself, does not vitalize by transmission. All that the vase would receive would be loss to the soul.

Further, in a strict sense, place is a bodiless thing and not a body. What need has it of soul? Again, the body would approximate the soul by its extremities but not by itself. There are other reasons against the soul being in the body as in a place. Its place, for instance, would be then transported with it and one would have a thing that carried around its own place. If, on the other hand, one conceives place as a space, the contention that the soul is in the body as in a place is even less acceptable. A space is necessarily empty. But the body is not a void. What the body is in is without doubt a void, but it is the body that is in the void.

More, the soul is not in the body as in a subject because what is in a subject is a condition of the subject, for example, its color or shape, while the soul is by itself.

The soul is not like a part in a whole because the soul is not a part of the body. If one were to say that it is a part of a whole animal, the same question would abide. In what manner is it in the whole? It is not as is wine in a vase, nor as the vase, or some other object, is in itself.

Neither is it in the body as a whole in its parts because it is ridiculous to say that the soul is a whole of which the body would be the parts.

Neither is it as form in matter. Form that is in matter is not separated from it and is posterior to matter. Further, the soul produces the form in the matter; so it is accordingly different from the form. And if one says "it is not a form generated in matter but a separate form" it is still not clear how this form is in the body.

In what sense, then, does everyone assert that the soul is in the body?

The soul is invisible and the body is visible. In seeing the body, we understand that it is animated because it moves and because it feels. We say, then, that it "has" a soul. From that it follows that we say that the soul is "in" the body itself.

But were the soul visible and sensible, if we saw it, wholly penetrated with life, going even to the limits of the body, we would no longer say that the soul is in the body. We would say that the body is the accessory in the principle, the contained in the containing, the fleeting within the perdurable.

21. What answer then will we give if someone, without asserting anything himself, poses the following questions? In what manner is the soul present in the body? Is it in its entirety present in the same manner or is each of its parts present in a different manner?

None of the modes of being-in-something that we have examined expresses fittingly the relationship of soul and body.

It is said that the soul is in the body as a pilot is in his ship. The comparison is good for indicating that the soul is separable from the body, but it does not draw into the clear the manner of union that is precisely the object of our investigation. As passenger, it is in the body only incidentally. In what way is it as pilot? The pilot is not in all of the ship as the soul is in all of the body.

Should one say that the soul is in the body as the skill is in an instrument, as, for example, the skill of the pilot would be in the tiller were this tiller animated and possessed of an inner skill that would accord it impulsion? Actually the difference is a great one since skill remains exterior to the instrument. Nonetheless let us conceive the soul on the model of a pilot whose soul would penetrate his tiller. Let it be in the body as in its natural instrument. Thus it moves itself at will. Does this advance us towards the solution? No, for one still does not know how the soul is in its instrument. And, although this manner of union would be different from the preceding, we wish still to discover the truth or at least to draw more closely to it.

Must one say that the soul is present in the body
22.   as fire is present in the air? The fire, although present *in* the air, is not present *to* it. Penetrating it
everywhere, it is not mixed with it. The fire remains fixed
and the air flows about. Since the air comes from the region
illuminated by light, it comes from there without keeping
anything. So long as it is under its radiation, it remains
luminous. Rather would it be better to say "the air is in
the light" than "the light is in the air."

That is why Plato is right, when it is question of the
cosmos, in not putting The Soul in the body but the body
in The Soul. There is, he says, a part of The Soul in which
the body is and a part where there is not body. For there
are powers of The Soul of which evidently it has no need
in order to live.

The same thing ought to be said of other souls. In fact
it is necessary to say that there are not other powers present
to the body than those that are necessary to it. And they
are present to it without being lodged in it nor in its parts.
For example, the sense power is present to all sentient
parts, and each power, according to the functions it exercises, is present to a different organ.

What I mean is this: Each part of a body that is
23.   animated and enlightened by a soul shares in this
soul in a different fashion; according to the aptitude of an organ for this or that function, the soul gives it a
corresponding power. Thus in the eyes is found the faculty
of seeing, in the ears that of hearing, in the tongue that of
tasting, in the body that of touching. Touch has for instrument the primal nerves, which both accord motor impul-
sions to the animal and have received this power; the
nerves have their origin in the brain; therefore one places
in the brain the principle of sensation and appetite and even
the entire animal. The principle has been suggested: there
where the organs have their source, there is the power that
uses them. But it were better to say this: there is the origin
of the activity of this power, because it is the origin of the
movement of an instrument that is necessarily based in
the power of the craftsman himself to put it into operation.
Or, rather, not his power (for the power is everywhere in
every instrument) but the action of this power whose origin
is the same as that of the instrument.

The faculties of sensation and appetite are in the soul.
To be capable of feeling and imagining, they have above
them reason which, by its lower part, is neighbor to their
higher parts. Thus the ancients have placed reason at the
summit of the animal, in the head, without, however, its
being in the brain. But it is lodged in this power of feeling;
therefore it is in the brain. The two basic faculties ought to
be given to the body and to the part of the body most able
to receive their action. And reason, which has no dealings
with the body, ought however to be in relation with these
two faculties that are a form of the soul and can receive
impressions from reason. The faculty of sensing is a faculty
of discernment. The imagination is a power that is, as it
were, intellectual. Appetite and impulse are obedient to
imagination and to reason. Hence reason is in the head,
not locally, but in the sense that the faculties that are in
the head use it. And we have just said in what way the
sense faculty is in the brain.

As to the vegetative faculty and the ability to grow and to
be nourished, they are not absent from any part of the body.
Nourishment is effected by the blood; blood is in the veins;
veins and blood have their origin in the liver; it is there,
then, that these two faculties are based. There also resides
the faculty of desire, for desire necessarily accompanies
that which engenders, that which nourishes, and that which
gives increase.

Finally, the blood, in becoming more subtle, lighter,
livelier, and purer, is fitting instrument of the irascible
power. The heart, therefore, which is the source whence
such blood is secreted, is the fitting seat of the bubbling
up of anger.

Where does the soul go when it leaves the body?
24. It is no longer here where there is no longer a
receptacle for it because it cannot remain in anything not naturally made for it. It departs when it is no
longer infatuated by the body that allured it. If it assumes
another body, it is in it and goes with it wherever its nature
has it be and be born.

But there are many places. The place where the soul is
ought to fit its inner dispositions and the overall pattern
that governs beings.

None escapes the chastisements that it is fitting to undergo because of evil conduct. The divine law cannot be avoided. It has within itself the power to achieve what it has determined upon. Without knowing it, the guilty one is transported to places where it is suitable that it serve its sentence. Carried by uncertain movement, drifting everywhere, it ends, after wanderings and much fatigue because of foolish resistance, by tumbling into its appropriate place. And there it offers itself willingly to an unwilled suffering.

Law prescribes the amount and duration of penalties. At the same moment that the penalty ceases, the power is given of escaping the place of chastisement thanks to the harmony that governs all things.

It is necessary to have a body in order to feel bodily chastisement. Pure souls, which are no longer subject in any way to the allurements of body, cannot in any way be the souls of any body whatsoever. Since they are not localized in any body, since they have no body, they are where their substance is, their being, and the divinity. They are in divinity with substance and being. Do you ask where? Look there where these realities are, but do not look with the eyes as though you were looking for bodies.

25.   Let us come now to memory. Does it function in souls when they are departed from earth? Does it remain solely in some of them? If so, do the souls remember everything or only some things? Finally, does memory exist forever or does it disappear a certain time after departure from the body?

If we would make our investigation as we ought, we should first of all understand what it is in us that remembers. I do not mean memory; I mean the principle in which memory resides. The definition of memory has been given elsewhere [10] and is repeated everywhere. But what is the nature of that which has memory? That is what it is necessary for us to lay hold of with exactness.

If the memory is memory of something acquired, is knowledge or impression, it cannot exist in impassible and nontemporal beings. Hence one must not ascribe memory to The One, nor to The Intelligence or Being in which time is not but only eternity. They have neither "before"

nor "after"; they remain always as they are in their identity
without undergoing the least change.

How can a being which is identical and forever like unto
itself have recollections? It does not have nor does it retain
at one moment a state different from that which it had
previously. It has not a succession of thoughts so that, in
the state or the thought which follows, it could remember
the state or the thought that preceded.

And yet what would prevent its knowing the changing of
other beings and for example the cycles of the world without itself changing? This is what would prevent it: if it
followed the changing of beings that are changeable, it
would think first of one thing and then of another; the act
of remembering comes from that which is thought of
different things. As to the thoughts it has about itself, one
must not say that it remembers them, for they have not
come to it in such a way that it has to lay hold of them
in order that they should not depart; if it did, it would be
fearful of seeing its own essence escape it.

For the soul as well, the words "to remember" ought not
to be used in the sense that one says it remembers its innate
ideas. When it is on earth, it possesses these notions without
having actual knowledge of them, and especially is this so
upon its arrival in the body. What of when it achieves
actual knowledge? The ancients seem to apply to this state
the names of memory and recall, but it is a type of memory
very different from that we are studying, and time has
nothing to do with memory taken in this sense.

But perhaps we are talking of these matters rather too
easily and without sufficient examination.

Do memory and recall pertain to the soul as such or to
a soul less enlightened or to the composite of soul and
body? In what conditions and at what moment does this
soul, if it is the soul, and this animal, if it is an animal,
receive memory?

We must, then, take up our inquiry again from the beginning: What is it that, in us, has memory? If it is the soul,
is it one of its faculties or one of its parts that remembers?
If it is the entire animal (certain authors think that it is
also what has sensation), how does it remember? What are
we to call this animal? Besides, is it the same in it that
perceives things sensed and things thought or is there a
faculty for each of them?

If there are two elements that cooperate in actual
26. sensation, the act of sensing ought to be like the
act of boring or weaving. In sensing, the soul is
the "craftsman." The body is the "tool." It is passive and
menial. The soul receives the impression produced in the
body or by the body as intermediary, or perhaps it makes
a judgment in accord with the bodily impression. The sensation is accordingly very much the common achievement
of soul and body. But memory does not necessarily pertain
for all of that to the composite of soul and body because
the soul has already received the impression which its memory either preserves or allows to escape.

One might imagine that the act of remembering de-
pended upon the composite because it is our bodily
constitutions that give us good or bad memories. But,
whether or not the body impedes the act of remembering,
this act does not pertain any the less to the soul.

Further, how can one accept the idea that the composite
and not the soul alone has memory of knowledge acquired
in the sciences?

If the animal is a composite in the sense that it is something different from the twin elements whence it comes, it
is absurd to say that the animal is neither a body nor a
soul. The animal is constituted without any change in its
constituents and without mingling to the extent that the
soul would no longer be in control in the animal. Further,
even were this so, memory would pertain no less to the
soul as in a mingling of wine and honey, the sweetness of
the mixture comes only from the honey.

But the objection will be made that it is the soul, doubtless, which has recollections but that is because it is in the
body and filled with impurity and, as it were, shot through
with bodily qualities so that it becomes able to fix within
itself impressions of sense objects; because of its residence
in the body, it receives these impressions and retains them.

These impressions are not magnitudes. There is no
pressure, as of a seal, or acceptance, as of wax. In reality
this impression in the soul is a type of intellection, even
in the case of sense objects. Where, in thinking, would there
be impression upon a body? What need is there of the
accompaniment of bodily thought or bodily quality? The
soul, further, necessarily remembers its own movements,
the desires it experiences and has not satisfied without the

desired object having attained to the body. How then could
the body testify concerning things that have not attained to
it? How could the soul use the body to remember what
the body is absolutely incapable of knowing? In truth, all
the impressions that come through the body terminate in
the soul; the others pertain to the soul alone if the soul is
to have a reality, a nature, and an activity proper to itself.
If this is so, it is necessary that it have, along with desire,
the remembrance of its desire, satisfied or not, since the
soul is not of those things that are in perpetual flux. Otherwise we could ascribe to it neither interior sense, nor awareness, nor the linking of impressions, nor understanding of
that which it experiences. And, if it has none of these qualities, it is not when it is in the body that it attains them.
Actually it possesses certain activities whose exercise
requires organs. But, when it arrives in the body, it bears
within it the faculties upon which it depends and the
activities themselves that belong to it alone. On the other
hand the body is an obstacle to memory. Actually, we see
oblivion result when one imbibes certain drinks, and often,
too, when the body is purged of them, we see memory
return. Since the soul remembers when it is alone, the
changing and fluid nature of the body must be the cause of
forgetfulness, not of memory. Thus it is that one should
interpret the River Lethe.

Our conclusion: this mode of being, memory, pertains to
the soul.

But to what soul?

27.   Is it to The Soul, called The Soul divine, the one
       that essentially constitutes us? Or is it to the other
soul, that which comes to us from the cosmos? Each of
them has recollections of which some are proper to it and
others are held in common with the other soul. When these
souls unite, they then have all the recollections at once.
When they separate, each of them, remaining alone, possesses rather its own recollections, although it keeps for a
time the recollections of the other. Such at least is the shade
of Hercules who is in Hades. This shade one must, I
believe, think of as recalling all the actions done during life
because this life pertains to it especially. The other souls
constituting the composite being, however, would have
nothing more to recount than the events of this earthly life

for, being of a composite, they would know only these events and such others as touched upon justice.

But Homer has not said what Hercules might be able to recount himself when separated from his shade. What would this godlike soul say once completely freed?

To the extent that it is under the attraction of earth, the soul recounts only what man has done or undergone. When time is far advanced and death at hand, it remembers its previous lives, even though some recollections have vanished through lack of appreciation. When freed of the body, it will remember things it could not remember in its present life. And, if it comes and goes in a new body, it will be able to recount the events of the life external to the body, those of the life it leaves as well as the numerous events of previous lives—although, again, with time it forgets many of the events it has encountered.

But what will it recall, once it is completely isolated? To know that, let us first of all search out the faculty by which remembering is effected in the soul.

28. Is it by the faculty of perception and sense? Or do we remember objects of desire with the desiring faculty and objects of anger with our irascible part?

Some will say that it is not one faculty that has pleasure and another faculty that recalls it. The desire of the object one has enjoyed reawakens when the object is remembered. If it is a different object, why then is desire awakened and why is it the same desire?

But, on that reasoning, what is to prevent one's ascribing to desire the sensing of its proper object and then desire itself to the faculty of sensing? One would then end by naming each faculty solely according to the element that predominates in it.

Should not one instead attribute sensation to each faculty but in a different way?

It is not desire that sees but the eye. Desire is awakened by sensation, by an influence conveyed by contiguity in such a fashion that desire unconsciously submits to the effect of sensation without being able to say what it is. Thus sensation perceives injustice and anger is stirred as if the shepherd of the flock saw a wolf whose scent and noise were sufficient to excite his dog, who has not, how-

ever, seen it. The desire that is satisfied keeps a vestige
of the past event not as a memory but as disposition and
affection. It is another faculty that was aware of the enjoyment and that keeps the memory of what happened. The
proof of this is that often memory of what is past does not
know the desires of the concupiscible part of the soul. Were
the memory in this part of the soul, it would know them.

29. Are we then to attribute memory to the faculty
of sense? Are we to say that memory and the faculty of sense are one and the same faculty?

If, as we said,[11] the shade of Hercules has memories as
does Hercules himself, it is because the sense faculty is twofold (if memory is something different from sensibility,
the remembering faculty is twofold). If memory is the
faculty of sense, given there is a memory of scientific
knowledge, it will be necessary that there be a sensation
of this knowledge. But then it will be necessary that another faculty be related to both.

Do we then suppose a common faculty of perception
and attribute to it the memory of both sense objects and
intelligible objects? If we perceived sense objects and intelligible objects by one and the same faculty, then that,
doubtless, would be to say something. But if they are two,
there would be no less than two memories. And if we attribute these two memories to each of the two levels of
soul, then we would have four memories.

But is it absolutely necessary that we remember objects
of sense by the faculty by which we sense them, that sensation and its remembrance come from the same faculty?
Is it necessary that the faculty by which we reflect be also
that by which we remember our reflections? Those who
reason best are not those who have the best memory. Nor
is there equal remembrance of equal sensations. Some
people have clear perception; others have a good memory
without clarity of perception.

On the other hand were memory distinct from the faculty
of sense, since memory bears upon objects accorded previously by sensation, it must also sense the objects of which
it will later have the recollection, must it not?

There is nothing against there being for recall an object

[11] §27.

sensed, that is, an image, and that memory and its reten-
tive powers pertain to imagination. Sensation culminates
in imagination and, when the sensation is no longer, the
culmination remains in the imagination. If then the image
remains with the objects absent, there is already remembrance however short the time that it remains present. If
it remains a very short time, memory is brief. If it lasts a
longer time, memory is augmented because the imagination
is the more robust. If the image changes with difficulty,
memory is strong.

Memory of sense objects, therefore, pertains to the
imagination.

As to the differences between memories, they come
either from the intrinsic difference of these faculties or
from the way of using them or from certain bodily constitutions that alter it and disturb it more or less. We will
return later to this question.[12]

30. But what of the remembering of intellectual concepts? Is there also an image of these concepts?
If (as Aristotle said) an image accompanies every
thought, the persistence of this image, which is like the
reflection of the concept, would explain the remembrance
of the known object. Otherwise, one must seek out something else. It is perhaps only because of the verbal formulation which accompanies thought that it pertains to imaginative perception. For thought is indivisible, and so long as
it is not expressed exteriorly but remains within, it escapes
us. Language, in developing it and making it pass from the
state of thought to that of image, reflects the thought as in
a mirror. And thus it is that thought is perceived, is made
determinate, and is recalled. Whenever the soul is moved
continually towards thought, it perceives it only if it is in
the condition indicated. For it is one thing to think; it is
another thing to perceive one's thought. We are always
thinking. But we do not always perceive our thought because the subject that receives the thoughts receives also,
alternately, sensations.

31. Since each soul has memory and memory pertains
to imagination, are there then two imaginations?
This might be when the two souls are separated.

[12] *See* IV, 6 [41], 3.

But in us, where they are joined in one and the same existent, how could there be two imaginations? In which of these two imaginations would remembrance be produced? If in the two of them, there would then be a double image of each object. (Let it not be said that the imagination of the higher soul represents only intelligible objects and the other sense objects. If that were so, we would be made up of two animated beings without any relation to each other.) If memory is in the two imaginations, in what do the two images differ? Why do we not perceive this difference? The reason is that one image agrees with the other; and, as the two imaginations do not exist apart and that of the higher soul dominates the other, a single image is produced—the lower accompanies the higher as a shadow or as a feeble flame an intense illumination. Or else they are in conflict and in discord, and the other manifests itself for itself.

But, actually, what is in the other soul escapes us. Speaking generally, the very duality of our souls even escapes us for they do the one thing and one serves as vehicle for the other. One of them sees all. Released from the body, it keeps certain memories but abandons others that relate it to the other soul. It is just as when we have left companions of lower social station for others more distinguished: we keep only a vague recollection of the first and recall very well the second.

32. How is there memory of friends, of children, of wife? How of fatherland and of all that an honorable man is able reasonably to recall.

The lower soul has a recollection accompanied with emotion. But man is able to remember without emotion. At the beginning, doubtless, the man feels emotion. Even The Soul itself feels the most noble of these emotions because it has some relationship with the soul. But it is fitting that the soul wish to act as The Soul does and to remember as it does. Especially is this so when it is itself refined: one becomes better through the education one receives from a higher being. Yet it is necessary that The Soul be willing to forget that which comes to it from the soul, the excellence of the higher is linked with a baseness in the lower that is kept down only by force.

The more it forces itself towards the intelligible realm, the more it forgets things here below because its life, upon

earth, is not filled with the memories alone of the better
things.

For it is beautiful, here below, to withdraw oneself from
the cares of men. It is necessary consequently to withdraw
oneself from the memory of such cares. In this sense one
can rightly say that the good soul is the forgetful soul. It
takes flight from multiplicity, reduces the multiple to The
One, abandons the indeterminate. It does not take with it
a mass of earthly memories; it is light, and it is wholly
alone. Even in the present life when it wishes to think and
to be in the intelligible realm it abandons to that end all
things else. Very few memories of this earth accompany
it into the intelligible realm, less indeed than when it is
only in the heavens.

The Hercules of Hades is able still to speak of his
bravery. But he esteems it a small thing now that he has
passed into a region more sacred and has arrived in the
intelligible realm: he is now endowed with a strength more
than Herculean for those battles which are the battles of the
sages.

SOURCES

For the key to abbreviations see *Guide to Sources,* page 223.

1 ¶1 Obedience . . . ourselves: *cf.* Plato, *Protagoras* 343 b;
  Alex. Aphrod., II, 1, p. 1, 3-5.
  ¶2 those who hold: *i.e.,* the Stoics; *cf. Stoic.,* I, n. 495 and II,
  n. 774; Diog. Laert., VII, 156.
  ¶4 As our body . . . The Soul of the universe: *cf.* Plato,
  Philebus 30 a 5-6.
  ¶5 Plato states: *cf. Timaeus* 90 c 8 - d 1.
  ¶6 "The Soul in its totality has the care of all that is inanimate": Plato, *Phaedrus* 246 b 6.

4 ¶2 Some people say: The Stoics, likely, are referred to here.
  ¶3 "distributed among bodies": Plato, *Timaeus* 35 a 2-3.

6 ¶9 "secondary and tertiary": Plato, *Timaeus* 41 d 7.

7 ¶1 passage in the *Philebus: i.e.* 30a-b.
  ¶3 clear in the *Timaeus: i.e.* 41 d 7.
  ¶4 "The Soul in its totality has the care of all that is inanimate": Plato, *Phaedrus* 246 b 6.
  "going . . . its wings": Plato, *Phaedrus* 246 b 7 - c 2.
  ¶5 As for . . . from it: *cf.* Plato, *Timaeus* 90 c 8 - d 1.

8 ¶3 We read: *cf.* Plato, *Republic* 620 a 2-3.

12 ¶1 They see: *cf. Orph.,* fr. 209.
   They descend: *cf.* Homer, *Iliad,* IV, 443.
   "Zeus has pity": Plato, *Banquet* 191 b 5.
   ¶2 From this . . . utterance: *cf.* Plato, *Republic* 617 b 6.

14 ¶2 the following myth: *cf.* Hesiod, *Works and Days,* 60-89.
   But the . . . in bonds: *cf.* Hesiod, *Theogony,* 521-528.

16 ¶3 "not of the gods": Homer, *Odyssey,* XVIII, 353.

19 ¶1 "indivisible and divisible": Plato, *Timaeus* 35 a 1.
   ¶3 Plato speaks: The quotations are from *Timaeus* 35a 1-3.
   ¶6 If desire . . . the heart: *cf.* Plato, *Timaeus* 70 a 7 - b 2,
   71 a 7.
   ¶7 The body . . . pursuits: *cf.* Plato, *Phaedo* 65 a 10 - b 1.

20 ¶3 Speaking . . . in a place: *cf.* Alex. Aphrod., II, 1, p. 14, 17.
   It is no more . . . vase: *cf. op. cit.,* II, 1, p. 14, 23.
   ¶4 If . . . as a space: *cf. Stoic.,* II, n. 506.
   ¶5 More . . . as in a subject: *cf.* Alex. Aphrod., II, 1, p. 14,
   24-25.
   ¶6 The soul . . . a whole: *cf. op. cit.,* p. 14, 5.
   ¶7 Neither . . . in its parts: *cf. op. cit.,* p. 14, 10.
   ¶8 Neither . . . in matter: *cf. op. cit.,* p. 13, 24.

21 ¶3 As passenger . . . incidentally: Aristotle, *On the Soul,* II,
   1; 413 a 9.
   The pilot . . . the ship: Alex. Aphrod., II, 1, p. 15, 9.
   ¶4 as the skill . . . instrument: *cf.* Aristotle, *op. cit.,* II, 1;
   412 b 12.

22 ¶2 That is why . . . in The Soul: *cf. Timaeus* 36 d 9-e 3.

23 ¶1 one places in the brain: *cf.* Plato, *Phaedo* 96 b 5-6.
   ¶2 Thus the ancients . . . head: *cf.* Plato, *Phaedo* 96 b 5-6.
   ¶4 Finally . . . of anger: *cf.* Plato, *Timaeus* 70 a 7-b 3.

24 ¶3-5 The divine law . . . with substance and being: *cf.* Plato,
   Laws 904 a - e.

25 ¶6 The ancients . . . recall: *cf.* Plato, *Phaedo* 72 e 5-7.
   ¶8 Do memory . . . as such: *cf.* Aristotle, *On the Soul,* I, 4;
   408 b 13-18.
   ¶9 certain authors: perhaps Aristotle, *On Dreams,* I, 4; 454 a
   7-11.

26 ¶6 There is no pressure . . . wax: *cf. Stoic.,* I, n. 484 and II,
   n. 343.
   River Lethe: *cf.* Plato, *Republic* 621 c 1-2.

27 ¶2 For the Hercules incident, *cf.* Homer, *Iliad,* XI, 601-2.
   ¶4 When freed . . . life.: *cf.* Plato, *Philebus* 34 b 11.

CONTEMPLATION

(III, 8 [30])

The small effort at professorial humor with which this treatise opens should—as should indeed all efforts at professorial humor—be taken very seriously.

Everywhere throughout the treatises so far, Plotinus' concern has been with the mystic's ascent to The One—with, in other words, the nature and goal of contemplation. Everything else that has been brought in, or left out, has been in, or out, solely on the basis of relevance to this overriding concern.

Now the reader will learn to his minor amazement that contemplation has been present not merely as a guiding idea but, to Plotinus' way of thinking, as the central reality. For all act is contemplative: that of vegetation by being and growing (his jesting remark at the outset), that of Plotinus by jesting (his jesting remark, from another aspect, at the outset) —*every* act.

One would expect a very attenuated notion of contemplation to result from such a position. Paradoxically, it is the richest of notions that results. Because he manages to eliminate the conventional dichotomy between action and contemplation, Plotinus is able to offer a contemplation that, in the strict sense, is productive.

By contemplation the mystic constructs his real self, achieves his authentic existence, quite as the contemplation of The Intelligence *is* The Intelligence and the contemplation of The Soul *is* The Soul.

This treatise is, perhaps, the best single instance of the mature thought and method of Plotinus. It repays an attentive reading. Even the bad joke at the beginning will repay any respectful receptiveness the reader may be able to muster.

162

1. If, before beginning serious investigation, we were jestingly to say that all beings are striving after contemplation—not merely those endowed with reason but unreasoning animals as well, even plants and the earth that begets them—and that they all, in their degree, attain to contemplation of reality and its refractions here below, who would listen to such nonsense? But we are here by ourselves and run no risk in treating our own doctrine jestingly.

Could it be true that in jesting we are contemplating? Yes. As do all who jest, in jesting we contemplate. One jests because one wants to contemplate.

Children and adults, jesting or serious, seem to have no other purpose except contemplation. To contemplation all actions tend, compulsive actions drawing it somewhat towards external objects, voluntary actions less so. In both instances contemplation is the motive. But of this more later.[1]

Now we would speak of the nature of that contemplation we attribute to earth, trees, and growing things in general—how things produced and begotten by earth can be ascribed to the act of contemplation, and how Nature, which is said [2] to lack reason and feeling, contemplates and produces all its effects through that contemplation which supposedly it does not possess.

2. Clearly, Nature does not have hands, or feet, or any natural or artificial tools. But it does need material to work on and to shape. All mechanical operations are excluded; [3] what sort of push or working of levers would produce its variety of colors and of forms? Doll-makers (to whose craft the operations of Nature are often compared) cannot give colors to objects without getting the colors from elsewhere. But the doll-makers do have, locked within them, an efficacy that goes not out yet guides their hands in all they make. A like indwelling efficacy must exist in Nature for what is not built with hands. It exists there, however, wholly immobile, having no need of parts whether movable or immovable. Only matter is mov-

---

[1] *See* §6.
[2] By the Stoics.
[3] Aristotelian mechanism is, again, sarcastically rejected here.

able. The efficacy that forms it is not. If it were, it would no longer be the first mover.

The objection may be raised that Reason is unmoved but that Nature is different from Reason and is moved. But if one means here the totality of natural things, then Reason will move, too. If, however, one means that a part of Nature is unmoved, this part will be Reason. For Nature is Idea, not a composite of form and matter. What need would it have of matter, cold or hot? The matter, the substratum upon which it acts, either possesses these qualities already or receives them when brought under Reason. Not fire, but Reason, makes matter fire. Reason is the maker in the realms of plant and animal. Nature is a rational principle that produces the Reason that accords something of itself to the substratum while itself remaining unmoved.

Reason that manifests itself in visible shapes is the lowest of its kind, inert, unproductive of another rational form. Above it is the productive Reason, doubtless the kin of the first that gives mere visible shapes, and it produces the form in the being engendered.

3. Being a productive agent and productive in this particular way, how does Nature achieve contemplation? Because it produces while remaining unmoved and within itself and because it is Reason, Nature is itself contemplation. Action conforms to Reason and hence is not Reason. And Reason is present to and presides over action and consequently is not action. Not action, yet Reason, Nature is contemplation.

The lowest reason proceeds from contemplation. It is contemplation in the sense that it is the object of contemplation. Higher reason is of two kinds: one that changes with beings and is not Nature but soul, and another that is in Nature and is Nature. This other kind, does it derive also from contemplation? Yes, for it, too, contemplates in a certain way, and it is produced by a contemplation and a principle that contemplates. What kind of contemplation does it have? Not the kind that results from discursive reason. (By discursive reason here I mean the deliberative process.) But why not, since it is life, reason, and productive? Because one plans only when one lacks. Nature does not lack for anything; it produces by the mere fact that it possesses; for it to be is for it to be productive. Because it is Reason, it is contemplation and object contemplated. Being all three—contemplation, object contemplated, and reason—it produces through the mere fact that it is all three.

Production, then, is a kind of contemplation that never becomes anything else, never does anything else, that is productive precisely as contemplative.

4. Were one to ask Nature why it produces, it might —if willing—thus reply: "You should never have put the question. Silently, as I am silent and little given to talk, you should have tried to understand. Understand what? That what comes to be is the object of my silent contemplation—its natural object. I am myself born of contemplation; mine is a contemplative nature. The contemplative in me produces the object contemplated much as geometricians draw their figures while contemplating. I do not draw. But, contemplating, I drop from within me the lines constitutive of bodily forms. Within me I preserve traces of my source and of the principles that brought me into being. They, too, were born of contemplation and without action on their own part gave me birth. But they are greater than I: they contemplated themselves and thus was I born."

What is the meaning here? That what we call "Nature" is a soul; that it was begotten by a higher soul of more powerful life; and that it contains its contemplation wordless within itself, with no deflection towards what is higher or lower. Abiding within its own realm, in self-repose and self-awareness, it sees because of this self-awareness the things that are below it to the extent they can be seen. Without further search, it produces at a stroke the object of its contemplation in all its splendor and beauty.

If one would predicate knowledge or sensation of Nature, they would resemble our knowledge and sensation only as those of a man who is asleep resemble those of a man who is awake. For Nature remains in repose while contemplating because its object is innate and remains interior and present because Nature is itself an object of contemplation—a contemplation both wordless and weak.

There is another that contemplates more clearly: of it Nature is only the copy. The result is that what Nature produces is weak; weakness of contemplation only begets weakness of object.

Similarly, it is men too weak for contemplation who seek that shadow of contemplation and reason which is action. Unable to give themselves to contemplation because weak of soul, they are unable to grasp the object of contemplation sufficiently and sate themselves. They want to see it. They seek to achieve by activity what they cannot obtain by thought. When they produce something, it is because they wish to see it, contemplate it, and perceive it, and they wish the same for other men.

Thus we find everywhere that doing and making are either a weak contemplation or the concomitants of contemplation: a weak contemplation, if after the action there is nothing to see; the concomitant of contemplation, if there is the ability to contemplate something better than what we have made.

Indeed, what man able to contemplate the true would prefer its image? There is proof of all this in the fact that the retarded children who have no capacity for scientific knowledge are reduced to practicing mechanical and manual crafts.

5.   That, then, is how the producing of things by Nature is a sort of contemplation.

Let us now consider The Soul, which is prior to Nature. It will be suggested how The Soul, by its contemplation, its love of knowledge and discovery, the birth pangs of its being filled with knowledge, its becoming itself entirely an object of contemplation, brings a further object of contemplation to birth, much as every science that is complete in itself brings a lesser science into existence in the student who achieves some knowledge of it although, in the student, the theorems of the science are unclear and unable to stand by themselves.

The higher part of The Soul, inhabitant of the supreme and, by its sharing in the supreme, filled and enlightened, stays there. The lower part shares in what the higher part has received and proceeds everlastingly from what is above it, life from life, an activity extending to everything and in everything present. Proceeding, The Soul's higher part stays in the supreme, which the lower part leaves. Detached from

its higher part, The Soul would no longer be present everywhere but only where its procession ceased. The part of The
Soul that leaves is not the equal of the part that remains.
Therefore: If The Soul must be present and exert its activity everywhere, and if antecedent must differ from consequent, and if, besides, activity proceeds either from contemplation or action and there is no action as yet because
contemplation precedes action, it necessarily follows that
the contemplation is weaker than that of the one preceding
yet is still contemplation. And action itself, derivative of
contemplation, seems to be the weakest of contemplations
because the begotten is always of the same kind as its begetter only weaker because the generic becomes effaced
in the descent.

All proceeds silently: The Soul needs no visible or external object for contemplation, and it engages in no action.
It is soul. It contemplates. The part that proceeds, different
from the higher and more directed towards the exterior,
does not, as prior, produce as does its prior. Yet, contemplation, it begets contemplation.

There is no boundary to contemplation or its possible
objects. "Does it extend here below?" Yes, because it extends everywhere. Where is it not that is itself in every
soul since it is not confined to a definite space? Yet it is
not in all things in altogether the same way, is not even
present in the same way to all parts of the soul. That is why
Plato says that the charioteer conveys what he has seen to
his horses, and they, benefited, clearly want to have what
they have heard of and have not received completely. Action in accord with this desire is action towards the object
of their desire, that is, contemplation and of the object
of contemplation.

6. The point of action is contemplation and the having an object of contemplation. Contemplation is
therefore the end of action.

Action seeks to achieve indirectly what it cannot achieve
directly.

When one has achieved the object of one's desires, it is
evident that one's real desire was not the ignorant possession of the desired object but to know it as possessed—as
actually contemplated, as within one.

Action always has some good or other in view—a good

for oneself, to be possessed. Possessed where? In the soul.
The circuit is complete: through action the soul comes back
to contemplation.

And what is there, then, in the soul, itself essential reasonableness, but an inexpressible reasonableness. And it is
there the more, the more reasonable it is. Then the soul
rests. It seeks no further. It is sated. Its vision remains all
within; it is sure of its object. The greater this assurance,
the more tranquil is the contemplation and the more unified
the soul. Knower and known are one. I mean this seriously.
Were they two, they would be different. They would lie,
as it were, side by side, in their duality unassimilable by the
soul, much as certain notions exist in the soul without producing effect. To learn, we must not allow ideas to remain
exterior to us, but fuse with them until they become part
of our existence. When this is done and our dispositions
correspond, the soul is able to formulate and make use of
them. It comprehends now what it merely contained before.
Using them, the soul becomes, as it were, different; only
upon reflection does it find them to be aliens.

Nevertheless, the soul itself is rational and a kind of intelligence, but an intelligence that sees an object different from
itself. It does not possess fullness and is deficient compared
with its prior. Yet it beholds in silence what it expresses in
words because verbal formulation is only of what it has
already seen. If it speaks, it is because it is deficient and
needs to inquire in order to know what it is it contains. (In
the case of practical activity the soul adapts to the external
objects the notions it possesses.) The soul is richer in content than nature is and so it is more at rest and more contemplative. But, as its possessions are not complete, it
wants to increase the knowledge of its object and the contemplation that comes from inquiry. Even while withdrawn
from its own higher part and involved in the variety of
things only to return to itself later, the soul contemplates
with its remaining higher part. But the soul that abides
within itself does this less. Thus it is that the wise man is
penetrated by reason and has wholly within himself what he
manifests to others. He contemplates himself. He achieves
unity and immobility not only in regard to external objects
but also in regard to the things within himself. He finds all
things within himself.

7. So everything derives from contemplation, and everything is contemplation.

This truth holds for the truly real beings as well as for the beings that they bring into existence by their contemplation and that are objects of contemplation either for sensation or for knowledge and opinion.

Actions, and desire as well, aim at knowledge. Begetting originates in contemplation and ends in the production of a form, that is, a new object of contemplation. All things, as images of their generating principles, universally produce forms and objects of contemplation. Begotten existences, being imitations of truly real beings, show that the purpose of generation is neither generation nor action but the production of works that are to be contemplated. Contemplation is aimed at by discursive reason and, below it, by sensation whose end is knowledge. Further, beyond discursive reason and sensation, is Nature, which, bearing within itself an object of contemplation and rational form, produces another rational form.

Such are the arguments that developed in the course of this inquiry or that we recalled from elsewhere. They ought now to be clear.

It should be clear as well that, since the supreme realities devote themselves to contemplation, all other beings must aspire to it, too, because the origin of all things is their end as well. Moreover, animals generate because of the activity within them of seminal reasons.

Generation is a contemplation. It results from the longing of pregnancy to produce a multiplicity of forms and objects of contemplation, to fill everything with reason, and never to cease from contemplation. Begetting means to produce some form and this means to spread contemplation everywhere. All the faults met with in things begotten or in actions are due to the fact that one strayed from the object of one's contemplation. The poor workman is the producer of bad forms. Lovers also must be counted among those who contemplate and pursue forms. But enough of this.

8. Contemplation rises from Nature to The Soul, from The Soul to The Intelligence. At each stage it is more intimately the contemplative's own. In a person already wise, knower and known are one since he aspires to The Intelligence.

Clearly, in The Intelligence, subject and object are one. This identity is more than a close association such as we find in the best of souls because "it is the same thing to think and to be." In The Intelligence we no longer have upon one side the object of contemplation and on the other that which contemplates. Were that so we would need another principle where this difference no longer exists. In The Intelligence the two things are one. This means that it is a living contemplation whose object does not inhere in something else; if it did, it would live, but not by it. Therefore if the object of contemplation is to be alive, it must no longer be with the life of a plant, or an animal, or any other animate existents. Doubtless, these beings are various kinds of thought: vegetative, sensuous, and psychic ways of thought. But they are thoughts because they are rational forms.

All life is thought, thought of greater or less obscurity as is life itself. But the life of which it is question now is a life of complete clarity. It is the highest life and the highest intellection identified.

The highest life is the highest thought: the lower life, the lower thought; the lowest of lives, the lowest of thoughts. Every life is of this sort and is thought.

Men readily distinguish the various kinds of life but do not do the same with thought: they call some things thought and others not because they do not try to find out what life really is.

This discussion, again, shows us that all beings are contemplations. If the truest life is life through thought and is identical with the truest thought, then the truest thought must be alive. Then contemplation and the object of this contemplation are alive and are life, and are identical.

Since the two are identical, how does it happen that their unity becomes multiplicity?

The Intelligence does not contemplate unity, for, even when it contemplates The One, it does not contemplate it as a unity. Otherwise there would be no intelligence. It begins by being one but does not remain one. Unconsciously it becomes multiple, as if pressed down by its own weight. It unfolds itself desirous of becoming all things, although it would have been better for it not to have desired this because thus it became the second hypostasis. It deploys itself like a circle which in its deployment becomes figure and surface, circumference, center, radii, higher and lower points—the higher, whence come the radii being the better, and the lower, whither the radii extend being the less good. The originating center is not equivalent to both center and circumference, nor the two to center alone. In other words, The Intelligence is not the thought of a single thing but is universal, and, being universal, it is the thought of all things. It must be all things and think all things. Each of its parts contains all things, and it is all things because otherwise The Intelligence would contain a part that was not intelligence. It would then be composed of non-intelligences and be a conglomeration of things that were waiting to become The Intelligence, to achieve completeness.

Therefore The Intelligence is infinite. When something proceeds from it, there is no impoverishment—neither for what proceeds, since it also is all things, nor for The Intelligence whence it proceeds, since The Intelligence is not composed of juxtaposed parts.

9. Such is the nature of The Intelligence, such the reason why it is not the first. Above it there must be a principle whose discovery is the ultimate object of all our previous discussion.

Multiplicity comes after unity; it is number, while unity is the source of number; multiplicity as such has as its source The One as such. This multiplicity is The Intelligence and the intelligibles taken together, both at the same time. They are two. Therefore must we find the principle prior to this duality. Could it be The Intelligence alone? The Intelligence is always bound to the intelligible; not bound to the intelligible, it cannot be The Intelligence. Then this principle is not The Intelligence and not the duality but prior to the duality and above The Intelligence. Could it be the intelligible alone? We have already seen that the intelligible is inseparable from The Intelligence. If this principle can be neither The Intelligence nor the intelligible, what can it be? It must be the principle from which derives The Intelligence and, with it, the intelligible.

But what is this principle and how are we to conceive it? It must be either a thinking being or not a thinking being. If it is a thinking being, it will be The Intelligence. If it is not a thinking being, it will be ignorant of even itself, and what is so estimable about that? To say that it is the Good or the most simple and absolute would be true but would not be clear or penetrating (as long as we do not have something upon which we can base our thought when we use such phrases).

The knowledge of other objects came about through The Intelligence, even that knowledge of a thinking thing. But by what immediate apprehension can we grasp this principle that is higher than The Intelligence?

We may answer that we apprehend it by that part of us which resembles it. For there is something of it in us. Or, rather, there is no place where it is not for those who can share in it. Because it is everywhere, we can anywhere receive something of it by directing to it that part of us which is capable of receiving it. For example, imagine a sound in a desert and a man located at any spot in that desert. Wherever it is that he listens to this sound, he will in one way hear all of it and in another way not.

What is it, then, that we grasp by directing our intelligence towards this principle?

First off, The Intelligence must, so to speak, turn back and, in spite of its duality, give itself over to the reality there; it must, if it wishes to look upon the first principle, cease to be entirely intelligence.

In itself, The Intelligence is the highest life and activity which comprehends all things, not by a movement that is still in progress but by a movement that already is achieved. The Intelligence is life, comprehends all things, and possesses all things in detail and not just in their general traits. If it did, it would possess them in an imperfect and vague manner.

Necessarily, therefore, it must proceed from a higher principle that, instead of being within the motion by which The Intelligence runs through all things, is the origin of this motion, of life, of The Intelligence, and of all things.

The originating principle is not the totality of things, but from it all things proceed.

The originating principle is neither all things nor any one of them. If it were, it could not beget all, but would be a multiplicity and not the origin of multiplicity. Indeed what begets is always simpler than what is begotten. Therefore, if this principle begets The Intelligence, it necessarily is simpler than The Intelligence. On the assumption that The One is also the totality of things, it would either be all things at once or each of them individually. If it were the totality of things, it would be posterior to them. If it were simultaneous with them, it would not be their source. But if it is prior, it is different from them.

The One must be an originating principle and, consequently, must exist before all things if they are to originate from it. If we assume that The One is each particular thing, then any one thing would be identical with any other thing and all things would be together and there would be no differentiation. Thus The One is no one of the totality of things. It is prior to all things.

What, then, is The One?

10. It is what makes all things possible. Without it nothing would exist, neither Being, nor The Intelligence, nor the highest life, nor anything else. What is above life is the cause of life. The activity of life, being all things, is not the first principle. It flows from it as from a spring. Picture a spring that has no further origin, that pours itself into all rivers without becoming exhausted of what it yields, and remains what it is, undisturbed. The streams that issue from it, before flowing away each in its own direction, mingle together for a time, but each knows already where it will take its flood. Or think of the life that circulates in a great tree. The originating principle of this life remains at rest and does not spread through the tree because it has, as it were, its seat in the root. The principle gives to the plant all its life in its multiplicity but remains itself at rest. Not a plurality, it is the source of plurality.

This is not surprising. Where is there place for surprise that the multiplicity of life issues from what is not multiple and that the multiple would not exist without the previous existence of that which is not multiple? The principle is not distributed through the cosmos. If it were, the cosmos would be annihilated and could not be born again unless the principle remained self-contained in its otherness.

That is why everywhere things are reduced to unity. For each thing there is a unity to which it may be reduced and there is for each unity that which is superior to it but is not unity as such. This continues until one reaches unity as such which cannot be reduced to any other.

To grasp the oneness of a tree, that is, its stable principle, or of an animal or of a soul or of the cosmos, is to grasp in each of these cases what is most powerful and of worth.

If at last we try to grasp the oneness that is found in the true realities and is their principle, source, and productive power, how can we all of a sudden become doubtful and believe that this principle is nothingness?

This principle is certainly none of the things of which it is the source. It is such that nothing can be predicated of it, not being, not substance, not life, because it is superior to all these things.

But if you manage to grasp it by abstracting even being from it, you will be struck with wonder. By directing your glance towards it, by reaching it, by resting in it, you will achieve a deep and immediate awareness of it and will at the same time seize its greatness in all things that come from it and exist through it.

11. Consider now the following. Since The Intelligence is a sort of seeing, that is, a seeing that is active, it really is a potentiality actualized. One therefore will have to distinguish in it both form and matter. Active seeing implies a duality, while before its actualization it was unity. Thus unity has become duality and duality has become unity. As our seeing needs the realm of sense for its actualization and perfecting, its seeing needs the Good.

If The Intelligence were itself the Good, why would it need to see or even to act in any way? Though other things act only for and by the Good, the Good has no such necessity: there is nothing for it except itself. After one has pronounced this word "Good," one should ascribe nothing further to it because any addition, of whatever sort, will make it less than it really is. Not even thought should be attributed to it. To do that would be to introduce a difference and thus make it a duality of intellection and goodness. The Intelligence needs the Good; the Good needs not The Intelligence. Upon attaining it, The Intelligence becomes like the Good because it is formed and perfected by it: see its trace, its imprint in The Intelligence and you can conceive the Good. Seeing this trace in itself, The Intelligence knows desire. The Intelligence desires at every moment and at every moment achieves its desire. The Good

knows not desire—what could it desire? Having no desire,
it fulfills no desire. It is not the same, then, as The Intelligence because The Intelligence is the quintessence of ap-
petition and desire.

The Intelligence is beautiful—of all things the most
beautiful. Dwelling in pure light and "stainless radiance," it
envelops everything with its own light. The realm of sense,
so beautiful, is only its reflected shadow. It abides in full
resplendence because it contains nothing dark to the mind
or obscure or indefinite. It knows beatitude.

Wonder seizes upon him who contemplates it, who enters
in and becomes one with it. Just as the view of the heavens
and the splendor of the stars leads one to think of their
author and to seek him out, so the contemplative who has
gazed upon the intelligible realm and been struck with the
wonder of it should seek out its author—should ask who
has given it existence, where this author is, and how he
authored it.

From whom comes such beauty as this, this procession
of plenitude? Not The Intelligence, nor Being, but their
prior. They come after it because they have need of both
thought and fulfillment. But they are close to that which
wants for nothing, which need not even think.

So high its rank, The Intelligence is authentic plenitude
and thought. Its prior is neither for if it were, it would
not be what it is—the Good.

SOURCES

For the key to abbreviations see *Guide to Sources*, page 223.

1 ¶1 not merely . . . as well: *cf.* Aristotle, *Nicomachean
Ethics*, X, 2; 1172 b 10.
¶4 which is said . . . feeling: *cf. Stoic.*, II, n. 1016.

5 ¶5 Plato says: *cf. Phaedrus* 247 e 5-6.

8 ¶2 "it is the same thing to think and to be": Parmenides in
Vorsokrat., fr. B 3.

9 ¶1 Above it there must be a principle: *cf.* Plato, *Republic*
509 b 9.

11 ¶2 The Intelligence needs . . . The Intelligence.: *cf.* Plato,
Republic 509 a 3.
¶3 "stainless radiance": Plato, *Phaedrus* 250 c 4.
¶4 Wonder seizes upon him: *cf.* Homer, *Iliad*, III, 342.

APPENDIX I

In the following excerpts the marginal references on the left indicate their sources; those on the right are cross references to the *Enneads* that appear in this translation.

PRE-SOCRATIC PHILOSOPHERS

These selections have been taken from *Ancilla to the Pre-Socratic Philosophers,* Kathleen Freeman's translation of *Die Fragmente der Vorsokratiker,* and the marginal numbers refer to the Fragments as numbered in Diels, fifth edition.

Heracleitus (fl.c. 500 B.C.)

60	The way up and down is one and the same.	(IV, 8 [6], 1)
84a	It rests from change.	(IV, 8 [6], 1)
84b	It is a weariness to the same [elements . . .] to toil and to obey.	(IV, 8 [6], 1)

Parmenides (fl.c. 475 B.C.)

3	For it is the same thing to think and to be.	(V, 9 [5], 5; V, 1 [10], 8; III, 8 [30], 8)

176

8   . . . But it is motionless in the limits of   (V, 1
[10], 8)
mighty bonds, without beginning, without
cease, since Becoming and Destruction have
been driven very far away, and true conviction has rejected them. And remaining the
same in the same place, it rests by itself and
thus remains there fixed; for powerful Necessity holds it in the bonds of a Limit, which
constrains it round about, because it is
decreed by divine law that Being shall not
be without boundary. For it is not lacking;
but if it were [spatially infinite], it would be
lacking everything. . . .

. . . But since there is a [spatial] Limit, it is
complete on every side, like the mass of a
well-rounded sphere, equally balanced from
its centre in every direction; for it is not
bound to be at all either greater or less in
this direction or that; nor is there Not-Being
which could check it from reaching to the
same point, nor is it possible for Being to be
more in this direction, less in that, than Being, because it is an inviolate whole. For, in
all directions equal to itself, it reaches its
limits uniformly. . . .

Anaxagoras (fl.c. 460 B.C.)

12   Other things all contain a part of every-   (V, 1
[10], 9)
thing, but Mind is infinite and self-ruling,
and is mixed with no Thing, but is alone by
itself. If it were not by itself, but were mixed
with anything else, it would have had a share
of all Things, if it were mixed with anything;
for in everything there is a portion of everything, as I have said before. And the things
mixed [with Mind] would have prevented it,
so that it could not rule over any Thing in
the same way as it can being alone by itself.
For it is the finest of all Things, and the
purest, and has complete understanding of
everything, and has the greatest power. All
things which have life, both the greater and
the less, are ruled by Mind. Mind took command of the universal revolution, so as to

make [things] revolve at the outset. And at
first things began to revolve from some small
point, but now the revolution extends over a
greater area, and will spread even further.
And the things which were mixed together,
and separated off, and divided, were all understood by Mind. And whatever they were
going to be, and whatever things were then
in existence that are not now, and all things
that now exist and whatever shall exist—all
were arranged by Mind, as also the revolution now followed by the stars, the sun and
moon, and the Air and Aether which were
separated off. It was this revolution which
caused the separation off. And dense separates from rare, and hot from cold, and
bright from dark, and dry from wet. There
are many portions of many things. And nothing is absolutely separated off or divided the
one from the other except Mind. Mind is all
alike, both the greater and the less. But
nothing else is like anything else, but each
individual thing is and was most obviously
that of which it contains the most.

Empedocles (fl.c. 450 B.C.)

26   In turn they get the upper hand in the   (V, 1
revolving cycle, and perish into one another   [10], 9)
and increase in the turn appointed by Fate.
For they alone exist, but running through
one another they become men and the tribes
of other animals, sometimes uniting under
the influence of Love into one ordered
Whole, at other times again each moving
apart through the hostile force of Hate, until
growing together into the Whole which is
One, they are quelled. Thus in so far as they
have the power to grow into One out of
Many, and again, when the One grows apart
and Many are formed, in this sense they
come into being and have no stable life; but
in so far as they never cease their continuous
exchange, in this sense they remain always
unmoved as they follow the cyclic process.

115 There is an oracle of Necessity, an ancient decree of the gods, eternal, sealed fast with broad oaths, that when one of the divine spirits whose portion is long life sinfully stains his own limbs with bloodshed, and following Hate has sworn a false oath—these must wander for thrice ten thousand seasons far from the company of the blessed, being born throughout the period into all kinds of mortal shapes, which exchange one hard way of life for another. For the mighty Air chases them into the Sea, and the Sea spews them forth on to the dry land, and the Earth [drives them] towards the rays of the blazing Sun; and the Sun hurls them into the eddies of the Aether. One [Element] receives them from the other, and all loathe them. Of this number am I too now, a fugitive from heaven and a wanderer, because I trusted in raging Hate. *(IV, 8 [6], 1)*

120 "We have come into this roofed cavern." *(IV, 8 [6], 1)*

PLATO

The Jowett translation has been used for the following selections. The marginal references given are according to the convention of referring to the pagination of the Paris 1578 edition of Stephanus.

Phaedo

64c Do we believe that there is such a thing as death? *(I, 6 [1], 6; I, 2 [19], 5)*

To be sure, replied Simmias.

Is it not the separation of soul and body? And to be dead is the completion of this; when the soul exists in herself, and is released from the body and the body is released from the soul, what is this but death?

Just so, he replied.

d There is another question, which will probably throw light on our present enquiry

if you and I can agree about it:—Ought the
philosopher to care about the pleasures—if
they are to be called pleasures—of eating
and drinking?

Certainly not, answered Simmias.

And what about the pleasures of love—
should he care for them?

By no means.

And will he think much of the other ways
of indulging the body, for example, the ac-
quisition of costly raiment, or sandals, or
other adornments of the body? Instead of
caring about them, does he not rather despise

e   anything more than nature needs? What do
you say?

I should say that the true philosopher
would despise them.

Would you not say that he is entirely concerned with the soul and not with the body?
He would like, as far as he can, to get away
from the body and to turn to the soul.

Quite true.

In matters of this sort philosophers, above
65   all other men, may be observed in every sort   (IV, 8
of way to dissever the soul from the com-   [6], 2;
munion of the body.   IV, 3
                                                                   [27], 19)

Very true.

Whereas, Simmias, the rest of the world
are of opinion that to him who has no sense
of pleasure and no part in bodily pleasure,
life is not worth having; and that he who is
indifferent about them is as good as dead.

That is also true.

What again shall we say of the actual
acquirement of knowledge?—is the body, if
invited to share in the enquiry, a hinderer or

b   a helper? I mean to say, have sight and hearing any truth in them? Are they not, as the
poets are always telling us, inaccurate wit-
nesses? and yet, if even they are inaccurate
and indistinct, what is to be said of the other
senses?—for you will allow that they are the
best of them?

Certainly, he replied.

Then when does the soul attain truth?—
for in attempting to consider anything in
company with the body she is obviously

deceived.

c

True.

Then must not true existence be revealed to her in thought, if at all?

Yes.

And thought is best when the mind is gathered into herself and none of these things trouble her—neither sounds nor sights nor pain nor any pleasure,—when she takes leave of the body, and has as little as possible to do with it, when she has no bodily sense or desire, but is aspiring after true being?

Certainly.

d

And in this the philosopher dishonors the body; his soul runs away from his body and desires to be alone and by herself?

That is true.

Well, but there is another thing, Simmias: Is there or is there not an absolute justice?

Assuredly there is.

And an absolute beauty and absolute good?

Of course.

But did you ever behold any of them with your eyes?

Certainly not.

Or did you ever reach them with any other bodily sense?—and I speak not of these alone, but of absolute greatness, and health, and strength, and of the essence or true nature of everything. Has the reality of them ever been perceived by you through the bodily organs? or rather, is not the nearest approach to the knowledge of their several natures made by him who so orders his intellectual vision as to have the most exact conception of the essence of each thing which he considers?

Certainly.

And he attains to the purest knowledge of them who goes to each with the mind alone, not introducing or intruding in the act of thought, sight or any other sense together with reason, but with the very light of the mind in her own clearness searches into the very truth of each; he who has got rid, as far as he can, of eyes and ears and, so to

e

66

(I, 6
[1], 5;
IV, 8
[6], 2;
I, 2
[19], 3)

speak, of the whole body, these being in his opinion distracting elements which when they infect the soul hinder her from acquiring truth and knowledge—who, if not he, is likely to attain to the knowledge of true being?

What you say has a wonderful truth in it, Socrates, replied Simmias.

b And when real philosophers consider all these things, will they not be led to make a reflection which they will express in words something like the following? "Have we not found," they will say, "a path of thought which seems to bring us and our argument to the conclusion, that while we are in the body, and while the soul is infected with the evils of the body, our desire will not be satisfied? and our desire is of the truth. For the body is a source of endless trouble to us

c by reason of the mere requirement of food; and is liable also to diseases which overtake and impede us in the search after true being: it fills us full of loves, and lusts, and fears, and fancies of all kinds, and endless foolery, and in fact, as men say, takes away from us the power of thinking at all. Whence come wars, and fightings, and factions? whence but from the body and the lusts of the body? Wars are occasioned by the love of money,

d and money has to be acquired for the sake and in the service of the body; and by reason of all these impediments we have no time to give to philosophy; and, last and worst of all, even if we are at leisure and betake ourselves to some speculation, the body is always breaking in upon us, causing turmoil and confusion in our enquiries, and so amazing us that we are prevented from seeing the truth. It has been proved to us by experience that if we would have pure knowledge of

e anything we must be quit of the body—the soul in herself must behold things in themselves: and then we shall attain the wisdom which we desire, and of which we say that we are lovers; not while we live, but after death; for if while in company with the body, the soul cannot have pure knowledge,

67

one of two things follows—either knowledge is not to be attained at all, or, if at all, after death. For then, and not till then, the soul will be parted from the body and exist in herself alone. In this present life, I reckon that we make the nearest approach to knowledge when we have the least possible intercourse or communion with the body, and are not surfeited with the bodily nature, but keep ourselves pure until the hour when God himself is pleased to release us. And thus having got rid of the foolishness of the body we

b

shall be pure and hold converse with the pure, and know of ourselves the clear light everywhere, which is no other than the light of truth." For the impure are not permitted to approach the pure. These are the sort of words, Simmias, which the true lovers of knowledge cannot help saying to one another, and thinking. You would agree; would you not?

Undoubtedly, Socrates.

But, O my friend, if this be true, there is great reason to hope that, going whither I go, when I have come to the end of my journey, I shall attain that which has been the pursuit of my life. And therefore I go

c

on my way rejoicing, and not I only, but every other man who believes that his mind has been made ready and that he is in a manner purified.

Certainly, replied Simmias.

And what is purification but the separation of the soul from the body, as I was saying before; the habit of the soul gathering and collecting herself into herself from all

d

sides out of the body; the dwelling in her own place alone, as in another life, so also in this, as far as she can;—the release of the soul from the chains of the body?

69c

The founders of the mysteries would appear to have had a real meaning, and were not talking nonsense when they intimated in a figure long ago that he who passes unsanctified and uninitiated into the world below will lie in a slough, but that he who

(I, 6
[1], 7;
IV, 8
[6], 1; 2;
V, 1
[10], 10)

(I, 6
[1], 6;
I, 2
[19], 3)

arrives there after initiation and purification
will dwell with the gods.

Phaedrus

246b   I will endeavour to explain to you in what   (IV, 8
way the mortal differs from the immortal   [6], 1; 2;
creature. The soul in her totality has the   VI, 9
care of inanimate being everywhere, and   [9], 9;
traverses the whole heaven in divers forms   V, 1
c   appearing:—when perfect and fully winged   [10], 2;
she soars upward, and orders the whole   I, 2
world; whereas the imperfect soul, losing her   [19], 6;
wings and drooping in her flight, at last set-   I, 3
tles on the solid ground—there, finding a   [20], 3;
home, she receives an earthly frame which   IV, 3
appears to be self-moved, but is really moved   [27], 1; 7)
by her power; and this composition of soul
and body is called a living and mortal creature. For immortal no such union can be
d   reasonably believed to be; although fancy,
not having seen nor surely known the nature
of God, may imagine an immortal creature
having both a body and also a soul which
are united throughout all time. Let that,
however, be as God wills, and be spoken of
acceptably to him. And now let us ask the
reason why the soul loses her wings!
    The wing is the corporeal element which is
most akin to the divine, and which by nature
tends to soar aloft and carry that which
gravitates downwards into the upper region,
which is the habitation of the gods. The
e   divine is beauty, wisdom, goodness, and the
like; and by these the wing of the soul is
nourished, and grows apace; but when fed
upon evil and foulness and the opposite of
good, wastes and falls away. Zeus, the
mighty lord, holding the reins of a winged
chariot, leads the way in heaven, ordering
all and taking care of all; and there follows
him the array of gods and demi-gods,
247   marshalled in eleven bands; Hestia alone   (I, 6
abides at home in the house of heaven; of   [1], 5; 7;
the rest they who are reckoned among the   IV, 8
princely twelve march in their appointed   [6], 1; 2;
                                                                    VI, 9

order. They see many blessed sights in the **[9], 9;**
inner heaven, and there are many ways to   **III, 8**
and fro, along which the blessed gods are   **[30], 5)**
passing, every one doing his own work; he
may follow who will and can, for jealousy
has no place in the celestial choir. But when
they go to banquet and festival, then they
b move up the steep to the top of the vault of
heaven. The chariots of the gods in even
poise, obeying the rein, glide rapidly; but the
others labour, for the vicious steed goes
heavily, weighing down the charioteer to the
earth when his steed has not been thoroughly
trained:—and this is the hour of agony and
extremest conflict for the soul. For the im-
mortals, when they are at the end of their
course, go forth and stand upon the outside
c of heaven, and the revolution of the spheres
carries them round, and they behold the
things beyond. But of the heaven which is
above the heavens, what earthly poet ever
did or ever will sing worthily? It is such as I
will describe; for I must dare to speak the
truth, when truth is my theme. There abides
the very being with which true knowledge
is concerned; the colorless, formless, intan-
gible essence, visible only to mind, the pilot
d of the soul. The divine intelligence, being
nurtured upon mind and pure knowledge,
and the intelligence of every soul which is
capable of receiving the food proper to it,
rejoices at beholding reality, and once more
gazing upon truth, is replenished and made
glad, until the revolution of the worlds brings
her round again to the same place. In the
revolution she beholds justice, and temper-
e ance, and knowledge absolute, not in the
form of generation or of relation, which men
call existence, but knowledge absolute in
existence absolute; and beholding the other
true existences in like manner, and feasting
upon them, she passes down into the interior
of the heavens and returns home; and there
the charioteer putting up his horses at the
stall, gives them ambrosia to eat and nectar
to drink.

Such is the life of the gods; but of other   **(V, 9**
                                                  [5], 2;

souls, that which follows God best and is likest to him lifts the head of the charioteer into the outer world, and is carried round in the revolution, troubled indeed by the steeds, and with difficulty beholding true being; while another only rises and falls, and sees, and again fails to see by reason of the unruliness of the steeds. The rest of the souls are also longing after the upper world and they all follow, but not being strong enough they are carried round below the surface, plunging, treading on one another, each striving to be first; and there is confusion and perspiration and the extremity of effort; and many of them are lamed or have their wings broken through the ill-driving of the charioteers; and all of them after a fruitless toil, not having attained to the mysteries of true being, go away, and feed upon opinion. The reason why the souls exhibit this exceeding eagerness to behold the plain of truth is that pasturage is found there, which is suited to the highest part of the soul; and the wing on which the soul soars is nourished with this. And there is a law of Destiny, that the soul which attains any vision of truth in company with a god is preserved from harm until the next period, and if attaining always is always unharmed. But when she is unable to follow, and fails to behold the truth, and through some ill-hap sinks beneath the double load of forgetfulness and vice, and her wings fall from her and she drops to the ground, then the law ordains that this soul shall at her first birth pass, not into any other animal, but only into man; and the soul which has seen most of truth shall come to the birth as a philosopher, or artist, or some musical and loving nature; that which has seen truth in the second degree shall be some righteous king or warrior chief; the soul which is of the third class shall be a politician, or economist, or trader; the fourth shall be a lover of gymnastic toils, or a physician; the fifth shall lead the life of a prophet or hierophant; to the sixth the character of a poet or some other imitative artist

VI, 9
[9], 8; 9;
11; I, 3
[20], 1;
4)

b

c

d

e

will be assigned; to the seventh the life of an artisan or husbandman; to the eighth that of a sophist or demagogue; to the ninth that of a tyrant;—all these are states of probation, in which he who does righteously improves, and he who does unrighteously, deteriorates his lot.

249   Ten thousand years must elapse before the soul of each one can return to the place from whence she came, for she cannot grow her wings in less; only the soul of a philosopher, guileless and true, or the soul of a lover, who is not devoid of philosophy, may acquire wings in the third of the recurring periods of a thousand years; he is distinguished from the ordinary good man who gains wings in three thousand years:—and they who choose this life three times in succession have wings given them, and go away at the end of three thousand years. But the others receive judgment when they have completed their first life, and after the judgment they go, some of them to the houses of correction which are under the earth, and are punished; others to some place in heaven whither they are lightly borne by justice, and there they live in a manner worthy of the

b   life which they led here when in the form of men. And at the end of the first thousand years the good souls and also the evil souls both come to draw lots and choose their second life, and they may take any which they please. The soul of a man may pass into the life of a beast, or from the beast return again into the man. But the soul which has never seen the truth will not pass into the human form. For a man must have intelligence of universals, and be able to proceed

c   from the many particulars of sense to one conception of reason;—this is the recollection of those things which our soul once saw while following God—when regardless of that which we now call being she raised her head up towards the true being. And therefore the mind of the philosopher alone has wings; and this is just, for he is always, according to the measure of his abilities, cling-

(IV, 8
[6], 1; 4;
VI, 9
[9], 8)

ing in recollection to those things in which God abides, and in beholding which He is what He is. And he who employs aright these memories is ever being initiated into perfect mysteries and alone becomes truly perfect. But, as he forgets earthly interests and is rapt in the divine, the vulgar deem him mad, and rebuke him; they do not see that he is inspired.

Thus far I have been speaking of the fourth and last kind of madness, which is imputed to him who, when he sees the beauty of earth, is transported with the recollection of the true beauty; he would like to fly away, but he cannot; he is like a bird fluttering and looking upward and careless of the world below; and he is therefore thought to be mad. And I have shown this of all inspirations to be the noblest and highest and the offspring of the highest to him who has or shares in it, and that he who loves the beautiful is called a lover because he partakes of it. For, as has been already said, every soul of man has in the way of nature beheld true being; this was the condition of her passing into the form of man. But all souls do not easily recall the things of the other world; they may have seen them for a short time only, or they may have been unfortunate in their earthly lot, and, having had their hearts turned to unrighteousness through some corrupting influence, they may have lost the memory of the holy things which once they saw. Few only retain an adequate remembrance of them; and they, when they behold here any image of that other world, are rapt in amazement; but they are ignorant of what this rapture means, because they do not clearly perceive. For there is no light of justice or temperance or any of the higher ideas which are precious to souls in the earthly copies of them: they are seen through a glass dimly; and there are few who, going to the images, behold in them the realities, and these only with difficulty. There was a time when with the rest of the happy band they saw beauty shining in

d

e

250

(I, 6 [1], 4; 5; 7; III, 8 [30], 11)

b

brightness,—we philosophers following in
the train of Zeus, others in company with
other gods; and then we beheld the bea-
tific vision and were initiated into a mystery

c   which may be truly called most blessed, cele-
brated by us in our state of innocence, before
we had any experience of evils to come,
when we were admitted to the sight of ap-
paritions innocent and simple and calm and
happy, which we beheld shining in pure
light, pure ourselves and not yet enshrined
in that living tomb which we carry about,
now that we are imprisoned in the body, like
an oyster in his shell.

The Banquet

"These are the lesser mysteries of love,
210 into which even you, Socrates, may enter; to
the greater and more hidden ones which are
the crown of these, and to which, if you pursue them in a right spirit, they will lead, I
know not whether you will be able to attain.
But I will do my utmost to inform you, and
do you follow if you can. For he who would
proceed aright in this matter should begin in
youth to visit beautiful forms; and first, if he
be guided by his instructor aright, to love
one such form only—out of that he should
create fair thoughts; and soon he will of

b   himself perceive that the beauty of one form
is akin to the beauty of another; and then if
beauty of form in general is his pursuit, how
foolish would he be not to recognize that the
beauty in every form is one and the same!
And when he perceives this he will abate his
violent love of the one, which he will despise
and deem a small thing, and will become a
lover of all beautiful forms; in the next stage
he will consider that the beauty of the mind
is more honorable than the beauty of the
outward form. So that if a virtuous soul have

c   but a little comeliness, he will be content to
love and tend him, and will search out and
bring to the birth thoughts which may im-
prove the young, until he is compelled to

(I, 6
[1], 5;
V, 9
[5], 2;
I, 3
[20], 2)

contemplate and see the beauty of institutions and laws, and to understand that the
beauty of them all is of one family, and that
personal beauty is a trifle; and after laws and
institutions he will go on to the sciences, that
he may see their beauty, being not like a
d   servant in love with the beauty of one youth
or man or institution, himself a slave mean
and narrow-minded, but drawing towards
and contemplating the vast sea of beauty, he
will create many fair and noble thoughts and
notions in boundless love of wisdom; until
on that shore he grows and waxes strong,
and at last the vision is revealed to him of a
e   single science, which is the science of beauty
everywhere. To this I will proceed; please to
give me your very best attention:

"He who has been instructed thus far in
the things of love, and who has learned to see
the beautiful in due order and succession,
211   when he comes toward the end will suddenly
perceive a nature of wondrous beauty (and
this, Socrates, is the final cause of all our
former toils)—a nature which in the first
place is everlasting, not growing and decay-
ing, or waxing and waning; secondly, not fair
in one point of view and foul in another, or
at one time or in one relation or at one place
fair, at another time or in another relation
or at another place foul, as if fair to some
and foul to others, or in the likeness of a face
or hands or any other part of the bodily
frame, or in any form of speech or knowledge, or existing in any other being, as for
example, in an animal, or in heaven, or in
b   earth, or in any other place; but beauty absolute, separate, simple, and everlasting,
which without diminution and without increase, or any change, is imparted to the
ever-growing and perishing beauties of all
other things. He who from these ascending
under the influence of true love, begins to
c   perceive that beauty, is not far from the end.
And the true order of going, or being led by
another, to the things of love, is to begin
from the beauties of earth and mount up-
wards for the sake of that other beauty, us-

(I, 6
[1], 1; 7;
VI, 9
[9], 3)

ing these as steps only, and from one going
on to two, and from two to all fair forms,
and from fair forms to fair practices, and
from fair practices to fair notions, until from
fair notions he arrives at the notion of ab-

d solute beauty, and at last knows what the
essence of beauty is. This, my dear Socrates,"
said the stranger of Mantineia, "is that life
above all others which man should live, in
the contemplation of beauty absolute; a
beauty which if you once beheld, you would
see not to be after the measure of gold, and
garments, and fair boys and youths, whose
presence now entrances you; and you and
many a one would be content to live seeing
them only and conversing with them without meat or drink, if that were possible—
you only want to look at them and to be

e with them. But what if man had eyes to see
the true beauty—the divine beauty, I mean,
pure and clear and unalloyed, not clogged
with the pollutions of mortality and all the
colours and vanities of human life—thither
looking, and holding converse with the true
beauty simple and divine? . . ."

Theaetetus

176   Evils, Theodorus, can never pass away;   (I, 6 [1],
for there must always remain something   6; I, 2
which is antagonistic to good. Having no [19], 1; 3)
place among the gods in heaven, of necessity
they hover around the mortal nature, and

b this earthly sphere. Wherefore we ought to
fly away from earth to heaven as quickly as
we can; and to fly away is to become like
God, as far as this is possible: and to become
like him, is to become holy, just, and wise.
But, O my friend, you cannot easily con-
vince mankind that they should pursue virtue
or avoid vice, not merely in order that a man
may seem to be good, which is the reason
given by the world, and in my judgment is

c only a repetition of an old wives' fable.
Whereas, the truth is that God is never in
any way unrighteous—he is perfect right-

eousness; and he of us who is the most righteous is most like him.

Parmenides

137c   Parmenides proceeded: If one is, he said, (V, 1 [10],
the one cannot be many?   8)

Impossible.

Then the one cannot have parts, and cannot be a whole?

Why not?

Because every part is part of a whole; is
it not?

Yes.

And what is a whole? would not that of
which no part is wanting be a whole?

Certainly.

Then, in either case, the one would be
made up of parts; both as being a whole, and
also as having parts?

To be sure.

And in either case, the one would be
many, and not one?

True.

But, surely, it ought to be one and not
many?

It ought.

d   Then, if the one is to remain one, it will
not be a whole, and will not have parts?

No.

But if it has no parts, it will have neither
beginning, middle, nor end; for these would
of course be parts of it.

Right.

But then, again, a beginning and an end
are the limits of everything?

Certainly.

Then the one, having neither beginning
nor end, is unlimited?

Yes, unlimited.

e   And therefore formless; for it cannot partake either of round or straight.

But why?

Why, because the round is that of which
all the extreme points are equidistant from
the centre?

Yes.

And the straight is that of which the centre intercepts the view of the extremes?

True.

138 Then the one would have parts and would be many, if it partook either of a straight or of a circular form?

(VI, 9 [9], 3; 6; V, 1 [10], 8)

Assuredly.

But having no parts, it will be neither straight nor round?

Right.

And, being of such a nature, it cannot be in any place, for it cannot be either in another or in itself.

How so?

Because if it were in another, it would be encircled by that in which it was, and would touch it at many places and with many parts; but that which is one and indivisible, and does not partake of a circular nature, cannot be touched all round in many places.

Certainly not.

But if, on the other hand, one were in itself, it would also be contained by nothing else but itself; that is to say, if it were really in itself; for nothing can be in anything which does not contain it.

b

Impossible.

But then, that which contains must be other than that which is contained? for the same whole cannot do and suffer both at once; and if so, one will be no longer one, but two?

True.

Then one cannot be anywhere, either in itself or in another?

No.

Further consider, whether that which is of such a nature can have either rest or motion.

Why not?

Why, because the one, if it were moved, would be either moved in place or changed in nature; for these are the only kinds of motion.

c

Yes.

And the one, when it changes and ceases to be itself, cannot be any longer one.

It cannot.

It cannot therefore experience the sort of motion which is change of nature?

Clearly not.

Then can the motion of the one be in place?

Perhaps.

But if the one moved in place, must it not either move round and round in the same place, or from one place to another?

It must.

And that which moves in a circle must rest upon a centre; and that which goes round upon a centre must have parts which are different from the centre; but that which has no centre and no parts cannot possibly be carried round upon a centre?

Impossible.

But perhaps the motion of the one consists in change of place?

Perhaps so, if it moves at all.

And have we not already shown that it cannot be in anything?

Yes.

Then its coming into being in anything is still more impossible; is it not?

I do not see why.

Why, because anything which comes into being in anything, can neither as yet be in that other thing while still coming into being, nor be altogether out of it, if already coming into being in it.

Certainly not.

And therefore whatever comes into being in another must have parts, and then one part may be in, and another part out of that other; but that which has no parts can never be at one and the same time neither wholly within nor wholly without anything.

True.

And is there not a still greater impossibility in that which has no parts, and is not a whole, coming into being anywhere, since it cannot come into being either as a part or as a whole?

Clearly.

Then it does not change place by revolv-

ing in the same spot, nor by going somewhere and coming into being in something;
nor again, by change in itself?

Very true.

Then in respect of any kind of motion the
one is immovable?

Immovable.

But neither can the one be in anything, as
we affirm?

Yes, we said so.

Then it is never in the same?

Why not?

Because if it were in the same it would be
in something.

Certainly.

And we said that it could not be in itself,
and could not be in other?

True.

Then one is never in the same place?

It would seem not.

b   But that which is never in the same place
is never quiet or at rest?

Never.

One then, as would seem, is neither at rest
nor in motion?

It certainly appears so.

Neither will it be the same with itself or
other; nor again, other than itself or other.

How is that?

If other than itself it would be other than
one, and would not be one.

True.

c   And if the same with other, it would be
that other, and not itself; so that upon this
supposition too, it would not have the nature
of one, but would be other than one?

It would.

Then it will not be the same with other, or
other than itself?

It will not.

Neither will it be other than other, while it
remains one; for not one, but only other,
can be other than other, and nothing else.

True.

Then not by virtue of being one will it be
other?

Certainly not.

But if not by virtue of being one, not by virtue of itself; and if not by virtue of itself, not itself, and itself not being other at all, will not be other than anything.

Right.

d

Neither will one be the same with itself.

How not?

Surely the nature of the one is not the nature of the same.

Why not?

It is not when anything becomes the same with anything that it becomes one.

What of that?

Anything which becomes the same with the many, necessarily becomes many and not one.

True.

But, if there were no difference between the one and the same, when a thing became the same, it would always become one; and when it became one, the same?

Certainly.

And, therefore, if one be the same with itself, it is not one with itself, and will therefore be one and also not one.

Surely that is impossible.

e

And therefore the one can neither be other than other, nor the same with itself.

Impossible.

And thus the one can neither be the same, nor other, either in relation to itself or other?

No.

Neither will the one be like anything or unlike itself or other.

Why not?

Because likeness is sameness of affections.

Yes.

And sameness has been shown to be of a nature distinct from oneness?

That has been shown.

140

But if the one had any other affection than that of being one, it would be affected in such a way as to be more than one; which is impossible.

(V, 1
[10], 8)

True.

Then the one can never be so affected as to be the same either with another or with itself?

Clearly not.

Then it cannot be like another, or like itself?

No.

Nor can it be affected so as to be other, for
then it would be affected in such a way as to
be more than one.

It would.

b   That which is affected otherwise than itself
or another, will be unlike itself or another,
for sameness of affections is likeness.

True.

But the one, as appears, never being
affected otherwise, is never unlike itself or
other?

Never.

Then the one will never be either like or
unlike itself or other?

Plainly not.

Again, being of this nature, it can neither
be equal nor unequal either to itself or to
other.

How is that?

Why, because the one if equal must be of
c   the same measures as that to which it is
equal.

True.

And if greater or less than things which
are commensurable with it, the one will have
more measures than that which is less, and
fewer than that which is greater?

Yes.

And so of things which are not commen-
surate with it, the one will have greater
measures than that which is less and smaller
than that which is greater.

Certainly.

But how can that which does not partake
of sameness, have either the same measures
or have anything else the same?

Impossible.

And not having the same measures, the
one cannot be equal either with itself or with
another?

It appears so.

But again, whether it have fewer or more

d measures, it will have as many parts as it has measures; and thus again the one will be no longer one but will have as many parts as measures.

Right.

And if it were of one measure, it would be equal to that measure; yet it has been shown to be incapable of equality.

It has.

Then it will neither partake of one measure, nor of many, nor of few, nor of the same at all, nor be equal to itself or another; nor be greater or less than itself, or other?

Certainly.

e Well, and do we suppose that one can be older, or younger than anything, or of the same age with it?

Why not?

Why, because that which is of the same age with itself or other, must partake of equality or likeness of time; and we said that the one did not partake either of equality or of likeness?

We did say so.

And we also said, that it did not partake of inequality or unlikeness.

141 Very true.

(VI, 9 [9], 3; V, 1 [10], 8)

How then can one, being of this nature, be either older or younger than anything, or have the same age with it?

In no way.

Then one cannot be older or younger, or of the same age, either with itself or with another?

Clearly not.

Then the one, being of this nature, cannot be in time at all; for must not that which is in time, be always growing older than itself?

Certainly.

And that which is older, must always be older than something which is younger?

True.

b Then, that which becomes older than itself, also becomes at the same time younger than itself, if it is to have something to become older than.

What do you mean?

I mean this:—A thing does not need to become different from another thing which is already different; it is different, and if its different has become, it has become different; if its different will be, it will be different; but of that which is becoming different, there cannot have been, or be about to be, or yet be, a different—the only different possible is one which is becoming.

That is inevitable.

c But, surely, the elder is a difference relative to the younger, and to nothing else.

True.

Then that which becomes older than itself must also, at the same time, become younger than itself?

Yes.

But again, it is true that it cannot become for a longer or for a shorter time than itself, but it must become, and be, and have become, and be about to be, for the same time with itself?

That again is inevitable.

Then things which are in time, and par-
d take of time, must in every case, I suppose, be of the same age with themselves; and must also become at once older and younger than themselves?

Yes.

But the one did not partake of those affections?

Not at all.

Then it does not partake of time, and is not in any time?

So the argument shows.

Well, but do not the expressions "was," and "has become," and "was becoming," signify a participation of past time?

Certainly.

And do not "will be," "will become," "will
e have become," signify a participation of future time?

Yes.

And "is," or "becomes," signifies a participation of present time?

Certainly.

And if the one is absolutely without participation in time, it never had become, or was becoming, or was at any time, or is now become or is becoming, or is, or will become, or will have become, or will be, hereafter.

Most true.

But are there any modes of partaking of being other than these?

There are none.

Then the one cannot possibly partake of being?

That is the inference.

Then the one is not at all?

Clearly not.

Then the one does not exist in such way as to be one; for if it were and partook of being, it would already be; but if the argument is to be trusted, the one neither is nor is one?

142 True. (VI, 9

But that which is not admits of no attribute or relation? [9], 3; V 1 [10], 8

Of course not.

Then there is no name, nor expression, nor perception, nor opinion, nor knowledge of it?

Clearly not.

Then it is neither named, nor expressed, nor opined, nor known, nor does anything that is perceive it.

Timaeus

27c   All men, Socrates, who have any degree of right feeling, at the beginning of every enterprise, whether small or great, always call upon God. And we, too, who are going to discourse of the nature of the universe, how created or how existing without creation, if we be not altogether out of our wits, must invoke the aid of Gods and Goddesses and pray that our words may be acceptable to them and consistent with themselves. Let

d   this, then, be our invocation of the Gods, to which I add an exhortation of myself to speak in such manner as will be most intelligible to you, and will most accord with my own intent.

(V, 1 [10], 6

First then, in my judgment, we must make
a distinction and ask, What is that which
always is and has no becoming; and what is
that which is always becoming and never is?
That which is apprehended by intelligence
and reason is always in the same state; but
that which is conceived by opinion with the
help of sensation and without reason, is always in a process of becoming and perishing
and never really is. Now everything that becomes or is created must of necessity be
created by some cause, for without a cause
nothing can be created. The work of the
creator, whenever he looks to the unchangeable and fashions the form and nature of
his work after an unchangeable pattern, must
necessarily be made fair and perfect; but
when he looks to the created only, and uses
a created pattern, it is not fair or perfect.
Was the heaven then or the world, whether
called by this or by any other more appropriate name—assuming the name, I am asking a question which has to be asked at the
beginning of an enquiry about anything—
was the world, I say, always in existence and
without beginning? or created, and had it a
beginning? Created, I reply, being visible
and tangible and having a body, and therefore sensible; and all sensible things are
apprehended by opinion and sense and are in
a process of creation and created. Now that
which is created must, as we affirm, of necessity be created by a cause. But the father and
maker of all this universe is past finding out;
and even if we found him, to tell of him to
all men would be impossible. And there is
still a question to be asked about him: Which
of the patterns had the artificer in view when
he made the world,—the pattern of the unchangeable, or of that which is created? If
the world be indeed fair and the artificer
good, it is manifest that he must have looked
to that which is eternal; but if what cannot
be said without blasphemy is true, then to
the created pattern. Every one will see that
he must have looked to the eternal; for the

28

b

c

29

(V, 9 [5],
5; VI, 9
[9], 3)

(IV, 8
[6], 1)

world is the fairest of creations and he is the
best of causes. And having been created in
this way, the world has been framed in the
likeness of that which is apprehended by reason and mind and is unchangeable, and must
b   therefore of necessity, if this is admitted, be
a copy of something. Now it is all-important
that the beginning of everything should be
according to nature. And in speaking of the
copy and the original we may assume that
words are akin to the matter which they
describe; when they relate to the lasting and
permanent and intelligible, they ought to be
lasting and unalterable, and, as far as their
nature allows, irrefutable and immovable—
c   nothing less. But when they express only the
copy or likeness and not the eternal things
themselves, they need only be likely and
analogous to the real words. As being is to
becoming, so is truth to belief. If then,
Socrates, amid the many opinions about the
gods and the generation of the universe, we
are not able to give notions which are altogether and in every respect exact and consistent with one another, do not be surprised.
d   Enough, if we adduce probabilities as likely
as any others; for we must remember that I
who am the speaker, and you who are the
judges, are only mortal men, and we ought
to accept the tale which is probable and
enquire no further.

Excellent, Timaeus; and we will do precisely as you bid us. The prelude is charming, and is already accepted by us—may we
beg of you to proceed to the strain?

Let me tell you then why the creator made
e   this world of generation. He was good, and
the good can never have any jealousy of
anything. And being free from jealousy, he
desired that all things should be as like him-
30   self as they could be. This is in the truest   (IV, 8
sense the origin of creation and of the world, [6], 1; 3)
as we shall do well in believing on the testi-
mony of wise men: God desired that all
things should be good and nothing bad, so
far as this was attainable. Wherefore also
finding the whole visible sphere not at rest,

but moving in an irregular and disorderly
fashion, out of disorder he brought order,
considering that this was in every way better
than the other. Now the deeds of the best
could never be or have been other than the
b fairest; and the creator, reflecting on the
things which are by nature visible, found
that no unintelligent creature taken as a
whole was fairer than the intelligent taken as
a whole; and that intelligence could not be
present in anything which was devoid of
soul. For which reason, when he was fram-
ing the universe, he put intelligence in soul,
and soul in body, that he might be the
creator of a work which was by nature
fairest and best. Wherefore, using the language of probability, we may say that the
world became a living creature truly en-
c dowed with soul and intelligence by the
providence of God.

   This being supposed, let us proceed to the
next stage: In the likeness of what animal
did the Creator make the world? It would
be an unworthy thing to liken it to any
nature which exists as a part only; for nothing can be beautiful which is like any imperfect thing; but let us suppose the world
to be the very image of that whole of which
all other animals both individually and in
their tribes are portions. For the original of
d the universe contains in itself all intelligible
beings, just as this world comprehends us
and all other visible creatures. For the Deity,
intending to make this world like the fairest
and most perfect of intelligible beings,
framed one visible animal comprehending
within itself all other animals of a kindred
31 nature. Are we right in saying that there is   (IV, 8
one world, or that they are many and in-   [6], 3)
finite? There must be one only, if the created
copy is to accord with the original. For that
which includes all other intelligible creatures
cannot have a second or companion; in that
case there would be need of another living
being which would include both, and of
which they would be parts, and the likeness
would be more truly said to resemble not

them, but that other which included them. In
b   order then that the world might be solitary,
like the perfect animal, the creator made not
two worlds or an infinite number of them;
but there is and ever will be one only-be-
gotten and created heaven.

Such was the whole plan of the eternal   (IV, 8
34   God about the god that was to be, to whom   [6], 1; V, 1
b   for this reason he gave a body, smooth and   [10], 2; 8)
even, having a surface in every direction
equidistant from the centre, a body entire
and perfect, and formed out of perfect bodies. And in the centre he put the soul, which
he diffused throughout the body, making it
also to be the exterior environment of it; and
he made the universe a circle moving in a
circle, one and solitary, yet by reason of its
excellence able to converse with itself, and
needing no other friendship or acquaintance.
Having these purposes in view he created the
world a blessed god.

c   Now God did not make the soul after the
body, although we are speaking of them in
this order; for having brought them together
he would never have allowed that the elder
should be ruled by the younger; but this is a
random manner of speaking which we have,
because somehow we ourselves too are very
much under the dominion of chance. Whereas he made the soul in origin and excellence
prior to and older than the body, to be the
ruler and mistress, of whom the body was to
be the subject.

35a   Out of the indivisible and unchangeable,   (IV, 3
and also out of that which is divisible and   [27], 4; 19)
has to do with material bodies, he com-
pounded a third and intermediate kind of
essence, partaking of the nature of the same
and of the other, and this compound he
placed accordingly in a mean between the
indivisible, and the divisible and material.

36d   Now when the Creator had framed the   (V, 1 [10],
soul according to his will, he formed within   2; 10; IV,
her the corporeal universe, and brought the   3 [27], 22)

e two together, and united them center to center. The soul, interfused everywhere from
the center to the circumference of heaven,
of which also she is the external envelop-
ment, herself turning in herself, began a
divine beginning of never-ceasing and rational life enduring throughout all time.

37c   When the father and creator saw the crea- (V, 9 [5],
ture which he had made moving and living,   2; V, 1
the created image of the eternal gods, he [10], 2; 4)
rejoiced, and in his joy determined to make
the copy still more like the original; and as
this was eternal, he sought to make the uni-
d verse eternal, so far as might be. Now the
nature of the ideal being was everlasting, but
to bestow this attribute in its fulness upon a
creature was impossible. Wherefore he
resolved to have a moving image of eternity,
and when he set in order the heaven, he
made this image eternal but moving according to number, while eternity itself rests in
e unity; and this image we call time. For there
were no days and nights and months and
years before the heaven was created, but
when he constructed the heaven he created
them also. They are all parts of time, and the
past and future are created species of time,
which we unconsciously but wrongly trans-
fer to the eternal essence; for we say that he
"was," he "is," he "will be," but the truth is
that "is" alone is properly attributed to him,
38 and that "was" and "will be" are only to be
spoken of becoming in time.

38b   Time, then, and the heaven came into be- (IV, 8
ing at the same instant in order that, having   [6], 2)
been created together, if ever there was to be
a dissolution of them, they might be dissolved together. It was framed after the pattern of the eternal nature, that it might
resemble this as far as was possible; for the
pattern exists from eternity, and the created
c heaven has been, and is, and will be, in all
time. Such was the mind and thought of
God in the creation of time. The sun and
moon and five other stars, which are called

the planets, were created by him in order to
distinguish and preserve the numbers of
time; and when he had made their several
bodies, he placed them in the orbits in which
the circle of the other was revolving.

39b   That there might be some visible measure
of their relative swiftness and slowness as
they proceeded in their eight courses, God
lighted a fire, which we now call the sun, in
the second from the earth of these orbits,
that it might give light to the whole of
heaven, and that the animals, as many as
nature intended, might participate in num-
c   ber, learning arithmetic from the revolution
of the same and the like. Thus, then, and for
this reason the night and the day were
created, being the period of the one most
intelligent revolution.

39e   Thus far and until the birth of time the   (V, 9 [5],
created universe was made in the likeness of   9; IV, 8
the original, but inasmuch as all animals   [6], 1)
were not yet comprehended therein, it was
still unlike. What remained, the creator then
proceeded to fashion after the nature of the
pattern. Now as in the ideal animal the mind
perceives ideas or species of a certain nature
and number, he thought that this created
animal ought to have species of a like nature
and number.

41   Now, when all of them, both those who   (IV, 8 [6],
visibly appear in their revolutions as well as   4; V, 1
those other gods who are of a more retiring   [10], 8;
nature, had come into being, the creator of   IV, 3 [27],
the universe addressed them in these words: 6; 7)
"Gods, children of gods, who are my works,
b   and of whom I am the artificer and father,
my creations are indissoluble, if so I will. All
that is bound may be undone, but only an
evil being would wish to undo that which is
harmonious and happy. Wherefore, since ye
are but creatures, ye are not altogether immortal and indissoluble, but ye shall certainly not be dissolved, nor be liable to the fate
of death, having in my will a greater and

mightier bond than those with which ye were bound at the time of your birth. And now listen to my instructions:—Three tribes of mortal beings remain to be created—without them the universe will be incomplete, for

c   it will not contain every kind of animal which it ought to contain, if it is to be perfect. On the other hand, if they were created by me and received life at my hands, they would be on an equality with the gods. In order then that they may be mortal, and that this universe may be truly universal, do ye, according to your natures, betake yourselves to the formation of animals, imitating the power which was shown by me in creating you. The part of them worthy of the name immortal, which is called divine and is the guiding principle of those who are willing to follow justice and you—of that divine part I will myself sow the seed, and having

d   made a beginning, I will hand the work over to you. And do ye then interweave the mortal with the immortal, and make and beget living creatures, and give them food, and make them to grow, and receive them again in death."

Thus he spake, and once more into the cup in which he had previously mingled the soul of the universe he poured the remains of the elements, and mingled them in much the same manner; they were not, however, pure as before, but diluted to the second and third degree. And having made it he divided the whole mixture into souls equal in number to the stars, and assigned each soul to a

e   star; and having there placed them as in a chariot, he showed them the nature of the universe, and declared to them the laws of destiny, according to which their first birth would be one and the same for all,—no one should suffer a disadvantage at his hands; they were to be sown in the instruments of time severally adapted to them, and to come

42   forth the most religious of animals; and as human nature was of two kinds, the superior race would hereafter be called man.

The Wallace translation has been used for the selections from *On the Soul*. Those from *Metaphysics* have been translated by the editor. The marginal references are given according to the convention of referring to the pagination of the Berlin 1831 edition of Bekker.

On the Soul

412a

Real substance is the name which we (IV, 3 [27], 21) assign one class of existing things; and this real substance may be viewed from several aspects, either, first, as matter, meaning by matter that which in itself is not any individual thing; or, secondly, as form and specific characteristic in virtue of which an object comes to be described as such and such an individual; or, thirdly, as the result produced by a combination of this matter and this form.

10 Further, while matter is merely potential existence, the form is perfect realization (a conception which may be taken in two forms, either as resembling knowledge possessed or as corresponding to observation in active exercise).

These real substances again are thought to correspond for the most part with bodies, and more particularly with natural bodies, because these latter are the source from which other bodies are formed. Now among such natural bodies, some have, others do not have life, meaning here by life the process of nutrition, increase, and decay from an inter-

15 nal principle. Thus every natural body possessed of life would be a real substance, and a substance which we may describe as composite.

Since then the body, as possessed of life, is of this compound character, the body itself would not constitute the soul: for body is not [like life and soul] something attributed to a subject; it rather acts as the underlying sub-

ject and the material basis. Thus then the
soul must necessarily be a real substance, as
the form which determines a natural body
possessed potentially of life. The reality,
however, of an object is contained in its perfect realization. Soul therefore will be a perfect realization of a body such as has been
described. Perfect realization, however, is a
word used in two senses: it may be understood either as an implicit state corresponding to knowledge as possessed, or as an explicitly exercised process corresponding to
active observation. Here, in reference to
soul, it must evidently be understood in the
former of these two senses: for the soul is
present with us as much while we are asleep
as while we are awake; and while waking
resembles active observation, sleep resembles
the implicit though not exercised possession
of knowledge. Now in reference to the same
subject, it is the implicit knowledge of scientific principles which stands prior. Soul therefore is the earlier or implicit perfect realization of a natural body possessed potentially
of life.

Such potential life belongs to everything
which is possessed of organs. Organs, however, we must remember, is a name that applies also to the parts of plants, except that
they are altogether uncompounded. Thus the
leaf is the protection of the pericarp and the
pericarp of the fruit; while the roots are
analogous to the mouth in animals, both
being used to absorb nourishment. Thus
then, if we be required to frame some one
common definition, which will apply to every
form of soul, it would be that soul is the
earlier perfect realization of a natural organic
body.

The definition we have just given should
make it evident that we must no more ask
whether the soul and the body are one, than
ask whether the wax and the figure impressed upon it are one, or generally inquire
whether the material and that of which it is
the material are one; for though unity and
being are used in a variety of senses, their

most distinctive sense is that of perfect realization.

10 A general account has thus been given of the nature of the soul: it is, we have seen, a real substance which expresses an idea. Such a substance is the manifestation of the inner meaning of such and such a body. Suppose, for example, that an instrument such as an axe were a natural body; then its axehood or its being an axe would constitute its essential nature or reality, and thus, so to speak, its soul; because were this axehood taken away from it, it would be no longer an axe, except in so far as it might still be called by this 15 same name. The object in question, however, is as matter of fact only an axe; soul being not the idea and the manifestation of the meaning of a body of this kind, but of a natural body possessing within itself a cause of movement and of rest.

The theory just stated should be viewed also in reference to the separate bodily parts. If, for example, the eye were possessed of life, vision would be its soul: because vision is the reality which expresses the idea of the 20 eye. The eye itself, on the other hand, is merely the material substratum for vision: and when this power of vision fails, it no longer remains an eye, except in so far as it is still called by the same name, just in the same way as an eye carved in stone or delineated in painting is also so described. Now what holds good of the part must be applied to the living body taken as a whole: for perception as a whole stands to the whole sensitive body, as such, in the same ratio as the particular exercise of sense stands to a single organ of sense.

25 The part of our definition which speaks of something as "potentially possessed of life" must be taken to mean not that which has thrown off its soul, but rather that which has it: the seed and the fruit is such and such a body potentially. In the same way then as cutting is the full realization of an axe, or actual seeing the realization of the eye, so also waking may be said to be the

413a full realization of the body; but it is in the
sense in which vision is not only the exercise
but also the implicit capacity of the eye that
soul is the true realization of the body. The
body on the other hand is merely the material to which soul gives reality; and just as
the eye is both the pupil and its vision, so
also the living animal is at once the soul and
body in connection.

It is not then difficult to see that soul or
certain parts of it (if it naturally admit of
partition) cannot be separated from the
5 body: for in some cases the soul is the realization of the parts of body themselves. It is,
however, perfectly conceivable that there
may be some parts of it which are separable,
and this because they are not the expression
or realization of any particular body. And
indeed it is further matter of doubt whether
soul as the perfect realization of the body
may not stand to it in the same separable
relation as a sailor to his boat.

430a 10 The same differences, however, as are   (V, 1
found in nature as a whole must be charac-   [10], 3)
teristic also of the soul. Now in nature there
is on the one hand that which acts as material substratum to each class of objects,
this being that which is potentially all of
them; on the other hand, there is the element
which is causal and creative in virtue of its
producing all things, and which stands toward the other in the same relation as that
in which art stands toward the materials on
which it operates. Thus reason is, on the one
hand, of such a character as to become all
15 things, on the other hand of such a nature as
to create all things, acting then much in the
same way as some positive quality, such as
for instance light: for light also in a way
creates actual out of potential color.

429a Thinking, we may assume, is like percep-   (I, 6 [1],9)
tion, and, if so, consists in being affected by
the object of thought or in something else of
this nature. Like sense then, thought or rea-
15 son must be not entirely passive, but recep-

tive of the form—that is, it must be potentially like this form, but not actually identical
with it: it will stand, in fact, toward its
objects in the same relation as that in which
the faculty of sense stands toward the objects
of perception. Reason therefore, since it
20   thinks everything, must be free from all admixture, in order that, to use the phrase of
Anaxagoras, it may rule the world—that is,
acquire knowledge: for the adjacent light
of any foreign body obstructs it and eclipses
it. Its very nature, then, is nothing but just
this comprehensive potentiality: and the reason—that is, that function through which the
soul is ratiocinative and frames notions—is
therefore, previously to the exercise of
thought, actually identical with nothing
which exists.

This consideration shows how improbable
25   it is that reason should be incorporated with
the bodily organism: for if so, it would be of
some definite character, either hot or cold,
or it would have some organ for its operation, just as is the case with sense. But, as
matter of fact, reason has nothing of this
character. There is truth, too, in the view of
those who say the soul is the source of general ideas: only it is soul not as a whole, but
in its faculty of reason: and the forms or
ideas in question exist within the mind, not
as endowments which we already possess,
but only as capacities to be developed.

Metaphysics

982b 12   It is because of wonder that men, ancient-   (I, 3
ly as now, philosophized. They wondered   [20], 1)
initially at the obvious problems of every
day, and then little by little they progressed
to the point of expressing difficulties of a
more demanding sort, *e.g.*, about phenomena
of moon, sun, stars, and in general the origin
of the universe.

1072a24   If then God is eternally in that blessedness (VI, 9 [9],
we men find only rarely, we wonder at such   9; V, 1

a marvel. But the marvel is greater even than   [10], 9)
this, for he is in a state of even greater
blessedness. Indeed, the state is his own, as
is the life itself since the act of thought is
life and he is that act so that his life is an
optimum and everlasting. We say, then, that
God is a living being, eternal, and infinitely
good, since life and eternity without inter-
ruption or pause is God's. Actually, this *is*
God.

1004a 34 It belongs to the philosopher to treat of   (I, 3
all this. If not the philosopher, then who can   [20], 4)
inquire whether "Socrates" and "Socrates
seated" are the same thing, or whether to
each thing there is a contrary and what this
contrary would be or in what sense to take it.
So it is with all questions of this sort. Since,
then, from one as one and from being as
being are there essential modifications of
unity (and not numbers or lines or fire),
it is clear that the role of philosophy is to
investigate their essence and attributes.

STOICS

The following selections have been translated by the editor. The marginal numbers
refer to the Arnim edition, *Stoicorum Veterum Fragmenta.*

II, 122 Dialectic, as Poseidonius says, is the sci-   (I, 3
ence of things that are true and things that   [20], 4)
are false and things that are neither one nor
the other, but, as Chrysippus points out,
strictly it treats as occasion offers of signs
and the signified.

II, 1175 Similarly, in the first book "On Justice" (IV, 8 [6],
[Chrysippus] quotes on this point the verses   5; 7)
of Hesiod: "Against them Cronus swings a
great whip; hunger and pestilence at the
same time; and the people perish," and he
asserts that thus act the gods in order that,
the wicked having been punished, others will

profit from the example provided and no
longer dare to do the like.

III, 29   Then, in the book "On Beauty," to prove   (I, 6
the statement that "only the beautiful is   [1], 6)
good," Chrysippus has recourse to an argument that goes like this: "The good is object
of choice; but what is chosen, pleases; but
what pleases, is praised; but what is praised
is beautiful." And, again: "The good is pleasant; the pleasant is splendid; the splendid is
beautiful."

III, 278   . . . As bodily beauty is a symmetry of   (I, 6
members proportionate to one another and   [1], 1)
to the whole, so beauty of the soul is nothing
other than the proportion of thought and its
parts with the totality of the soul or with one
another.

III, 472   The correspondence that, in his opinion,   (I, 6
holds between the condition of the body and   [1], 1)
that of the soul Chrysippus was able to
demonstrate from the fact that the health of
the soul is identical with its beauty. With
respect to the body, he defined the matter
exactly, placing health in the symmetry of
the elements and beauty in the symmetry of
the parts of the body. He proved this, clearly, in terms of an earlier discourse where he
had affirmed that bodily health consisted in
a proportion of cold and hot, of dry and
wet. All these, obviously, are strictly bodily
elements while beauty, according to him,
consisted not in the symmetry of elements
but in the symmetry of parts.

III, 605   Thus, only the sage is seer inasmuch as he   (IV, 3
knows how to interpret signs coming from   [27], 11)
gods or daimons and affecting human life.
For that reason the forms of the diviner's art
are in him and the strict interpretation of
dreams, the examination of the flight of birds
and the way of sacrifice and all that pertains
to such matters.

III, 650   If, as they say, love is nothing other than   (I, 3
the impulse of the creative imagination, on   [20], 2)

the other hand beauty shows itself in the youth, the sage is a lover and will be enamored of things worthy of love and able to say the lofty and the graceful.

III, 671   Yes, the evil man drags his soul sorrowfully through the entire span of life with no reason for joy such as naturally comes solely from justice, wisdom, and the other virtues that reign along with them.

(I, 6 [1], 7)

APPENDIX II

A PLOTINUS GLOSSARY

The terminology of Plotinus presents a challenge to the contemporary reader whether he approaches the *Enneads* with some philosophic awareness or with none. If he is as yet an uninitiate in philosophy, he will be inclined to read into many of the repeated, quite technical and personal expressions of his author the meanings which the expressions have in ordinary conversation today but which they never had for Plotinus. If on the other hand he is not unfamiliar with Plato and Aristotle among the ancients and, say, Whitehead and Heidegger among the moderns, he will be fair game for delusive overtones from the words Plotinus uses. For the modern reader the words of Plotinus should not have a ring of familiarity about them; directly they have, it is a good indication that one is missing the point. Yet they should have some meaningful resonances; otherwise understanding is quite out of the question. Hence this small glossary of the more treacherous terms as they appear in the present version.

Hypostasis: It has been thought well merely to transliterate the Greek term since by his use of it Plotinus intends none of the conventional English renderings of the word, *e.g.*, substance, actual existence, argument, person, etc., but "transcendent source" of reality.

Primal Hypostases: They are three (V, 1 [10], 1) and only three (II, 9 [33], 1–2) in number: The One, The Intelligence, and The Soul.

Divinities: The three hypostases; not, however, three gods;

216

the sole Absolute—The One—and two derivatives, The Intelligence—a One-in-Many (VI, 6 [34], 13)—and The Soul—a One-and-Many (V, 1 [10], 8)—are less entities perhaps than they are spiritual attitudes.

The One: The first hypostasis (V, 1 [10], 1), transcending essence (V, 6 [24], 6) and existence (V, 5 [32], 6), beyond number (V, 5 [32], 4) and name (VI, 9 [9], 5)—its designation "The One" being only the denial of all multiplicity (V, 5 [32], 6)—it is The First (V, 1 [10], 1), the source of everything (V, 1 [10], 7) and everything's goal (V, 5 [32], 1). It is the *Good* (II, 9 [33], 1). From it proceeds the second hypostasis,

The Intelligence, which is to The One as a circle is to its center (III, 8 [30], 8), is undivided (IV, 1 [21], 1) yet multiple (*ibid.*), is actual vision (III, 8 [30], 10) and desire (III, 8 [30], 11). It is *Being* (V, 3 [49], 5). From it proceeds the third hypostasis,

The Soul, which is to The Intelligence as matter is to form (III, 9 [13], 5), is the maker of the cosmos (IV, 3 [27], 5). Its refraction through matter is *Nature* (IV, 4 [28], 13).

Reason proceeds from The Intelligence into The Soul without itself becoming a fourth hypostasis (II, 9 [33], 1), and informs matter (III, 8 [30], 2).

Ideas: Not thoughts (V, 9 [5], 7), but substances (V, 8 [31], 5) and intelligences (V, 9 [5], 8) whose totality constitute The Intelligence (*ibid.*) and are its terms (VI, 2 [43], 8); the models of things (VI, 5 [23], 8), they give order to the multiplicity of sense.

Demiurge: Platonic maker of the cosmos assimilated imperfectly into the Plotinian schema: in IV, 4 [28], 10 it is The Soul, and in V, 1 [10], 8 it is The Intelligence.

The intelligible realm: The region "above" (IV, 3 [27], 32); The Intelligence and the objects of its knowing (III, 3 [48], 5); model of the region "below" (V, 8 [31], 12).

The realm of sense (V, 1 [10], 4), which is incorruptible (V, 8 [31], 12) yet multiple (III, 2 [47], 1), is the cosmic body of The Soul (II, 9 [33], 7).

Seminal reasons: Productive agents of The Soul, whence they come into lower and vegetative souls (II, 3 [52], 18); invisible

(V, 1 [10], 4), they are divided by matter (IV, 9 [8], 5); they hold the chief place in beings (VI, 1 [42], 9) and produce the sensory in bodies (VI, 3 [44], 16).

Daimons: Eternal beings, intermediary between the divinities and man (III, 5 [50], 6), charged with the chore of chastising (IV, 8 [6], 5) the

Individual human soul, which is all things (III, 4 [15], 3), is itself an intelligible realm (III, 4 [15], 3), and has the same powers as The Soul (III, 4 [15], 6), differs from another human soul according to the body it has and the previous life it has led (IV, 3 [27], 8), and is not necessarily linked to the body it occupies.

Before-After: Not temporal but logical referents with respect to origin (V, 1 [10], 6).

Above-Below: Not spatial but ontological referents with respect to proximity to, or distance from, the intelligible.

APPENDIX III

Sᴇʟᴇᴄᴛᴇᴅ Aɴɴᴏᴛᴀᴛᴇᴅ Bɪʙʟɪᴏɢʀᴀᴘʜʏ

EDITIONS

Moser, G. H., and Creuzer, F., *Plotini Opera Omnia,* I-III. Oxford: Typographicum Academicum, 1835.

Although the text leaves much to be desired according to contemporary standards, this pioneering edition is still of value to the student because of its notes, index, and critical apparatus.

Henry, Paul, and Schwyzer, Hans-Rudolf, *Plotini Opera,* I-II. Paris: Desclée De Brouwer, 1951, 1959.

To be completed in three volumes, this magisterial work has already proved itself indispensable. Volume II provides a magnificent bonus: the Arabic versions of Plotinus, translated into English by G. Lewis, opposite the relevant Greek.

TRANSLATIONS

Bréhier, Emile, *Plotin: Ennéades,* Texte établi et traduit, I-VI (in seven volumes). Paris: "Les Belles Lettres," 1924–38.

The introduction and the long prefatory notes to each *Ennead* make this a singularly gracious and reliable guide to the thought of Plotinus. The translation is more than admirable; the Greek text upon which it is based, somewhat less.

Turnbull, Grace H., *The Essence of Plotinus.* New York: Oxford University Press, 1934.

Selections, abbreviated and in some instances corrected, from the earlier MacKenna version (see below), in which the editor has made Plotinus' thought relatively simple without falsifying it unduly.

Cilento, Vincenzo, *Plotino: Enneadi,* I-III (in four volumes). Bari: Laterza, 1947–9.
The unusual combination of a poet's flair and a scholar's sobriety mark these pages. Of exceptional worth are the textual discussions, with full attention to variant readings, that are had in the notes. Volume III, Part 2, contains as well the annotated Plotinus bibliography of Bert Marien, which has 1463 entries.

Armstrong, A. H., *Plotinus.* London: G. Allen, 1953.
Brief selections grouped about the themes "The Hypostases," "The One," "The Intelligence," "Soul," "Self," and "Return" that were chosen and newly translated by a master, they are strongly recommended to those especially interested in Plotinus' view of the cosmos.

Harder, Richard, *Plotins Schriften,* Neuarbeitung mit griechischen Lesetext und Anmerkungen, I, II and V (in seven volumes). Hamburg: Meiner, 1956–62.
This, although still incomplete in its revised version, is the best translation there is, and it is difficult to imagine a better. The volumes of critical commentary, after Harder's death continued by Rudolf Beutler and Willy Theiler, are of uniform excellence.

MacKenna, Stephen, and Page, B. S., *Plotinus: The Enneads,* 3rd ed. London: Faber and Faber, 1962.
This is rather a Plotinian rhapsody than a translation—and an Irish rhapsody at that with the pipes of Pan always in the middle distance. Yet, paradoxically, it is in its general tonality absolutely faithful: every *Ennead* is authentically Plotinus although few sentences are. This edition is immeasurably enriched by the Introduction of Paul Henry.

STUDIES

Heinemann, Fritz, *Plotin.* Leipzig: Meiner, 1921.
The author's main contention, that there is a perceptible evolution of doctrine in the various treatises of the *Enneads,* has not been generally accepted. But the acuity of his textual analyses as he goes about establishing his unacceptable conclusion has proved to be a continuing boon to Plotinian scholarship.

Arnou, René, *Le désir de Dieu dans la philosophie de Plotin.* Paris: Vrin, 1921.

This doctoral dissertation from the Sorbonne was epoch-making in its day; it has lost none of its value in the meantime.

Bréhier, Emile, *La philosophie de Plotin*, 2e éd. Paris: Boivin, 1928. English translation: *Philosophy of Plotinus*, trans. by Joseph Thomas. Chicago: University of Chicago Press, 1958.
Limited to a characteristically perceptive discussion of the three hypostases and of the sense realm and matter, this small book will aid the student particularly by the comparisons it institutes between the doctrine of Plotinus and that of ancient India.

Theiler, Willy, *Die Vorbereitung des Neuplatonismus*. Berlin: Weidmann, 1930.
Important chiefly for its discussion of the influence of Philo of Alexandria, this monograph has never been equaled in value.

Henry, Paul, *Plotin et l'Occident*. Louvain: Spicilegium, 1934.
Plotinus as he has come down to us in the West through the writings of Firmious Maternus, Marius Victorinus, Augustine, and Macrobius is presented with largeness of view and meticulous regard for detail that always characterizes the work of Père Henry.

Henry, Paul, *Les états du texte de Plotin*. Paris: Desclée De Brouwer, 1938.
It is adventure in the history of ideas to pore over this assessment, through quotations and scattered references, of the presence of Plotinus in the writings of the generations immediately succeeding his own.

Arnou, René, "Contemplation chez les anciens philosophes du monde gréco-romain: 4. La contemplation chez Plotin," *Dictionnaire de spiritualité*, II (1950), 1727–38.
Plotinian mystical doctrine in its historical context.

Arnou, René, "L'acte de l'intelligence en tant qu'elle n'est pas intelligence," in *Mélanges Joseph Maréchal*, II. Paris: Desclée De Brouwer, 1950, 248–62.
The philosophic doctrine, born of his mystical experience, that was Plotinus' chief contribution to the obscurantism of Neoplatonism.

Schwyzer, Hans-Rudolf, "Plotinos," *Paulys Realencyklopädie der classischen Altertumswissenschaft*, XXI (1951), 471–592.
The best summary treatment of the general doctrine of Plotinus together with an evaluative survey of Plotinian scholarship of that date.

Les sources de Plotin. Entretiens sur l'Antique Classique, V. Vandoeuvres-Geneva: Fondation Hardt, 1960.

Ten brilliant papers, together with the discussions they occasioned, by the best of contemporary Plotinus scholars, E. R. Dodds, Willy Theiler, Pierre Hadot, Henri-Charles Puech, Heinrich Dörrie, Vincenzo Cilento, R. Harder, H. R. Schwyzer, A. H. Armstrong, Paul Henry.

APPENDIX IV

GUIDE TO SOURCES

Alex. Aphrod.   Alexander Aphrodisiensis, *De Anima*, I. Bruns, ed. "Commentaria in Aristotelem Graeca," *Supplementum Aristotelicum*, II, 1. Berlin: Reimer, 1887.

Diog. Laert.   Diogenes Laertius, *De Clarorum Philosophorum Vitis, Dogmatibus et Apophthegmatibus Libri Decem*. C. G. Cobet, ed. Paris: Didot, 1878.

Eus.   Eusebius Pamphili, *Praeparatio Evangelica*, I-II. K. Mras, ed. Berlin: Akademie-Verlag, 1954, 1956.

Orph.   *Orphicorum Fragmenta*. O. Kern, ed. Berlin: Weidmann, 1922.

Stoic.   *Stoicorum Veterum Fragmenta*, I-IV. H. von Arnim, ed. Leipzig: Teubner, 1903-1924.

Trag.   *Tragicorum Graecorum Fragmenta*. A. Nauck, ed., 2nd. ed. Leipzig: Teubner, 1889.

Vorsokrat.   *Die Fragmente der Vorsokratiker*. Greek and German by H. Diels; 7th ed. by W. Kranz. Berlin: Weidmann, 1954.

N.B. Citations from the works of Plato and Aristotle follow the convention of referring to the pagination of the Paris 1578 edition of Stephanus and the Berlin 1831 edition of Bekker, respectively; references to lines in Plato are according to the Oxford 1905-1913 edition of Burnet.